Inside the Future

Surviving the Technology Revolution

Henry C. Lucas, Jr.

PRAEGER

Westport, Connecticut
London

Library of Congress Cataloging-in-Publication Data

Inside the future : surviving the technology revolution / Henry C. Lucas, Jr.
 p. cm.
 Includes bibliographical references and index.
 ISBN 978–0–313–34826–6 (alk. paper)
1. Information technology—Social aspects. 2. Technological innovations—Social aspects.
3. Technology—Social aspects. I. Title.
HC79.I55L834 2008
303.48'3–dc22   2007048576

British Library Cataloguing in Publication Data is available.

Library of Congress Catalog Card Number: 2007048576
ISBN: 978–0–313–34826–6

First published in 2008

Praeger Publishers, 88 Post Road West, Westport, CT 06881
An imprint of Greenwood Publishing Group, Inc.
www.praeger.com

Printed in the United States of America

The paper used in this book complies with the
Permanent Paper Standard issued by the National
Information Standards Organization (Z39.48-1984).

10 9 8 7 6 5 4 3 2 1

TO

*Dean Howard Frank and
my colleagues at the Smith School,
University of Maryland*

Contents

Part III How to Survive

Preface

I truly believe this is a century unlike any other because this is a century in which every-thing physical and analog will become digital, mobile, virtual, personal.[1]
—Carly Fiorina, former Chairman and CEO, Hewlett-Packard

The gains in productivity will be staggering for those countries, companies and individuals who can absorb the new technological tools.[2]
—Thomas L. Friedman, author columnist, *New York Times*

The fundamentals of business and the economy are changing in every market, in every industry and in every nation. The 21st century has brought new business processes and models, participation in new markets, radically different organizational structures, and changes in our daily lives. New business models enabled by information technology are challenging the recorded music industry, providers of video content like Hollywood and the TV networks, newspapers, politicians, stock markets, stock brokers and mortgage companies, to name a few. We are expected to perform more of our own services online, and we are forming new kinds of social groups via online communities. There is a charge for talking to an airline reservations agent—we are supposed to use the airline's Web site and not bother its staff!

Academics in the information systems field have largely ignored these profound changes in the economy to focus on more narrow topics that are easier to publish in academic journals. We have seen enrollments drop in traditional Information Systems courses, not just due to the dot-com debacle or a perceived lack of IT jobs, but because we are not teaching how to deal with the huge transformations the technology enables. I am concerned that it is not just academics who are missing this revolution in technology, but that the population at large is unaware of the full magnitude of the transformations going on around us.

To address these issues, the Robert H. Smith School of Business formed a partnership with Maryland Public Television (MPT) to produce a one-hour documentary on how information technology is revolutionizing organizations, markets, industries, and our personal lives. The purpose of this book is to expand on the themes of the documentary and provide a significant amount of additional material to supplement the TV program. The major goals of the book are to:

- Convince the reader that technology is truly transformational.
- Suggest a framework for understanding these transformations.
- Provide examples of how technology is changing everything.
- Suggest how you should respond to the technology revolution, both at work and at home. We all want to survive this revolution and end up flourishing because of it.

The book begins with a set of rules which describe how technology is changing the nature of work and leisure activities. Each chapter revisits the rules as it provides examples of how they apply. The second chapter presents a framework for understanding how new technologies disrupt existing models and how this conceptual view of change helps us predict the likely outcome of ongoing transformations.

The second section of the book presents evidence for transformations, beginning with everyday events like going to the office, listening to music, or reading the newspaper. Chapter 4 looks at the power of online communities, a new phenomenon enabled by the Internet. Never has word of mouth (or "word of mouse") spread so rapidly to so many people. The United States is largely a service economy, and in Chapter 5 we look at how technology has the potential to transform services.

Governments exist to help improve people's lives; they provide a variety of services and a great deal of information. E-government helps to make government more transparent and efficient as we see in Chapter 6. We still are a major manufacturing nation, and Chapter 7 examines some transformations in this sector. The Internet and World Wide Web are very significant transformational technologies; to realize their full potential we need to all be connected at broadband speeds. Chapter 8 looks at the companies competing for the digital pipeline to your home and the implications for those who are being left out of the technology revolution. Chapter 9 tackles the health care industry in the United States, an industry that cries out for a whole series of transformations, including those enabled by technology.

We educators have a long history of resisting change, and Chapter 10 looks at the potential for transforming education. There are ways technology can help, but I am afraid that technology alone will not be enough to move education to a whole new level.

Chapter 11 looks at one company in depth: Eastman Kodak. Managers at Kodak were quite happy with the status quo of high profit margins on film; they chose to ignore the advent of digital photography until too late. We try to understand what happened at Kodak to prepare the reader to avoid suffering a similar fate. Chapter 12 takes a look at our rules of the revolution and summarizes the evidence that supports them.

The last section of the book is about how to survive and flourish in the technology revolution—how to lead the transformation instead of being transformed by the technology. Chapter 13 talks about change because a transformation can be thought of as a massive change that brings us to a whole new level. The final chapter offers suggestions for the reader on how to take advantage of what is going on around us, both at work and at home.

Finally, each chapter contains a sidebar on "surviving" the technology revolution. These sidebars preview some of the key points in the chapter, and they suggest to you how to avoid falling behind the revolution. The objective is for you to become a leader and to use IT-enabled transformations to the greatest advantage.

NOTES

1. Carly Fiorina, Commencement Address, Robert H. Smith School of Business, University of Maryland, May 22, 2006.

2. Thomas L. Friedman, *The World Is Flat: A Brief History of the Twenty-First Century* (New York: Farrar, Straus and Giroux, 2005), 45.

Acknowledgments

I would like to thank Dean Howard Frank of the Smith School of Business at the University of Maryland, who shares our vision of technology and who has transformed the school during his years as Dean. Howard supported this project intellectually and financially from the beginning and has provided leadership throughout its development.

Frank Batavick of Maryland Public Television was the director and producer of the documentary. He has helped with the book project as well, and he is responsible for creating a first-rate TV program that gets across the message of technology-enabled transformation to the viewing audience. Bob Cringely, our narrator, skillfully interviewed scores of people for the program, and many of their observations are found in this book. I want to thank my son Jonathan, who used his experience as a screenwriter to offer helpful advice throughout the project, and my son Scott, the other Professor Lucas, who offers the view of the humanities. I also thank my wife, Ellen, for her encouragement and enthusiasm for this project.

I want to thank Kimberly Holiday for her help in getting the screen shots ready for the printers and Ruth Zuba for her all around cheerful work on the book. I gratefully acknowledge Tim Tagaris for permission to use his photograph of the Lieberman/Bush Kiss float (Figure 4.1); Carolyn Seeley for her help obtaining permission to use the two figures from Ebay (Figure 4.2 and Figure 4.3); my colleague, Galit Shmueli, for permission to use a screen shot from her blog (Figure 4.4); Markos Moulitsas for his permission to use the screen shot from the Daily Kos (Figure 4.5); Donna Bigler from the Montgomery County Office of Public Information for permission to use the screen shot from the Montgomery County Webpage (Figure 6.5); Young-seok Yoon, director of the Seoul's Metropolitan Government's City Marketing Division, for permission to use Figure 6.6; John Wiley & Sons for permission to use the reproduction of Figure 7.1, "Cisco's Business Model," from *Informational Technology Strategic Decision Making for Managers* (Lucas, 2004); Emily Ripps for her assistance in obtaining permission to use the selections from Cisco (Chapter 7); Jackie Lustig from OLPC for permission to use the picture of the XO laptop (Figure 8.1); Susan White at King Features Syndicate for her help in obtaining permission to use the Jimmy Margulies cartoon (Chapter 10); Tad Dearden at Harvard Business School Publishing for permission to use selections from the 2005 Gavetti interview with former Kodak CEO, George Fisher (Chapter 11); Randomhouse Publishers for quotations from Alecia Swasy's *Changing Focus* (Chapter 11); and Janice De Gross of *MIS Quarterly* for permission to use the LaPointe & Rivard case studies (Chapter 11).

PART I

Introduction to a Revolution

1

Rules of the Revolution

The extraordinary technological developments of the twenty-first century have brought organizations of every size an unprecedented ability to transform themselves. The fundamentals of business and the economy are changing in every market, in every industry, and in every nation. These transformations result in radically different business processes and models, participation in new markets, the creation of new relationships among organizations, and radically different organizational structures. A technology transformation can be a major opportunity for an organization, or it can be a tremendous threat to its survival and to the future of its employees and the community around it. This same technology is transforming our personal lives. Social networks change the nature of personal and group relationships. People choose what music and what video content they wish to enjoy when and where. Online communities and phenomena like blogs are changing the political landscape forever. Each of us needs to understand the implications of this revolution in technology, and we must develop a strategy for coping with it.

Why should anyone want to read a book about information technology (IT)-enabled transformations? One might say, "I don't see much different in my life as a result of the technology—I go to work, travel, and watch TV just the way I used to. What's the big deal here?"

The revolution in technology has been a silent, well-kept secret. Humans are very good at incorporating modest amounts of change in their lives and not noticing that anything has happened. The first airline reservations systems appeared in the 1960s, and the airlines deployed these systems to travel agents in the 1970s. If you are old enough to have been traveling in the 1960s, the changes in making a reservation were dramatic. When you talked to an airline agent, that person could tell you for sure if a seat was available on a particular flight and could actually make a reservation on the flight with your name on it, something not possible using prior, manual methods. On your first trip you were probably surprised and then pleased by this level of service. But within a few months, you stopped noticing and just expected that any airline would now provide a computerized reservations system, or CRS. When the Internet came along and travel services like Travelocity and Expedia appeared, suddenly you were making your own reservations and comparison shopping online: no more airline or travel agents. Making your own reservation probably took more time, but you were in control of the process. How long did it take for you to decide that online was the preferred way to make a reservation?

The airlines figured out that they could save a lot of fees they paid to Travelocity and other travel sites by setting up their own Web sites to sell seats on their planes. Today the airlines want to charge you a fee if you talk to an agent rather than use their Web site to make your reservation. And of course the logical extension is to have you print out your boarding pass at home and avoid the lines at the check-in counter at the airport.

Because this revolution has been largely silent, and because changes can happen very quickly, we all risk being left behind if we are unprepared. For some aspects of the revolution, being left behind is not a major problem; one just misses out on some benefits. You can still find a lot of music that is not at iTunes and may be just as happy with CDs and living without a portable music player. But it is far more serious when a transformation affects something crucial like one's employer. At a company like Kodak that missed the transformation to digital photography, tens of thousands of people lost their jobs. *It is dangerous to ignore the revolution in information technology that is enabling huge transformations of organizations, markets, industries, and our daily lives. If you fall behind, you may never catch up.*

How extensive is the technology revolution? We interviewed Carly Fiorina, former CEO of Hewlett Packard, about the nature of IT-enabled transformations. Her comments:

> I agree with the central thesis, which is that information technology has transformed business, but actually info tech is transforming life. It impacts everybody. And the easiest example I can use is to ask [readers] to think about the impact of the iPod on the music industry. It's a piece of technology in the hands of consumers, but what its done is totally transform that industry and the expectations of an individual consumer . . . . Now a consumer says, "I want to listen to what I want to when I want to on the device I choose." Put another way, whether in business or in life, it used to be that IT was kind of this special department, big iron and really complicated. Only geeks got it and . . . you knew it was in the back room working somehow, but really, if you weren't a geek, you didn't want to learn much more about it. We've come to the place now where technology in the hands of an individual means that anyone can communicate with anyone else anywhere in the world virtually, for free. Anyone can get any piece of info they want at any time on virtually any device, and ultimately the individual is more and more in charge—whether [it's] the

individual consumer or the individual employee or the individual citizen. That's incredibly exciting, but it puts huge stress on institutions, industries, and businesses because when the individual has more and more power, the institution has less and less.

WHAT HAS BEEN TRANSFORMED?

The transformation described above, and in more detail in later chapters, took place over 40 years, which is pretty gradual. Yet, if we look back to the 1960s, the technology has enabled dramatic changes in the way an airline operates. If this were the only example, there would not be enough material to talk about. But the point is that there are many, many examples of technology-enabled transformations, and these changes affect all of us in a myriad of ways. This book presents many stories of technology transformation across a variety of settings to convince you that there is something going on here. Our examples include:

- The transformation of everyday events
  - The virtual office
  - The airline trip
  - Buying online
  - Listening to music when and where we want to
  - Picking up video content on different devices, while at home or on the go
  - Reading the newspaper, placing an ad, and looking for a job

- The power of online communities
  - Giving feedback to Web sites and rating products and vendors
  - Joining an online community
  - Creating a community around a blog

- Transforming services
  - The new way of trading stocks
  - Tracking packages in real time
  - The age of customer self-service

- A more responsive government
  - Immediate answers to questions
  - Completing transactions online instead of in person

- Transforming manufacturing
  - The 21st century supply chain
  - The virtual manufacturing company
  - Creating highly efficient organizations
  - Radio Frequency Identification (RFID) and its coming impact

- The digital highway to your house
  - The race is on. Who will win?
  - Cable, Digital Subscriber Line (DSL), Worldwide Interoperability for Microwave Access (WiMax), and power line broadband

- The critical condition of healthcare
  - The $2 trillion opportunity
  - How IT can improve the quality of care and the efficiency of administration
  - The electronic medical record
- The challenge for education
  - Students are ahead of the faculty
  - Is the online experience comparable to in person?
  - Do we need to change our approach from "do your own work" to "search the net" for prior work that applies?

These are the major transformations we will discuss in later chapters. We tend not to notice a lot of the transformations going on around us because they have often taken a long time, like the airline example. Many of the changes brought on by technology are a secret to observers. For example, customers of a virtual manufacturing firm that outsources all production may not notice that a contract manufacturing company in Asia made the products they purchased from the American firm. One objective of the book is to provide enough evidence to convince readers that there are many technology-enabled transformations taking place and that they need to consider what is happening in making personal and professional decisions.

SOME NEW RULES

The technology revolution comes with rules that describe new directions in products, services and leisure activities. The rules that follow apply to advanced, post-industrial economies as well as some developing countries.

Rule: *Every process is becoming digital, mobile, and virtual (Carly Fiorina).*

Carly Fiorina, former CEO of Hewlett-Packard, made this comment in a talk at the Smith School of Business at the University of Maryland. It is a strong statement, and if this rule has few exceptions, it is dramatic and far-reaching. Carly has lately expanded this rule. It is now "digital, mobile, virtual, and personal."

Her comments during a 2007 interview emphasize the impact of this rule:

> Going back to the music industry or photograph or traditional media, these are all industries that have in fact been turned on their heads by individuals or technology. My way of saying this is that every process that used to be physical or analog is becoming digital, mobile; you can carry it around—it's virtual and personal. That's a big transformation. That's a historic transformation, and we're at the beginning of that transformation, not the end.

Carly offered a great example of a process that follows this rule. For over 100 years, photography has been a physical, chemical process. When the digital camera came along, it changed the nature of photography forever, much to the detriment of Kodak. A digital camera is a computer with a lens, and it added tremendous mobility to photography. You could take a picture and immediately view it. You could load the picture on a computer and send it instantly anywhere in the world. The process became virtual in the sense that a person located miles away could take a picture and transmit it to someone else to view. For example, a repair facility could photograph a faulty product and send the picture to an engineer thousands of miles away.

Mobility is being encouraged through the use of handheld personal digital assistants (PDAs) and cell phones to access corporate applications. Sales teams can use their handhelds to check and update client lists while medical staff members use them to access patient records, and warehouse workers check inventory levels. AT&T is working on an application in which its sales staff will use PDAs to create customer accounts and review contracts. The sales representative will be able to offer instant discounts by checking the customer's purchase history. The coming U.S. Census will feature hand-held devices so that mobile workers can access central databases (*Wall Street Journal,* 6/12/2007).

We will see in subsequent chapters that much manufacturing in the United States is virtual. Companies in this country design products and take orders for them but employ contract manufacturers, often located in foreign countries, to make the products. This process has been going on for years, but information technology has reduced the time required to communicate information between the order taker and the actual manufacturer, making this approach more appealing. With high-speed data communications and worldwide connectivity, response times can be fast enough to keep stock-outs to a minimum and satisfy customer demand.

There are also examples of individuals in virtual locations. The individual who works from home "telecommuting" has a virtual presence at a physical site. At Accenture, consultants reserve an office in the city they will be visiting; they do without a permanent, assigned office. One could say that online communities are a virtual version of a physical community of people who meet together.

Rule: *Products and services that can become digital will, and their physical representations will disappear.*

We have an Edison phonograph that my grandmother bought around 1900, and I am old enough to remember 45 rpm records with a single song in each side. From 1900 until the 45 rpm recording, the technology did not change much: the plastic records grew smaller, and the playback devices went from mechanical to electrical. The first big change in recorded music media was the CD, which recorded in a digital rather than analog format. This technology provided very clear sounds, though some audiophiles maintain that analog recordings have more richness. It also made it possible to create copies that are identical to the master copy. Reproducing zeros and ones is a lot easier than trying to faithfully copy an analog tape or record.

We are headed toward a time in which the physical media of a record, tape, CD, or DVD will disappear. Digital files stored on computers and mobile devices like MP3 players and iPods will replace them. Consumers will be able to access all of recorded music online and all movies ever made and download them to whatever device is most convenient, or they will create play lists and have the music streamed to a listening device. (This rule will not be greeted positively at Blockbuster.)

Rule: *Physical products will be marketed with information components.*

My favorite example of this rule comes from the automotive industry. The automakers were asleep when cell phones came along. For better or worse, consumers use a large number of cell phone minutes in their cars; the automakers could have entered the lucrative cell phone business had they figured this out. General Motors has tried to go beyond this early mistake with its highly successful OnStar system. OnStar is a telematics application that uses cellular and satellite technology to provide a variety of services to subscribers. A customer subscribes to OnStar, which is an ongoing information component of his or her car. OnStar at its basic level provides an immediate connection with an OnStar representative who can unlock the doors on your car, or call the police and an ambulance in case of an accident. The system automatically notifies an OnStar representative if the car's air bags deploy so that he or she can summon aid. A Global Positioning System (GPS) receiver provides the exact location of the car.

Rule: *Organizations are shifting as much work to consumers as possible: the age of customer self-service is here.*

There is a story about the early days of telephony on what led to automatic dialing. At first an operator completed all telephone calls. A subscriber wishing to make a call picked up the phone and turned a handle to signal the operator. The operator asked the caller the name of the party he or she was calling and made a physical connection between the two. Phone company engineers, looking at the growth in telephones and calls, soon calculated that at the current growth rate, every man, woman and child in the United States would have to be a telephone operator in a few years. Clearly that was impossible. The answer was to develop automatic dialing equipment so that people could complete local calls (at first) themselves by dialing numbers on their handsets. But wait, did this not turn every man, woman and child in the United States into a telephone operator? Eventually automatic local dialing extended to long-distance within the United States and then to international calls as well.

The advantages of self-service for the service provider are pretty compelling. No longer is it necessary to have expensive employees providing a service, and often these services represent unpleasant, repetitive labor. But why do people not object to having work forced on them? In the case of dialing the telephone, the workload on the individual was pretty minimal, and it was faster to dial than wait for the operator. In the case of making your own travel reservations, in many instances I have found that more time is required, but the ability to search for different schedules and fares makes it worthwhile. Given that the cost of labor is continually increasing, and that many of the jobs being replaced are not particularly attractive to workers, customer self-service is a trend that is going to grow in the future.

Rule: *People want freedom to set their own schedules and to work and engage in leisure activities from a location of their choosing.*

Computing began with large, mainframe computers that could easily fill a room. These mammoth machines needed a lot of power and air conditioning. The development of the minicomputer reduced these requirements, and individual departments bought their own computers. But they were certainly not portable. In 1981 IBM introduced its personal computer (PC), which gave computing power to the people. It was not long until vendors began to make portable PCs that could run on a battery for a few hours. Heavy portables gave way to notebook computers weighing a few pounds and eventually to personal digital assistants and devices like the Blackberry. For the mass market, various kinds of music players came along to play cassette tapes and then CDs. The ability to share music on the Internet led to MP3 players so that the listener could download a song and take it with him or her. And of course, the iPod has been a phenomenal success for portable or fixed location listening.

Vendors who offer video content have gotten the message. The TV networks have started providing copies of popular shows for downloading to portable devices after the shows appear on the network. The industry is scrambling to figure out what kind of entertainment to make specifically for smaller, portable devices. The message is that consumers want to determine what to watch, when, and where. They do not want to be bound to a fixed schedule determined by a network or cable company scheduler.

Rule: *Technology enables powerful online communities: power to the people.*

In the early days of networking you could use proprietary networks like AOL and Prodigy. These services turned out to be very popular with elderly individuals who had trouble getting out. They could make friends online and carry on a social relationship, despite the fact that there was no face-to-face interaction. The Internet expanded the creation of chat rooms and community Web sites to the point that virtual communities are as common as physical groups who meet in person.

The power of online groups appealed to the first Internet merchants. The two biggest obstacles to electronic commerce at first were a secure payments mechanism and customer trust in the online merchant. Online stores also wanted to take advantage of the medium; what benefits could they offer that a physical store could not? The answer was to tap into online groups. On eBay, buyers rate sellers, so the next time someone is thinking about buying from a seller, he or she can consult the ratings to see how satisfied past customers have been. Amazon features a large number of product reviews so that the buyer can get the opinions of others before deciding to purchase. With blogs, you can create your own community, or participate in an online community by adding to other people's blogs.

Rule: *Some services are better bundled, some are better unbundled, and the market will choose the winners.*

There are many examples of the Internet forcing vendors to unbundle goods and services. Online stock brokers offered a different pricing model from full-service brokers. This latter group provided a bundle of services including a stock trade, research, advice, estate planning, and similar benefits. Online brokers focused solely on the stock trade and charged commissions that were a fraction of the full-service brokers'. As a result, the full-service brokers had to respond and offer their own online trading, priced to compete with the electronic brokers. Online brokerage is an example of unbundling.

On the other side, the OnStar service above is an example of bundling. You obtain a set of benefits for subscribing to the service, and there are different bundles of services available. GM made an early decision to include the hardware needed in the vehicle to participate in OnStar as standard equipment. With this approach, the service could be turned on if the dealer was successful in selling OnStar to the buyer. There would be no need for the delivery of the car to be delayed for installation.

Since the technology makes it simple to offer voice mail, call waiting, and similar services, telecommunications companies tend to offer various bundles to encourage subscribers to buy from them. The bottom line is that some bundles will go away and new bundles will appear.

Rule: *Technology will speed up every process, reducing cycle times and driving inefficiencies out of the economy.*

Says Thomas Friedman in *The World Is Flat,* "The gains in productivity will be staggering for those countries, companies and individuals who can absorb the new technological tools." This rule is one of the most obvious. When you can communicate data quickly anyplace in the world, it is possible to dramatically reduce cycle and response times. TAL, a firm in Asia which we discuss in Chapter 7, handles the forecasting, manufacture, and stocking levels of men's branded dress shirts at Penney's. How can a firm located thousands of miles away be responsive to U.S. shoppers? Penney's stores communicate their sales instantly to TAL, which in turn uses the data to schedule production. By knowing inventory and the products that have sold, TAL can keep targeted stock levels in each store. If there is a problem, TAL uses air freight rather than surface transport to be sure there are enough shirts in stock. How about productivity? Penney's no longer keeps warehouse and store inventories of men's dress shirts, saving capital and labor in the process.

Rule: *Local markets will become national and international.*

The beauty of the Internet and Web is that a firm can look like a global powerhouse when it operates out of a mud hut in Africa or a cinder block house in South Asia. There are many examples on the Web of artisans and small business operators whose products are now sold on a national or international level. One of the major impetuses for getting Internet access to rural areas in places in developing countries is to allow farmers to check crop prices and choose the best time to take their products to market.

Rule: *Technology will continue to accelerate globalization.*

Most developed countries believe in globalization as a solution to many of the problems of poverty. As we have seen with offshore manufacturing, technology greatly facilitates globalization. However, the end results of globalization are at times confusing. Asian countries have booming economies as a result of being more involved with the global economy; on the other hand, South America has had fewer benefits so far from globalization, and parts of Africa seem to be experiencing negative growth.

Regardless of one's feelings about globalization, it is a trend that will continue unless governments enact major barriers to trade and commerce. Why is this so? Businesses, at least in Western-style economies, are continually striving to increase efficiency and reduce costs. In a competitive economy, if a firm fails at these efforts, it is unlikely to remain in business. While a great new product may ensure high sales, eventually those sales will attract new entrants, and the incumbent firm will have to compete on costs as well as sales. The vast majority of IT applications is justified based on cost reduction or increased efficiency, and the presence of global networks leverage these applications worldwide.

Rule: *The spoils go to innovators and those who can execute.*

This rule seems almost too obvious to state, but it is widely ignored. I worked with a company for a number of years, and managers there always received my recommendations with enthusiasm. They just never executed much in the way of improvement programs. If management literature is any indication, and I think it is, one of the most underdeveloped topics is execution. How do you motivate managers and other employees to take action?

On the innovation side, OnStar has captured the largest market share of any automotive telematics provider; the others are not even close. The iPod, combined with iTunes, has been a runaway success, and it is responsible for the resurgence of Apple. As I reflect on most of the applications of information technology I have studied, the biggest returns have come from the most innovative applications. It is not necessarily the case that the technology is cutting-edge, or that others have access to the same technology. Instead, those developing the application have figured out how to use the technology in an innovative way. Think about Amazon, eBay, Monster.com, Google and other new businesses enabled by the Internet.

Rule: *The rapid development of new technology-based business models is responsible for a hyper-competitive economy.*

The U.S. and other Western, post-industrial economies have always been highly competitive. Automakers, brokerage firms, airlines, aircraft manufacturers, and many others compete fiercely with each other. It has always seemed to me that the benefits of this competition generally go to consumers in the form of new products and services, lower prices, and higher quality. When the Iron Curtain fell, state-owned industries that had never needed to compete, unsurprisingly, turned out to be totally uncompetitive with industry in other countries and largely became extinct. Technology contributes to enhancing one's competitive position, and we have seen how it can dramatically speed up the pace of events.

The disruptions from IT-enabled transformations are happening much more quickly now than disruptions from other sources in the past. The recording industry, newspapers, stock brokerage, retailing, manufacturing, education, and others are all struggling to figure out how to operate in today's environment as new entrants, new ideas, and new products appear daily.

Rule: *Individuals, organizations, and countries who resist technological change and fail to adapt will be left behind.*

There are those who reject the demands of a competitive economy and who oppose globalization, sometimes for good reason. However, there are too many forces operating to stem the tide; hundreds of thousands of businesses and millions of employees work in organizations that operate in a hyper-competitive economy. These organizations utilize technology to compete, and there is every indication that they will continue to do so. With half of U.S. capital investment going to information technology, technological change and transformation is going to continue as a major force in the economy.

Carly Fiorina comments:

Charles Darwin said it is not the strongest of the species that survives, nor the most intelligent, but those most adaptive to change. And the truth is in this kind of era, in a twenty-first century that is global and technology intensive, it's not necessarily size or . . . traditional barriers to entry in a business that count anymore, its all about adaptability. How fast can a business adapt? In some ways that's true of people as well. The people who succeed and thrive and prosper are those who can adapt as opposed to getting stuck in their ways.

Tourists who visit some of the more remote South Seas islands come back describing cultures that are very different from ours. People have few possessions and share land and goods as a community. It is unlikely that those in developed countries will move in that direction. The United States, Eastern and Western Europe, Russia, and many countries in Asia have chosen to strive for economic growth to improve living conditions for their citizens. Developing countries who aspire to improve their living conditions need access to technology in order to compete in the world economy. Efforts to bring some of the benefits of the Internet to rural Africa and developing Asian countries are aimed at helping to achieve integration with the world's economy. As we will see, projects like the "One Laptop per Child" effort offer the possibility for a dramatic upgrading of the technological capabilities of millions of people.

From my years of working with and observing technology, I have become a firm believer in this last rule. Resisting the technology is unwise and potentially catastrophic for individuals, organizations, and nations.

PREVIEW

The coming chapters present evidence of IT-enabled transformations across a wide variety of domains. The idea is to provide sufficient examples so that the reader will see that transformations are taking place and will think about the consequences. The book attempts to answer the question of what the reader should do in response to the evidence. How do you keep from falling behind the technology revolution? How do you survive? What are the implications of this transformation for individuals? How should managers and organizations respond? What are the implications for policy-makers and public officials?

2

A Framework for Transformation

It is easy to talk about transformation, but harder to describe exactly what constitutes one. It is a little like the struggles of the Supreme Court with obscenity. To paraphrase Justice Potter Stewart in 1964: "I shall not today attempt further to define the definition of an [IT-enabled transformation], but I know it when I see it." This chapter explores the notion of an IT revolution and whether or not we can claim that it has led to the transformation of anything, much less our claims that IT is transforming the world around us.

While our focus is on technologically-enabled transformations, it is important to recognize that technology is only an enabler. It does not determine the nature of an innovation or the outcome of implementing it. Technology did not initiate eBay—Pierre Omidyar used the capabilities of the Internet to build eBay. The technology did not create the application, but the existence of the technology influenced the development of eBay's business model. Technology works in conjunction with complementary innovations, strategies, new business models, and work processes to produce a transformation.

IS THERE AN IT REVOLUTION?

Future historians will compare the widespread adoption of information technology during the last half of the twentieth century with the Industrial Revolution 150 years earlier. Alfred Chandler, in his book *A Nation Transformed by Information* (2000), describes how he changed his thinking about the importance of information:

> [W]e realized that what we were considering was not an industrial revolution, but an information revolution—a revolution that evolved from the industrial world of the twentieth century. *Moreover, this information revolution has transformed the industrial world of the nineteenth and twentieth centuries as profoundly as the First and Second*

Surviving

This chapter offers a lens for viewing IT-enabled transformations. This framework is designed to help you see a transformation coming and prepare for it. What are the skills and competencies needed to survive and flourish while undergoing a major transformation?

In this chapter, we distinguish between competence-enhancing and competence-destroying changes. Here's a good example of both: We visit a commercial printing company that experienced three major technological discontinuities. The first was the introduction of MacIntosh computers and graphics software in the prepress operation, where documents are prepared for printing. This change eliminated the old, time-consuming and error-riddled process using film to produce the output for making a printing plate. The second discontinuity was the introduction of digital film-to-plate machines. The plate making equipment could accept the output of the Macs directly, making it easy to generate new plates and correct errors. The last technology the firm implemented was a private network, which allowed it to prepare prepress materials at one location and run the print job at another, providing great flexibility for the company.

The changes were competence-enhancing for the printing firm. It has flourished during a time when there has been relentless pressure on profit margins and many companies are leaving the industry. The basic technology required the firm to change its business processes, but technology dramatically improved the processes without destroying them.

However, for the original prepress workers, the changes were competence-destroying. These workers could not adapt to the Macs and ended up leaving the company.

Industrial Revolutions transformed the earlier commercial world of the eighteenth century. (Chandler and Cortada, p. 3; italics added)

He continues to discuss the impact of information on the economy:

Our authors (1) review the changing technological underpinnings—or, to use a modern term, infrastructure—of the means of transmitting information, (2) consider the changing nature of the recipients of the information flows, and (3) analyze the ways in which the recipients *used these flows to shape and reshape U.S. business, society, and culture.* (Chandler and Cortada, p. 4; italics added)

It is my belief that information technology is doing even more than reshaping business, society and culture: it is dramatically transforming organizations, markets, industries, and the way we live.

Figure 2.1
IT-Enabled Transformations

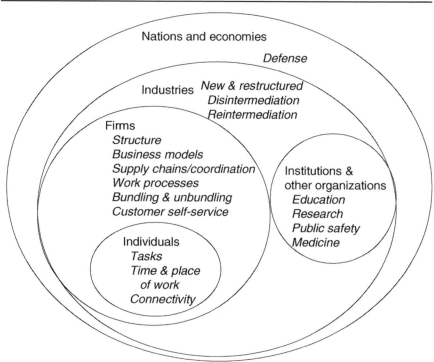

The Industrial Revolution is associated with the first development of new business models: the mass production of goods in centralized factories. The substitution of water and steam power for animal power made possible the construction of huge factories, and production moved from the home workshop to large cities. The physical landscape changed during the Industrial Revolution as entrepreneurs grouped factories in cities to take advantage of centralized services and transportation, triggering a mass exodus from rural areas to cities.

Figure 2.1 shows some of the changes that are associated with the widespread adoption of information technology. The figure begins with the most micro-level changes in the tasks undertaken by individuals and the nature of work. Many individuals spend time in firms which have a structure, follow a business model, and have work processes among other features. In addition to firms, there are other institutions and organizations including government entities and non-profits like educational institutions and charities. Firms and other organizations belong to industry groups which exhibit changes from IT.

Technology also affects nations and economies, also shown in Figure 2.1. More specifically, information technology is associated with transformations in:

1. *The tasks that individuals perform at work and at leisure.* From the factory to the office to leisure-time activities, the tasks individuals perform differ dramatically from the days of little or no technology. Factory workers monitor automated equipment instead of performing manufacturing operations themselves. Thousands of college professors, managers, and office workers are their own secretaries, keyboarding papers, reports, memos, and correspondence. Millions of people download music from iTunes and play it on their iPods.

2. *Time and place of work.* Technology makes it possible to change the location of work for a large number of people, and it enables work to take place any time during the day. For the first time since the Industrial Revolution, rural areas are gaining population. Many knowledge workers telecommute at least part of the week.

3. *Connectivity.* Electronic mail has dramatically changed the nature of communications through its asynchronous nature and our ability to communicate easily across time zones. Email has introduced efficiencies in communication and has led to a decrease in the number of letters and the volume of first class mail in the United States. Email enables virtual work on a global scale. Cellular communications provide constant phone access. In the near future, cellular and other hand-held devices will become a primary means for connecting to the Internet, especially when the user is traveling.

4. *The way in which we structure organizations.* One of the most exciting contributions of technology is the way it enables organizations to develop innovative new structures. Companies can use IT to become virtual, assigning projects to task forces scattered around the world who communicate electronically. The technology encourages firms to outsource work because they can instantly route orders to a manufacturing or fulfillment partner. A company can easily concentrate on its core competence and use technology to make it easier to distribute work to partners.

5. *New business models.* The Internet has provided the impetus for the creation of new business models like the portal, auction sites, and Web travel services to name a few. IT also enables models like lean production at Dell and mass customization at Lands End. Many of these models involve the creation of a new marketplace.

6. *Coordination and the operation of supply chains.* Technology has made it possible for supply chain partners to share information on product demand and availability. The customer's purchase in a store creates a scanner record that the retailer transmits to a supplier. The supplier can share this and other information with its suppliers, creating much more efficient supply chains. Wal-Mart is famous for its innovative use of technology to help keep its prices down.

7. *All types of work processes from manufacturing to service to office work.* Work flow software lets service companies automatically route and track documents. Bar coding and radio frequency identification devices enable manufacturing control systems to keep track of the location of work in process. Sophisticated systems use this information to plan and schedule production in a factory.

8. *Unbundling.* The Internet creates a platform for new entrants to force incumbents in an industry to unbundle. Electronic brokerages forced full-service brokers to unbundle research and other services and to offer customers the option of trade execution only. The Internet and peer-to-peer technology is forcing the recorded music industry to unbundle individual songs from albums and make them available for sale.

9. *Self-service and the nature of customer service.* Organizations are making a concerted effort to have customers interact with them directly using technology to provide better service and to reduce labor costs. Students register for classes, obtain class material, and receive their grades online. Shippers use the Internet to track goods in transit. We make airline reservations on the Internet and check in at the airport at an automated kiosk or print a boarding pass at home from the airline's Web site. Customers entering their own orders and paying for goods or services online is becoming a common practice.

10. *Education and the nature of research.* The Internet is truly transforming education. Students of all ages use it to locate material. Schools use classroom support systems like Blackboard and WebCT to distribute materials, host discussion groups on class tropics, and communicate regularly with students. This technology has created an industry of online schools and education.

11. *Medicine.* Technology is responsible for remarkable changes in the practice of medicine ranging from advanced imaging systems to instruments for minimally invasive surgery. Technology has the potential to transform the practice of medicine as well through electronic patient record systems, online prescriptions, all digital imaging, and automated insurance to physician to patient links.

12. *The emergence of new industries and the restructuring of old ones.* Electronic commerce has been responsible for the creation of new businesses. Before the Internet there were no portals or search engine companies. Auctions took place physically in a single location, though a remote bidder might be able to bid by phone. eBay has changed the way in which individuals and organizations shop. eBay Motors has created a national used car market, something that would have been extremely difficult to accomplish before the Internet.

13. *Disintermediation and re-intermediation.* The Internet has provided the opportunity to disintermediate businesses like the travel agent, who no longer receives a commission from the airline and must charge for its services. Various Web travel services constitute a new intermediary made possible by technology.

14. *Individual national economies and the global economy as a whole.* The impact of IT on an economy is difficult to measure. A Brookings study by Litan and Rivlin (2000) estimated that the Internet has contributed 0.25 to 0.50 percent to growth in the economy in year 2000 prices. Anecdotal stories of Internet adoption in developing countries suggest that there are significant economic and social benefits possible from the technology.

15. *The nature of defense.* For better or worse, it is clear that information technology has transformed warfare, including smart weapons, battlefield displays, avionics, the electronic control of weapons, and the collection of intelligence, to name a few.

WHAT CONSTITUTES A TRANSFORMATION?

The technology field is associated with much exaggeration, from vendor promises to the inflated expectations of the dot-com Internet stock market bubble. Is this notion of an IT revolution and transformation more of the same? How does one determine the difference between a true transformation and incremental changes? Webster's definition of transformation is: "to change in composition or structure . . . to change the outward form or appearance . . . to change in character or condition." In the selection quoted earlier, Chandler and Cortada (2000) characterize a transformation as something that will "shape and reshape the economy."

In the organization studies field, "punctuated equilibrium" offers one theoretical lens for understanding the nature and effects of transformational change. This approach describes how industries experience long periods of stability punctuated by major changes in the technology (Tushman and Anderson, 1986; Anderson and Tushman, 1990). An example of a major transformation is the change in the airline industry as a result of moving from propeller aircraft to jets. While most observers would agree that the aircraft example is a major discontinuity, technology transformations are often more difficult to identify. They have tended to occur over a long period of time without a well-defined beginning and end point.

In an empirical study of punctuated equilibrium, Romanelli and Tushman (1994) defined a revolutionary transformation as one that occurred when they found changes in three major organizational conditions-strategy, structure, and power-within any two-year time period. A more recent study (Dehning et al., 2003) of excess stock market returns related to news of company investments in transformational technologies defined technology transformations as events that:

- Fundamentally alter traditional ways of doing business by redefining business capabilities and/or (internal or external) business processes and relationships.
- Potentially involve strategic acquisitions to acquire new capabilities or to enter a new marketspace.
- Exemplify the use of IT to dramatically change how tasks are carried out ... is the move recognized as being important in enabling [the] firm to operate in different markets, serve different customers, ... or gain considerable competitive advantage by doing things differently.

These definitions for a revolutionary transformation require interpretation and judgment; there are no quantitative measures or numeric cutoffs. Consider the example of substituting jet aircraft for propeller-driven planes. This change did not create a radically new business model; airlines still moved passengers and freight from one location to another. However, the dramatic increase in system capacity and the demand for travel due to lower flight times and lower fares led to a huge increase in the volume of activity at each airline. Airline business models evolved over time as the industry grew and became more competitive. The tasks workers performed also changed, partially from the introduction of information technology to handle the increasing volume of reservations and other transactions. The technology moved to the Internet and enabled the airlines to substitute customer self-service for making reservations and for check-in at the airport. For customers, the time and place of work changed as managers and consultants traveled more frequently to other locations than their home base. The ability to move goods quickly around the world affected supply chains as air freight provided insurance for just-in-time production systems.

Change is a continuum ranging from incremental advances on one end to radical transformation on the other. One important research task is to define what constitutes a transformation. How do we map change to the various points on the continuum? What kind of major changes are required for observers to agree that a transformation has taken place? What kind of indicators measure change? Can we define change generically, or does each domain and proposed transformation require its own measures?

For the examples in this book, you will have to decide whether or not you think the massive changes described constitute a transformation. I believe they do. If you are in doubt, you might consult the definitions above and ask if the transformation described fundamentally alters ways of doing business and uses information technology to dramatically alter how tasks are carried out. Has the technology changed the way people live and work?

A FRAMEWORK FOR IT-ENABLED TRANSFORMATION

Reviewing the process by which a transformation takes place contributes to our understanding of the role of technology in transforming leisure, work, organizations, and the economy. Figure 2.2 is a description of the IT transformation process. It is important to remember that the figure refers to the application of IT to create new businesses, services, entertainment, and other innovations. It is a complete development and change effort, not just the technology, that leads to a transformation.

The model begins on the left-hand side with a distinction made by Tushman and Anderson (1986) between competence-enhancing and competence-destroying change. A competence-enhancing change enables individuals to make use of prior knowledge and skills to use technology in new ways. A competence-destroying change happens when the skills to operate the core technology are quite different from pre-technology days; current workers and processes are not able to cope with the changes.

Concentrating first on the top row of the figure, in the case of a competence enhancing transformation, we would expect to see one or all of the following:

- A reduction in average costs
- New business processes
- Changes in the structure of work
- Different products or services offered
- The voluntary adoption of new business models
- A new organization structure.

The result of the transformation could be a brand new business, a new competitive position, and a higher market share. The final impact of the transformation in most cases will be dramatic new benefits for customers.

Figure 2.2
The IT Transformation Process

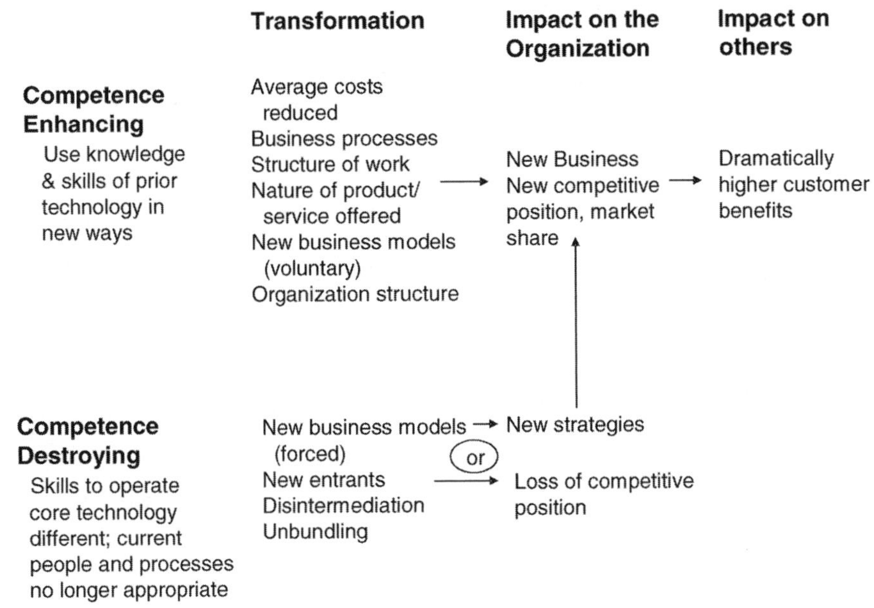

	Transformation	Impact on the Organization	Impact on others
Competence Enhancing Use knowledge & skills of prior technology in new ways	Average costs reduced Business processes Structure of work Nature of product/ service offered → New business models (voluntary) Organization structure	New Business New competitive → position, market share ↑	Dramatically higher customer benefits
Competence Destroying Skills to operate core technology different; current people and processes no longer appropriate	New business models → New strategies (forced) (or) New entrants ———→ Loss of competitive Disintermediation position Unbundling		

Competence-destroying technology follows a slightly different path. In this case, the firm may be forced into adopting a new business model, possibly by new entrants that take advantage of the technology. The incumbent firm may be affected by disintermediation or forced unbundling. This firm has two choices: It can lose its competitive position and eventually go out of business, or it can adopt new strategies to compete.

This framework is oriented toward business organizations because often transformations start there, or they end up having a major impact on business. A college student named Shawn Fanning started Napster, a file sharing program for music. This grass-roots program did not involve a business at first, but it soon had a major impact on all of the firms involved in the recorded music industry.

SUMMARY

This chapter presents a framework for thinking about IT-enabled transformations. One of its major features is the distinction between competence-enhancing and competence-destroying changes. It is clear that transformations are not uniformly positive for everyone affected; they can have a very negative impact on individuals who cannot adapt to major changes. You want to think about how a transformation could affect you and develop a strategy for being sure it turns out to be competence-enhancing and not competence-destroying.

REFERENCES

Anderson, P., and M. Tushman. "Technological Discontinuities and Dominant Designs: A Cyclical Model of Technological Change." *Administrative Science Quarterly* 35, no. 4 (December 1990): 604–633.

Bakos, Y., H. Lucas, G. Simon, S. Viswana, and B. Weber. "The Impact of E-Commerce on Competition in the Retail Brokerage Industry." *Information Systems Research* (December 2005): 352–371.

Chandler, A., and J. Cortada, eds. *A Nation Transformed by Information.* New York: Oxford University Press, 2000.

Dehning, B., V. Richardson, and R. Zmud. "The Value Relevance of Announcements of Transformational Information Technology Investments." *MIS Quarterly* 27, no. 4 (December 2003): 637–656.

Duliba, K., R. Kauffman, and H. C. Lucas, Jr. "Appropriating Value from CRS Ownership in the Airline Industry." *Organization Science* 12, no. 6 (November–December 2001): 702–728.

Kashan, R., R. Agarwal, S. Johnson, and H. C. Lucas, Jr. "Technological Discontinuities: The Transformation of EarthColor." Robert H. Smith School of Business Working Paper, 2004.

Romanelli, E., and M. Tushman. "Organizational Transformation as Punctuated Equilibrium: An Empirical Test." *Academy of Management Journal* 37, no. 5 (October 1994): 1141–1166.

Tushman, M., and P. Anderson. "Technological Discontinuities and Organizational Environments." *Administrative Science Quarterly* 31, no. 3 (September 1986): 439–465.

PART II

Evidence for Transformations

——— 3 ———

Transforming Everyday Events

The evidence for transformations should be visible in everyday activities. This chapter looks at changes that are here now, or that we will encounter in the near future. Some of these changes are a sharp jolt, a major discontinuity in the way people live. But most of the changes are so gradual that we may not notice them. Comparing the "before" and "after" leads to the conclusion that we have experienced a major transformation.

HEY DUDE, WHERE'S MY OFFICE?

An executive who has been promoted usually gets a bigger, better office with the promotion. When someone makes it to the level of the CEO, he or she should have the best office in the place—unless you happen to be CEO of Accenture, the global technology consulting firm. Bill Green, Accenture's CEO, does not have the best office in the company. In fact, he does not have an office at all! Accenture is a virtual company.

Accenture has no operating headquarters and lacks formal branches. Bill Green lives in Boston. Accenture's CFO lives in Silicon Valley and the chief technologist's home base is Germany. The head of HR is located in Chicago. The 129,000 consultants (with growth of 40,000 more expected) who work for the company spend much of their time in client offices, or they avail themselves of leased Accenture offices in over 100 worldwide locations. Accenture has operated this way for 17 years, ever since it split off from the now defunct accounting firm, Arthur Andersen. The partners could not agree on a single location for headquarters, and decided that they would live wherever they wanted to and would meet regularly.

What makes a virtual office possible? Technology is a big help. Accenture employees log on to the company's Web site to record where they are working each day. Employees can access their files, email, and desktop from anyplace in

---

Surviving

This chapter shows how processes are becoming digital, mobile, and virtual, and how products are going digital.

We will see many examples of customer self-service. If you want to gain the benefits of the technology revolution, you have to get comfortable serving yourself on different Web sites. One of the benefits from doing so is that you can set your own schedule for working and leisure. If you wake up at 3 a.m. and want to make a plane reservation or put in a stock trade, you can do so.

We see tremendous advantages accruing to individuals and organizations that can innovate. Unfortunately, we also see those who resist change being left far behind. If people fall behind the changes described in this chapter, they miss opportunities as consumers of goods and services. If you work for a company in one of the industries described here, the consequences of missing the technology revolution are far more serious. The recorded music industry, magazines, and newspapers are experiencing great turmoil. Would things have been different if managers there saw the revolution coming and devised a way to join it?

---

the world. Consultants use Accenture's internal Web site to share files and documents, and the firm uses videoconferencing for meetings. Travel vendors for the company track employee movements so that they can be located if necessary.

Employees of a virtual firm have to make an effort to communicate. Every six weeks, Accenture's 23-member executive leadership team meets in a different city. Mr. Green talks daily with many of his direct reports by phone, and every other Friday he discusses business with the heads of Accenture's five operating groups. There are global phone conversations at 1 p.m. London time, which shares the pain since that time is midnight in Australia, 9 p.m. in Beijing and 5 a.m. in California.

Executives do not rely totally on email and phone calls; when there is a difficult problem, they often travel to handle it face-to-face. When a project is in trouble or there is a downturn in business, managers meet physically with the affected employees. Mr. Green tries to have breakfasts and dinners with Accenture executives who happen to be in the same city as he is that day.

There is a cost to this kind of business, and much of that cost is wear and tear on employees. First, as Green said, you cannot go down the hall to the coffee pot and ask someone about their weekend and follow-up with a business question. In the 12 months prior to an interview with Green in June 2006, he had flown 165,000 miles. Accenture employees are in a constant state of jet lag.

On the positive side, the company saves the overhead of a large headquarters, and consultants spend a lot of time with clients, building relationships. Accenture says that nearly 85 percent of the company's largest clients have been with the firm for 10 years or more. With the constant travel, all levels of Accenture employees mix together. As Green put it, "We get information that we'd never get if we were stuck back at a headquarters" (*Wall Street Journal*, 6/5/2006).

A small consulting company, Point B, decided to start out as a virtual firm so that people could work in the cities where they lived rather than endure the constant travel of the typical consultant. Tim Jenkins is a co-founder of the company. In an August 2007 interview he talked about how they started:

> So our idea was, let's just get rid of the office space. It's just . . . overhead and it doesn't add any value to the client. In 1995, when we started, that was just beginning to get possible. The Internet was becoming ubiquitous, laptops were getting very functional, and Microsoft had released Windows 95, which allowed, kind of, the multi-tasking we really needed . . . on the road. Microsoft also had released some email software that . . . communicates effectively. We also used some telephony software that allowed our folks to be found wherever they were, and we pretty much ran the firm on laptops and without paper, even from 1995.

But you have to make up for the social parts of an office culture:

> I think you don't eliminate offices in order to save money necessarily because you end up having to invest in culture and bringing people together. So the office has one good aspect in that people get together and get to know each other. When you don't have [an] office and your people are spread all around, you have to invest in other ways of getting them together and building those connections. We do a lot more get-togethers in more . . . [of a] semi-formal nature to get people to know each other and to learn from each other. And we make quite a bit [of] investment there, probably more than we would've spent on [an] office base. But as a result, we created a great network within the firm even though most people don't see each other day to day, even week to week. And even when we have multiple associates at one client, they may not see each other because they're spread throughout the client's organization.

Jenkins talked about one challenge, sharing knowledge in the firm:

> We created a system whereby any associate can essentially query either the subset of the firm or the entire firm, and then both the query and all the responses to it are captured for posterity and they're searchable. So, one, the associates get immediate responses to their queries from the experts within the firm, and then two, the data about who had that information is captured. So in the future people can do a quick search and go directly to those people as opposed to having to bother the firm with a query. We call it our knowledge exchange, and it's worked quite well for us for the last few years.

Accenture and Point B are not alone. Companies have large, globally dispersed workforces and they want to bring talent and skills together from around the world to solve problems. In one instance IBM needed to quickly develop a pilot product for a Korean bank after a competitor entered the picture. The contract could be worth up to $100 million. A manager in Palo Alto, Willy Chiu, answered an alert from the head of Asian operations for IBM in Tokyo. He responded by opening up chats with 18 colleagues on his laptop. IBM's country manager in Seoul volunteered to take the lead in mobilizing resources. Chiu asked a team in Beijing to free up staff to work on the project, and received notice that they would be made available. A banking expert from England offered to provide references from a similar project in Spain (*BusinessWeek*, 8/20 & 27/ 2007).

One way to be virtual and reduce travel is through video-conferencing systems. The newest devices now create a "telepresence" using broadcast quality cameras and rows of 50-inch plasma screens; they can cost up to $500,000 each (*Wall Street Journal*, 9/28/2006). (For those with a smaller budget, high-definition video conferencing systems are available for a fraction of the price.) This technology makes it possible to have conferences in which it appears that all participants are almost in the same physical location, and it can drastically reduce travel and increase the number of spontaneous meetings.

The virtual firm has been around for at least 20 years, and it is becoming more prevalent with globalization and the movement of jobs around the world. The head of development for the new Boeing 787 Dreamliner has to manage 100 suppliers with thousands of employees at 100 sites in different countries. The vice president of customer support for EarthLink has a home base in Atlanta, but oversees employees at call centers in India, the Philippines, Canada, and other countries. Communications technology has enabled a new form of organization that is dramatically different from traditional structures for managers and employees (*Wall Street Journal*, 6/5/2006).

Russell Wilcox, head of E-Ink gives his vision for how organizations are changing:

> Maybe in the last decade you want to push decision making closer to the field because the people in the field have all the information and the executive doesn't, so you want them to make the decision. What's happening as this gets more complicated is that nobody has the information, and so it's not the executive at all. What you want is the person in the field to not only have the ability to make the decision, but also have the ability to get all the information they don't have. Nowadays, you don't need to know as much because you can instantly get it, and you can find out in five minutes through the Internet a summary on any topic. So, use information technology to put information access in the field. So not only is the decision made there, but all the relevant information is instantly available there . . . then let the person in the field figure out what information they need. Make it easy for them to learn instantly and then they can make a more effective decision. Not just at the executive level but all throughout the organization.

These kinds of technologies have profound implications for the nature of work, for both the employee and the manager. Employees take more initiative and operate with more autonomy than in the classical hierarchical organization. Managers have to create an environment for collaboration and provide resources to the staff. Managers operate by influencing others more than by issuing orders and directives. Are we preparing students to work in this kind of environment when they enter the workforce?

MORE OR LESS FRIENDLY SKIES?

In the 1950s flying was an expensive exclusive way to travel, though slow by today's standards. There were far fewer flights than today, and planes could hold a smaller number of passengers than a modern jet. What happened when a passenger named Mary made a reservation circa 1955?

Mary arrives at a downtown ticket office in her home city, Chicago. There she asks about flights to Washington, D.C. A reservations agent for the airline looks at a schedule and gives her the information about what flight the agent's airline has. To find out about other airlines, she might ask this agent, or better yet, she could phone other airlines or go to a travel agent. Mary selects a flight, and the agent calls the airline's reservations center to request a reservation.

At the reservations center there is a manual system for keeping track of reservations and flights. It must have looked something like the following: Flights were posted around the room, and clerks made hash marks to indicate that a seat had been sold. *There was no record of the passenger's name. Proof that you should be on the flight was the fact that you had a ticket with that flight and date on it.*

The reservations center responded that there was a seat available, and the agent sold the seat to Mary, writing out a ticket by hand for her. Mary in turn wrote a personal check to the airline. The day of the flight Mary went to the airport in Chicago and presented her ticket, and the agent let her through to board the aircraft.

Given the volume of air traffic, this system worked pretty well though it would have been easy for a plane to be oversold if a clerk forgot to write down a reservation or if he or she put the hash mark on the wrong flight. One of the major drawbacks with this system is the difficulty of expanding the process to handle more flights and larger airplanes. And of course, this expansion is exactly what was needed when jet planes began to replace propeller aircraft. The major airlines first developed computerized reservations systems (CRS) in the 1960s to solve the problem of booking flights as they converted to jet fleets.

Thinking about the framework for IT-enabled transformation, the technology applied in the airline industry is both competence-enhancing and competence-destroying. It has enhanced the competence of airlines and their employees at the expense of the travel agent. This technology has also created changes in the daily lives of travelers.

In the 1970s, several airlines, led by United and American, diffused CRS technology to travel agents. At one point the agents were booking some 80 percent of all flights and were receiving commissions from the airlines for this service. This technology was competence-enhancing; it streamlined work processes and leveraged the ability of travel agents to do business.

In the 1990s, the Internet presented entrepreneurs with a low-cost network with the ability to reach a substantial number of travelers. The response was the creation of a number of Web travel services that used the airlines' CRSs to search for the best prices and/or schedules for their customers. Soon the airlines developed their own sites to reduce their ticketing costs, especially the fees paid to the CRS vendors. Discount airlines who do not list with the CRS vendors also rely upon the Web; some 57 percent of Southwest's ticket revenues come from the Internet.

What has been the impact on the travel agent? Due to the post-9/11 depression in the industry, airlines stopped paying commissions to travel agents. The agents have been forced to implement fees, so the cost of their service is obvious to the traveler. The individual travel agent has been unable to develop systems comparable to those on the Web; it does not have the capital or technology skills to compete. (Some of the large chains like Rosenbluth have been able to invest in IT to remain competitive.[1]) The discount airlines have effectively disintermediated the travel agent and the CRSs by refusing to pay to list their flights on the systems the agents use for making reservations.

What are the changes for individual travelers? If Mary wants to make a trip from Chicago to Washington D.C. today, the process is entirely different. First Mary looks at Travelocity on the Web and enters the city pair for travel along with her preferred dates. Travelocity will either search for the lowest fare or search by schedule so that Mary can choose the times of her flights. Mary sees that United flies this route, and she brings up another copy of her browser to see if United's own Web site has any special fares.

Seeing that it does, Mary books her flight using a credit card to pay for the tickets. At this point she has an electronic or e-ticket. The only record is on the reservations computer and a confirming email message that Mary has saved. The night before she is to leave, Mary logs back onto the United site and prints a boarding pass. The next morning at the airport, she takes her carry-on bag directly to the security line and shows her preprinted boarding pass to go through the line. As the plane boards at the gate, the United gate agent scans the bar code on her boarding pass so that the airline can confirm that passengers have boarded the plane.

Compared to the 1950s, today's process for making a reservation and boarding the aircraft is totally different, as is the technology that is behind today's procedures. Are these changes really a transformation? Are they competence enhancing for the passenger? For the airline there is no question that the technology has been transformational. The airlines cannot operate without their reservations systems, especially with the security requirements of modern air travel. Technology keeps an accurate record of each passenger's name on a flight and any special requirements for that passenger. Other systems plan the route of the plane and report its progress back to the airline.

Using the database of the reservations system, the airlines practice yield management. An analyst looks at the historical pattern of ticket sales for a flight and compares it with the same flight that is scheduled in the future. The analyst's job is to try and maximize the revenue from a flight, which is accomplished by changing the number of seats available in different fare categories. If a flight has low bookings compared to its historical record, the analyst might increase the number of discount fares on that flight.

Are today's passengers better off from the airlines' application of technology? Mary has more choices in making a reservation and can easily obtain information about all of the airlines that serve a particular route. She can search for the best price, or at least a low price, on different Web sites. With carry-on luggage she can avoid the long lines at check in, or with her e-ticket she can go to special kiosks to check luggage. If she is unable to print a boarding pass in advance, the e-ticket kiosk will print one for her once she enters a credit card to provide identifying information. I find that this process takes more time than calling a travel agent, but it is nice to be in control when making a reservation, and I can do all of this 24 hours a day, seven days a week.

The airlines have done a great job of promoting customer self-service. We now are all travel and ticket agents, and the airlines are saving a great deal of money as a result. (If you want to talk to a reservations agent or you want a paper ticket, you are likely to have a surcharge to cover the labor and materials.)

SHOP UNTIL YOU DROP

If someone is looking for a contrast between physical and electronic processes for achieving the same end, look no farther than retailing and electronic commerce. E-commerce is a little over a decade old, and as Figure 3.1 from the U.S. Department of Commerce shows, it represents a very small part of total retailing in the United States. For the first quarter of 2007 total retail sales were estimated to be $999.5 billion, while e-commerce sales were $31.5 billion, or 3 percent of the total. So why should anyone get excited about e-commerce? The answer is in the trend and the growing appeal of this way of shopping.

Every reader is familiar with the physical process of shopping. You go to a store, maybe a mall with many stores, and look for the product that you want to buy. If the buyer wants a product that is likely to be in stock, he or she just shows up at the store. If there is some doubt about the item being there, the buyer might call a series of stores until finding one that has the item. Then the buyer gets into the car for a drive to the store; parks; finds the item; if clothing, probably tries it on; makes the purchase; and drives home. Maybe this buyer has multiple items to purchase, and so the scene repeats itself many times that day.

While it is dangerous to simplify and divide the world into two kinds of people, this approach may be justified when it comes to retailing. The world has two types of people: those who love to shop and those who don't. What is the

Figure 3.1

Estimated Quarterly U.S. Retail E-commerce Sales as a Percent of Total Quarterly Retail Sales, 4th Quarter 1999–1st Quarter 2007

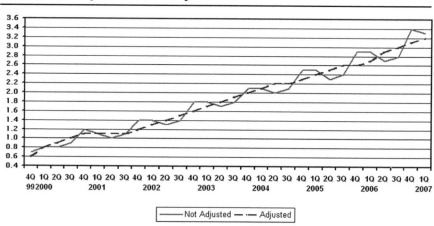

Source: U.S. Department of Commerce.

alternative for the non-shopper and maybe the dedicated shopper who has limited time for the physical process? During the dot-com boom in the 1990s, e-commerce was one of the most exciting business prospects. While the boom ultimately died, the victim of a lot of hype and unsound business models, e-commerce has thankfully survived.

The electronic counterpart of physical shopping is a totally different process. The buyer goes directly to the Web site of a merchant he or she wants to visit, or the buyer might use a comparison shopping agent to find the lowest price on a desired product. If it is clothing, there are size guides to help choose the appropriate size. Some sites let the customer see how the item looks on a model with the customer's measurements. When the customer finds the desired item, it goes into an electronic shopping basket. When finished, there is an electronic checkout where the buyer reviews all of the items in the basket and pays with a credit card. The merchant ships the products to the customer by the customer's choice of carriers.

Is online shopping the same experience? Not at all. First, the physical shopper will probably not visit multiple stores looking for the best price. An online shopper can, in a short time, look at a number of merchants online to find the best price. The online shopper also spends far less time because the physical visit to the store is eliminated. Is the buyer getting the same goods online as in the store? Here the answer is a surprising "no." Why not? The items being purchased are the same, but the shopper in the physical store has immediate use of her purchases and gratification from that. The online shopper has to wait for delivery and must delay gratification. (Of course, if you are in a big hurry, most online merchants will ship overnight at a significant additional cost.)

There are a couple of points worth noting with this example. First, e-commerce is a small part of overall retail sales in the United States. This is an example of a transformation that is occurring slowly, and one which will probably never be 100 percent. There will still be physical stores in the future, but online shopping has been growing and is going to continue to grow in the future. Second, e-commerce presents a real dilemma for the traditional merchant with physical stores. What if the electronic sales cut into store sales, eventually forcing the merchant to close those stores? The experience to date suggests that online sales expand the total sales of the enterprise, but this kind of cannibalization is something to watch. The other side of the dilemma is that the merchant's customers expect to be able to shop online, so there may be no choice. Here is an example where it does not make sense to resist the trend; e-commerce is here to stay.

COULD YOU PLEASE TURN THAT DOWN?

Shawn Fanning wanted to share music with his friends, so he wrote a file sharing program named Napster for the Internet and released it on June 1, 1999 to about 30 friends. Within days 10,000–15,000 people downloaded the program, and by the end of the year there had been a million downloads. By the fall of 2002 there were 32 million users and growth was one million a week. Growth peaked in February of 2000 at more than 80 million users, and 1.5 million logged on at one time. There were 2.5 billion songs per month downloaded before a court shut down the service based on a suit by the Recording Industry Association of America (Moon and Herman, 2002). Universities had to prohibit the use of Napster because it was consuming all of their network capacity.

Napster employed a server, a computer that kept track of what songs were available for sharing on Napster users' computers. The court found that this index encouraged the infringement of copyrights on recorded music. However, by the time Napster closed for business, other file sharing programs were available that did not employ an index. Instead, a user wanting a particular song sends a request over the network to all computers logged on with the program running. The first one responding is the source of the download for the requested song.

Several of our revolutionary rules apply here. First, what Napster did was to make possible an unbundling of the music album. Listeners complained that they only wanted one or two songs on an album, but were forced to buy a CD for $15 or more with the songs they wanted and many that they did not care to hear. Napster made it possible to order music by the song, and, of course, it was free. The Internet facilitates unbundling, especially for digital goods like music.

Did Napster have an impact? The sales of CDs have been falling, though it is hard to assign causality. Some of my students argue that the quality of the music released is mainly to blame (see Figure 3.2). Album sales are 30 percent below their levels when Napster appeared, and ten times as many songs are

Figure 3.2
CD Sales and Legal Downloads

CD Sales

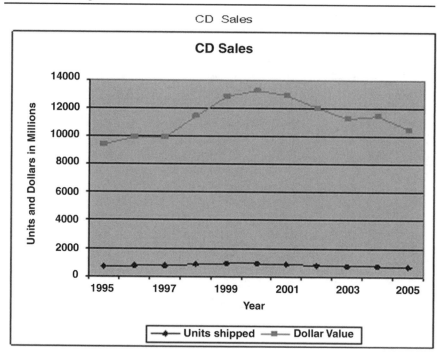

Digital Downloads

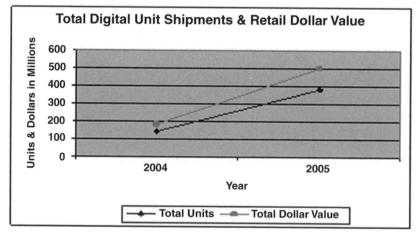

Source: Recording Industry Association of America.

downloaded from file sharing services as are bought from legal sites like iTunes (*New York Times,* 11/28/2005). The Recording Industry Association of America (RIAA) claims that recording companies are losing $4.2 billion per year due to music piracy (*Technology Review,* May/June 2006).

One of our rules says that it is not wise to resist the march of technology; transformations are going to happen. The RIAA did not follow this rule. Instead, it brought suit against the file sharing services and eventually against users of those services. It issued subpoenas to Internet service providers to try and determine who was using the file sharing software and then sued the individuals. Of course, their research on users was not always accurate, and the RIAA filed a suit against an elderly woman in New England who did not have a computer and had never heard of Napster. All told, the RIAA has launched more than 28,000 suits since 2003 (*Technology Review,* May/June 2006).

I am not sure what my colleagues in marketing teach, but my guess is that they do not recommend threatening and suing your customers. In line with the rules in Chapter 2, what might the recording industry have done differently? First, they might have seen that the Internet was a natural vehicle for distributing digital content, and that music had made the transition from analog medium to digital when CDs first appeared. A little market research would have revealed that a large number of their customers wanted to buy single songs rather than entire albums, and that a lot of their customers were college students with high-speed Internet connections in their dorm rooms. If executives in the industry had thought long and hard about these facts and tried to forecast what might happen in the future, they might have reached a reasonable conclusion that a lot of music, maybe all of it, would be delivered on demand over the Internet in the not-too-distant future. At that point, the appropriate action would have been to buy Napster and set it up as a legal download site, charging a modest amount for buying music by the song.

The last rule that applies here is that the spoils go to the innovator. While Fanning and Napster are back as a legal service, the real innovator since file sharing software is Apple. A number of legal services started for downloading during Napster's day, but they were reportedly difficult to use, and more importantly, they did not have access to all the recording studios' music. Each site had permission to distribute music from a group of different recording companies, so the user might have to visit multiple sites and have multiple monthly memberships to download the music he or she wanted. Many people did not bother and continued to use the successors to Napster to share music.

Apple and Steve Jobs saw a great opportunity, and they designed the innovative iPod, a product that has experienced phenomenal success. To go along with the iPod hardware, Apple started iTunes, a site where users can find almost any music they want and can download it for $.99 a song. There is still a lot of sharing going on, but there is now an easy-to-use alternative in the shape of iTunes and an iPod, and Apple continues to innovate with new versions of the iPod coming out on a regular basis. There are also complementary products so that you can use your iPod with large speakers as a home stereo system, and several automakers provide connections to their car audio systems for an iPod. iTunes downloaded its one billionth song in February 2006. Apple has sold over 100 million iPods in total through the first quarter of 2007 (www.apple.com). Apple claims a 76 percent market share in the United States for the iPod, the sale of 1.5 billion songs, and 88 percent of the U.S. legal music download market from iTunes (*Wall Street Journal,* 10/4/2006).

The recorded music business has gradually (and grudgingly) come to the conclusion that it needs a new business model. At first it treated the Internet as a competence-destroying change. Today, the industry is trying to take advantage of the Internet and turn it into a competence-enhancing innovation. EMI Music has announced plans to back a new record label that abandons the industry's traditional royalty payment to become more "artist-friendly." Instead of paying artists to produce music and then taking the profits from the CDs, the company will split profits with artists (Knowledge@Wharton, 7/26/2006). The industry has begun to realize that the barriers to entry for producing recorded music are suddenly much lower with digital technology.

The recorded music industry is also seeing that it can take advantage of multiple channels. Why not sell music on the Internet as well as on CDs, especially if you can collect fees for downloads? Some experts think that the future is music by subscription where listeners will have music streamed to portable devices over the Internet. As wireless Internet access becomes more freely available, this model may take off (Knowledge@Wharton, 7/26/2006). If so, the recording companies want to be the ones selling the subscriptions!

WAKE UP, RADIO

The music industry wasn't the only business caught napping by Napster and other channels for online music. Radio has been facing its own crisis with the amount of time people tune into the radio during the week having fallen by 14 percent in the last decade. Clear Channel Communications, one of the largest operators, and CBS are both talking about selling off some of their stations. Walt Disney got out of the radio business entirely in the summer of 2006.

Critics of the radio industry observe that it has come to the realization it needs an online strategy very late in the game. Digital radio revenues are growing fast, but they only represented $87 million of total industry revenues of $20 billion in 2005. The competition is not just from the Internet, but XM and Sirius satellite radio have attracted some 11 million subscribers, and most auto makers offer one of these radios as an option in their new cars.

What kind of new business models is the radio industry offering? Clear Channel has an agreement with BMW to provide real-time free traffic updates for the navigation systems in the maker's new cars. It will also send radio signals to AT&T wireless phone users, providing both streaming and on-demand content. CBS is streaming more than 70 of its stations live and has started

KYOURadio.com for listeners to contribute their own Podcasts (*New York Times,* 9/15/2006). Anyone selling digital content had better develop a strategy for the Internet very quickly.

ON THE WISDOM OF INVESTING IN A VIDEO STORE

The people who have video content, Hollywood, TV networks, cable companies, satellite TV services, and even amateurs have watched what has happened to the music industry with great interest. It appears that most of these individuals have come to the conclusion that Rule 1, every process will become digital, mobile, and virtual, applies to them. One thing is clear: consumers want to choose what content to watch, and they want to decide on the video device, the time, and the place of viewing. The question is how to respond.

What has saved video content providers up until now? Video has not experienced the same trials and tribulations as music yet because of limits on current technology and the fact that no one is sure what the winning technology and business model for video will be. It is also not clear what kind of content users want and what devices they want to use for viewing it.

On the technology side, video content has a lot more bits than music, so that it is feasible to download a movie only if the user has a high speed or broadband line. At the time of Napster's rise, not very many people had broadband at home. While you might listen to music at work where you have a high-speed connection, you probably would have trouble watching a movie at work. Even with a broadband line, a full-length movie takes a while to download unless you use a program like Bittorrent that downloads in parallel from multiple copies of a video file on different computers. Finally, most homes have a television in one room and a computer in another, and the two are not connected. You could watch a downloaded video on the PC or burn it to a DVD and play it on your DVD player/TV. Apple released a product in 2007 that allows the wireless transmission of a movie from a PC to a TV set, and other approaches to an Internet connection to a TV set are being developed.

The first on-demand views came courtesy of the video store. In the beginning, Hollywood fought videotape players arguing that they would lead to rampant copyright violations. It turns out now that the studios make more money from DVD sales than from the box office, reinforcing our rule that resisting technological transformations is unwise. Today, on-demand refers to a service from a cable or satellite TV provider in which the viewer can order specific movies for immediate or delayed viewing. TiVo made it possible for consumers to shift the time of viewing (and eliminate commercials) by recording shows as broadcast and storing them for future viewing. This technology proved so popular that all of the cable providers now rent digital video recorders (DVR) that provide the same functions as TiVo. A device called a SlingBox enables a viewer in a remote location like a hotel room to access shows at a home location using a PC and the Internet. TiVo and DVRs allow time shifting for viewing while the SlingBox provides place-shifting.

The discussion above has focused on movies, but there is a wide variety of possible video content available. There are TV shows, news clips, home videos, commercials, infomercials, and content that a producer might create for a specific device like a video iPod. On the device side there is the conventional television monitor, a computer and its monitor, a portable device like a PDA or iPod, or even a cell phone. There is a lot of experience with full length movies playing on a TV monitor as well as with movies on a PC. It is not clear what kind of content is most appropriate for PDAs and cell phones, but it will probably be much shorter than a half-hour TV show or full-length movie.

MTV is experimenting with what kind of content to make available on a cell phone screen for the 18-year-old viewer. The MTV network has a over a billion dollars in ad revenue each year and is a highly recognized brand. A new executive vice president for multiplatform production, news and music is trying to figure out what kind of content to produce for laptops, PDAs, iPods and game players. There is an expectation that in the future people will no longer watch scheduled shows on channels, and that mobile TV could be a $27 billion market by 2010 (*New York Times Magazine*, 5/28/2006).

Other content providers are experimenting now with new approaches to providing their products. The major TV networks are distributing shows through iTunes shortly after they have aired on affiliated stations. CBS is offering rentals of "Survivor" for $.99 and wants to make its shows available on as many different platforms as possible, including cell phones. NBC is thinking about producing original content specifically for the Internet.

In the fall of 2006, Apple and Amazon.com announced plans to offer movie downloads on their sites. Consumers can buy or rent videos over the Internet instead of going to the video store in person, or waiting for a DVD to arrive in the mail from a subscription service. Amazon has all of the major movie studies lined up to provide content except for Walt Disney, which is going with Apple. While there are some disputes on prices, the cost to the studio of having a movie downloaded is a lot less than the cost of selling a packaged DVD; for one thing, there is no packaging and no need for a DVD.

For whom will this technology be competence-enhancing or competence-destroying? This transformation in video content is potentially competence-enhancing for the creators of content; they will have a greater variety of distribution channels and the opportunity to develop a group of new products. Traditional businesses like video stores will have to find a way to offer their content online; it is difficult to understand why people would drive to a video store if they could download a movie from home. A service like Netflix also has to be concerned; even though its product comes to a subscriber's home, the time between ordering and receiving the video is much longer than a digital download takes. Netflix will most certainly be in the downloading business early on. Last but not least is Wal-Mart, which accounts for about 40 percent of the $17 billion of annual DVD sales. Downloaded movies could prove competence-destroying for this part of Wal-Mart's business. Wal-Mart is asking the studios for lower

DVD prices so that it can be competitive with downloads at Apple and Amazon (*Business Week*, 9/11/2006). Of course, there is nothing that prevents Wal-Mart from entering the online download business to compete with other sites.

And if you are not happy with professionally produced videos, there is always YouTube. Visitors to this site post and watch home videos, a new business enabled by the Internet. In less than two years the site has grown to the point of providing 100 million daily videos (*Business Week*, 9/18/2006). As of this writing, Google, the owner of the site, is trying to figure out how to make money from this success, with the most likely outcome being some kind of advertising model.

The interest is there, the key players are aware that there is a transformation going on, and now the challenge is to figure out business models that will work in this new environment. *Every process will become digital, mobile, and virtual.* For the consumer, the benefits of the transformation are already being felt: more choice, more variety, and greater flexibility in buying and viewing video content.

COULD I BORROW YOUR PAPER WHEN YOU'RE DONE?

Newspapers have been around for hundreds of years. The United States views the press as a vital component of democracy, informing citizens of the news and offering a counter view to those in power. But newspapers are in a state of upheaval because of multiple threats from IT-enabled technology, especially the Internet. Papers are losing subscribers and their circulation is falling, reducing revenues. At the same time, they are losing advertising to Internet businesses, further reducing revenue. The end result is that newspapers are cutting back on employees and reducing the amount of content they publish.

The irony is that many newspapers are quite profitable, with an average margin of 20 percent, higher than pharmaceutical companies. Yet their stock prices are falling, and investor discontent led to the sale of Knight Ridder in 2006. Confusion over technology was one of the reasons that the *Wall Street Journal* finally agreed to be acquired by Rupert Murdoch's News Corporation. Newspaper stocks are declining because analysts and investors do not see opportunities for growth or even for maintaining the status quo. Most people seem to think that conditions will become worse in the industry and that a solution to the industry's problems is not in sight. A few prominent papers are losing a lot of money. For example, the *San Francisco Chronicle* lost $330 million between 2000 and 2006, over $1 million a week. The *Pittsburgh Post-Gazette* lost $20 million in 2006 (*BusinessWeek*, 7/23/2007). Are these papers the trend-setters?

Why are papers losing circulation? The decline has been between 2 percent and 3 percent a year, and paid circulation has dropped from about 30 percent of revenue in the 1980s to 20 percent in 2005. One reason for these problems is that newspapers have tended to have a monopoly in their markets. Many newspapers started or bought television stations when this technology appeared in order to control their local markets. The business model was to build a huge audience and sell ads with fees based on circulation numbers and to capture any advertising that went to television via their TV properties. Today newspapers face a variety of competitors with a strategy that does not seem to be working any more.

There are many sources of news. Cable news and news Web sites have up-to-the-minute reports that are more recent than a printed newspaper can hope to provide. The Internet is providing free access to news, thus disintermediating newspapers, which charge for content while standing between the news and those who consume the news. Young workers listen to music on their iPods instead of reading newspapers on the morning commute to work. Newspapers have Web sites, but only a few have had any success in charging for access. The reader who looks at the news on a Web site is not necessarily going to buy the paper either.

Where has the advertising gone? Placing an ad in a newspaper or on TV is using a blunt instrument. A lot of people see the ad, but most of them are probably not at all interested in the product. They are a captive audience, but not a targeted audience. Ford Motor Company wants to advertise to a person who is thinking about buying a car, not to thousands of people who will not buy a car for the next two or three years. If a person browsing the Web enters the name of a car, or "automobile," or goes to a car "infomediary" like Edmunds.com, Ford would like to send that person a message. The person viewing the ad has self-selected and demonstrated a potential interest in its product. In addition, companies using paid search only pay if the visitor to the site clicks on their ad. So a percentage of general product advertising that might have been placed in a newspaper has migrated to the Web, especially to search engines like Google. Internet advertising has grown to a $17 billion industry, nearly 6 percent of the $285 billion spent in the United States on advertising in 2006 (*Wall Street Journal*, 5/25/2007).

While we are on the subject of cars, local newspapers have always had a thriving business in advertisements for used cars. I mistakenly thought that the used car market would always be local; the buyer wants to see the car and kick the tires. eBay proved that idea wrong; observing a lot of cars being sold on eBay, the company set up a separate auction site called eBay Motors. In doing so, it created a national used car market. Buyers will bid on cars and travel to bring them home or pay to have them shipped home. eBay facilitates buyer trust in a number of ways, particularly through seller feedback so that a buyer can see if a seller has good ratings from past buyers. The majority of sellers on eBay are auto dealers who want to sell on a continuing basis; they are very concerned with their feedback scores. The Web is a much richer medium for advertising a car for sale than a newspaper. Auto listings on eBay, for example, usually include many photographs of the cars and lengthy descriptions of the vehicle. The site often has "car fax" data which shows the history of ownership and repairs. eBay Motors is a Web business that is siphoning revenue from the local newspaper.

Another source of lucrative revenues for newspapers is help-wanted ads from companies seeking to hire staff. Craigslist and Monster have been eating away at this revenue stream as well. Ads on these sites can be accessed worldwide, and they are more economical to run than print ads in several newspapers would be. In 2000, the *San Jose Mercury News* had $118 million in help-wanted ads; by 2005 this number had dropped to $18 million as high tech companies in Silicon Valley saved money by turning to the two Web sites mentioned above, among others, for advertising. In February of 2007, ad revenues continued to show declines compared with the same month a year earlier. *USA Today* experienced a 14 percent decline, while the *New York Times* had a 7.5 percent drop, and the *Wall Street Journal* went down 10 percent (*New York Times,* 3/26/2007). In the first quarter of 2007, revenue for every major ad category was down, with the sharpest drop for classified ads (which may have been due to economic woes in real estate as much as to the Web) (*Wall Street Journal,* 7/18/2007). The Internet combined with economic conditions is severely impacting the printed news business.

Jim Buckmaster, CEO of Craigslist, said in an August 2007 interview that he thinks many of their ads would not have appeared in newspapers:

> Most probably, 90 percent or more of classified ads on Craigslist never would've seen the light of day in print because print classifieds are too expensive for many other things that people use Craigslist for. It's been very empowering for people … just the fact that there are 25 million classified ads being posted on our site every month. Probably 99 percent of those wouldn't have been posted, but once you drop the cost to zero, people start using it for all kinds of things.

It is not clear that newspapers would agree that ads on Craigslist would not have appeared in their pages, since they have seen their classified ad revenue shrink dramatically.

What's a newspaper to do given the extent of disruptive technology it faces? The answer is not at all clear. Some suggest that newspapers should focus more on local news, since the Web tends to pay less attention to local matters. This model has been successful for the *Annapolis Capital,* which has moved local news to the first page and national and international news to interior pages. Other experts suggest that newspapers offer more feature articles and less hard news. A model for engaging readers and keeping them as loyal readers and subscribers is not readily apparent (*Knowledge@Wharton,* 3/27/2006).

Some analysts have suggested that Rupert Murdoch's interest in purchasing the *Wall Street Journal* was part of a vision of a digital future for delivering the news. In this scenario, video will be a bigger component of the news, and it will stream across a variety of fixed and mobile display devices. Murdoch can tie together his Fox News in the U.S. and Sky News outlets around the world, the online *Wall Street Journal,* and a business TV channel he is planning to launch (*New York Times* 5/13/2007).

The technology has turned everyone into a potential author and publisher. David Berlind of ZDNet commented:

The media business as a whole has had to embrace a lot of the newer technology just to survive in this world. It's been the equivalent of dealing with a society of people where they've each been handed their own printing press and each becomes a source of information. When the blogosphere came along earlier this decade, that's when people were really empowered with great publishing tools, really the equivalent of a printing press—and that's when we suddenly found that our audience members could easily change the channel, and we were going to have to really embrace this technology and use it to our fullest benefit, moving forward to stay relevant with those audience members. Part of that has been the willingness to use the social technologies to also engage them in a dialogue. In other words, it's not just about broadcasting anymore. It's about conversation . . . and we have been very successful, in terms of embracing social networks and platforms and actually using them, in getting our content out.

This experience suggests to the newspaper industry that it think about the entire media experience and how to build an online community of readers and potential contributors.

Another strategy for the newspaper industry lies with "e-ink" and e-readers—lightweight devices with clear display screens and long battery life. The idea is that the newspaper could be continuously updated during the day and pushed to your mobile reading device. "Bluntly put, there's not much future for the once-a-day distribution of highly perishable information, printed with ink on thin sheets of expensive, chemically treated wood pulp" (*IEEE Spectrum,* February 2007). Would you carry an e-ink device in your purse or briefcase; would you use it on a train or plane to get the news?

We talked to the head of E-Ink, a Cambridge company that has the lead in creating a paper substitute that has electronic ink. The page can be erased and rewritten instantly creating a portable newspaper or document of almost any kind. The process works on thin plastic so you can envision having a real electronic, one-page newspaper that contains the same content as today's multipage paper. Russell Wilcox describes the future:

> There are products, like the Sony Reader, which are electronic book products. The screens are only . . . about as big as a paperback. But you can receive news RSS feeds, internet, fresh news coming to your device, and more and more devices like that are going to hit the market. By next year you'll see larger screens, and I hope by the year after you'll actually see screens 12" and above diagonal, about the size of your laptop. [It] is flexible—there's no glass—so you can . . . carry something so large the same way you'd carry a manila folder and be able at any moment to pull out a big surface for reading. You could ask what's the difference between an electronic book and an electronic newspaper, and I do think the size is what's important. [The format of a newspaper] is effective is because it's a panorama of news. So you're scouting what's out there, and you see a headline that attracts your eye, and you dive in and you read. So the larger we can make this display, the more like reading a real newspaper it will become. To get things very large, we want to move away from traditional glass displays to plastic displays, and E-Ink is the leading

technology in making displays out of plastic that you could drop or even roll like a pencil.

On the future of newspapers, Wilcox opines:

> The business premise behind a newspaper is, "I'm going to give you information of the day and alongside I can sell you ads." The reason the Internet has just wiped out the market capitalization of newspapers—Google is worth all the newspapers put together many times that—is because their business premise is much more powerful: "I'm not going to just give you the news of the day, but I'm going to give you all human information and alongside that I'm selling you ads." That's why Google is so much more powerful. That's why the newspaper of the future is going to be just the news of the day if you're a news organization, or it's going to be some packaging of all human information or some mix of that.

The newspaper story is one of competence-destroying change. The industry by and large has not been able to develop an effective strategy to deal with this disruptive technology. Our two rules—that processes become digital, mobile, and virtual, and products that can become digital, will—apply forcefully here. Newspapers are one bundle, and both consumers and advertisers are forcing unbundling as they turn to specialized sites for finding used cars and jobs and as they look for specific kinds of information.

WHAT ABOUT YOUR PERSONAL LIFE?

Have you every forgotten something and struggled to bring back a memory? Technology is very good at storing data, and that data can be words, pictures, sounds, or video content. A project at Microsoft Research called MyLifeBits is creating a digital chronicle of Gordon Bell's life. (Bell is one of the researchers and also is a computer pioneer, having designed the very successful VAX computer system for DEC.) When the project says "everything," it is not exaggerating. Bell wears a camera around his neck to make a record of what he sees during the day; the system allows him to re-live an event with sounds and images. Every word one has read, whether on a Web site, in an email, or an electronic document, can be recalled through a few keystrokes. For Bell, the system records all the photographs he takes, his conversations, each Web site visited, every email sent and received, and so on. A co-worker at Microsoft, Jim Gemmell, estimates that Bell has something like 50,000 photos and 80,000 Web pages that he has recorded, along with hundreds of thousands of emails, documents, and so on. A $600 disk drive can today hold a terrabyte (one trillion bytes) of data, which can store everything that an individual reads, all the music he or she listens to, and eight hours of speech and ten pictures a day for sixty years. As the technology progresses, in ten years he or she will be able to carry that same mount of information on a flash memory chip in a cell phone (*Scientific American,* March 2007).

As new technology appears, hundreds of uses appear for it, including birders and batters. The Colorado Rockies baseball players have iPods in the dugout, but they are not just for music. A player can download a clip of how he performed against the opposing team's pitcher the last time at bat. He can study his prior performance for clues on how to get a hit his next time at bat. It used to be that birdwatchers used binoculars and a notebook. The technologically enabled birder goes into the field today with a digital camera, a Palm device with a bird-species database, and an iPod containing bird songs. The U.S. government estimates that 46 million Americans observed, fed, or photographed birds in 2001, spending $6 billion in the process. One birder, spotting a rare find, sent text messages to colleagues using his Blackberry; a half dozen showed up in time to see the bird (*Wall Street Journal*, 2/26/2007).

LIVING IN A VIRTUAL WORLD

Second Life is a three-dimensional virtual world in which some three million participants assume roles, with each person being represented by an avatar. An avatar can be an accurate representation of a user's personality or a complete fantasy. The avatars can walk, run, and fly. Participants own property, build houses, start businesses, and buy and sell products and services. The system operates like a massive multiplayer game with no script; the avatars interact with each other in whatever way they choose.

Companies are establishing a presence on Second Life to help understand what customers really want. For example, a clothing manufacturer can have customers design a pair of jeans. Cisco is using Second Life with executive briefings and technical support on a virtual campus; the company views this effort as another way to reach customers. A number of people have started businesses at the site using Linden dollars (Linden Labs developed Second Life). They offer real-estate and retail products among others that create a virtual economy in Second Life. There is a conversion rate from Linden to U.S. dollars, so it is possible to earn money on Second Life. Second Life is not small; between 10,000 and 30,000 avatars are in the virtual world at a time, but the site is sparsely populated as of yet (*Information Week*, 2/24/2007).

Electric Sheep is a company that builds applications in virtual worlds like Second Life. Its CEO, Sibley Verbeck, talked about the nature of virtual worlds in an interview:

> Virtual worlds are ... the first communication medium that allows anyone in the world to feel like they're in a place together and to interact with that place, co-operatively, competitively, or just meeting each other. It is going to radically change how we do business, how we're entertained, the service economy ... by allowing the people who are individuals or small companies, or large companies anywhere in the world, to really interact in the most human way they've ever been able to interact before.

As an example of what you can do in a virtual world, Verbeck goes on:

> You might watch NASCAR through the virtual world, but then you could get in and drive some of the cars, you know, or you could maybe even be in an Indy 500, and you would have your own vehicle that's not there in real life but ... gives you the perspective of being on the track, and we can do these kinds of things. That car might be branded so that your avatar, as you're in it, and that car might all be advertising Pepsi or whatever brand.

As another example, Electric Sheep helped Starwood test the design of a new hotel chain in a virtual world:

> All we had is one artist's rendering, but what we could do was make a hotel that looked like that. In a totally free-form fashion people could walk through it, go into the kitchen, go into the restaurant, go into the rooms and then say, "Oh, this would be a little better" or "It would be a little more user-friendly or might work better if we did it this way," and we just moved things around, dragging these objects around to make the kitchen bigger. There are very important design choices that came out of actually seeing and taking tours of it with all of the parties who've managed hotels, who could look at it from different perspectives, who are not used to necessarily thinking from a architectural or a design point of view. But once you could really live it, through this virtual environment, more like real life than looking at any drawings or seeing any other renderings on a computer, you could have some "aha" moments where you could see things that need to be changed.

Verbeck thinks that e-commerce will move to virtual stores where you can better see the merchandise than you can currently on Web sites.

> I predict that five years from today, we'll see more retail sales to consumers through virtual worlds than on the Web. Virtual worlds can recreate a lot of the real world shopping experience of talking to someone who's there in the store, of going shopping with friends, just to explore, or just browsing, window shopping that may lead to purchasing. There will come a point when you can get an avatar of your dimensions and try on clothing. ... I think five years from now people will be using virtual worlds, both on their high-definition television screen and on their computer, and on their mobile handset, videophone, etc. So in all of these ways it will be used to meet with, communicate with, shop with ... people who are elsewhere.

And what about virtual worlds as a new communications medium?

> I think we'll finally see a lot of remote business communication that feels like being in a meeting with people where you're really comfortable just hitting a button, turning something on. Your avatar is sitting there, you see everyone else around you, and you really feel like you're in a meeting with them. [For a] conference call, it's sometimes hard to keep track of who's speaking; it's much easier when the audio is sounding like it's in a 3D environment because people are positioned around

the room, and you hear them from your right and left, and you can look at them and they can see you, and you can bring up something visual to show them, all in this environment. It just feels much more human.

SUMMARY

What rules have we seen illustrated in this chapter? Consider the following:

Rule: *Every process is becoming digital, mobile, and virtual.*

Virtual offices, online news and advertising, airline transactions, e-commerce

Rule: *Products and services that can become digital will, and their physical representations will disappear.*

Music, video content, newspapers

Rule: *Organizations are shifting as much work to consumers as possible: the age of customer self-service is here.*

Airlines, e-commerce

Rule: *People want freedom to set their own schedules, to work and engage in leisure activities from a location of their choosing.*

Music, TV content, airline transactions, virtual offices

Rule: *Some services are better bundled, some are better unbundled and the market will choose the winners.*

Record albums, newspapers

Rule: *The spoils go to innovators and those who can execute.*

Apple iPod and iTunes, eBay, Amazon

Rule: *Individuals, organizations, and countries who resist technological change and fail to adapt will be left behind.*

Recording industry, newspaper industry

NOTE

1. In 2003 American Express purchased Rosenbluth's corporate travel division.

4

The Power of Online Communities

People are forming virtual communities. They're not physical communities. They're virtual communities and yet they are as real as meaningful as important to those people as going . . . to the clubhouse down the street used to be to us. Those are historic changes that I think are going to impact not just how we think of business. I think they are impacting how we think about our role in the world as human beings, how we think of interacting with others . . . . Technology continues to creep inexorably further and further and further into our lives, and it cannot be stopped; it will not be stopped . . . although it can be resisted.

—Carly Fiorina interview, 2007

Members of online communities collaborate across time and space independent of geographical barriers. Online communities have different rules and norms from physical communities. They often exist around a single idea or topic, like a community of people who drive the same model car. Online communities are possible because of information technology. They first appeared on the old French Minitel system, which is based on telephone technology, then on mass market information services like AOL and Prodigy, and then on the Internet. An online community is virtual by definition, and these communities have powerful influence on organizations and society.

Rule: *Technology enables powerful online communities: power to the people.*

The term "online community" covers a wide variety of endeavors on the Internet. There are groups that collaborate in order to do work. For example, open source software developers work together to create software that is in the public domain. There are family groups and support groups for many kinds of problems

Surviving

The online community is a new phenomenon brought to us courtesy of the Internet and personal computers. Like any community, participation is voluntary and one has to see benefits to continue as a member. It is hard to imagine a candidate posting a question to a portal like Yahoo and getting almost 40,000 responses, yet that is exactly what happened in the 2008 presidential primary campaign.

Companies are using these technologies to create communities of people who use their products. So the community provides opportunities to a variety of people, and it is clear that they have a great deal of influence on different events. A politician who ignores online communities does so at great risk. Bloggers also create an online community, though less formal than a MySpace or Facebook.

Email and blogs reinforce each other so that messages and news events that might have been ignored before the technology suddenly explode onto the national scene. Would Don Imus's racist and sexist description of the Rutgers women's basketball team have cost him his job before the existence of online communities? Those who are unaware of the existence of online communities or who minimize their influence are in for a surprise.

like alcohol or drug addiction. There are professional groups and thousands of special interest groups.

Groups meet in "chat rooms" where members post to a common message board. There are listservs where a sender dispatches one message that goes to everyone who has subscribed to the listserv. One of the newest technologies for creating a community is the Web log or blog. Individuals maintain their own blogs using software available free from places like Google; the owner posts his or her thoughts on any topic he or she likes. Other people can read the blog and post comments to it.

Why are online communities so popular? What do participants find there that is lacking in other communities? One answer may come from senior citizens who have been very active in online communities since the early days of networking. If a person has limited mobility, using a computer and a network to communicate with others is an attractive option. The online community provides social interaction, especially for an elderly person who is pretty much stuck at home if he or she lives in a cold, snowy northern climate in the winter. The ease of communications and the asynchronous nature of interactions make it easy to join an online community. A person can interact with hundreds or even thousands of individuals who have at least one common interest.

Wikipedia, the collaborative, online encyclopedia, discusses the motivation for participation in a virtual community after noting that its editors and contributors form such a community. This source quotes earlier work by Kollok

(1999), who suggests that there are three reasons people participate in these communities: anticipated reciprocity, increased reputation, and sense of efficacy. Social psychology suggests a fourth motivator, which is the need for a sense of community.

Reciprocity seems to be a likely explanation for many participants in online communities, especially those that offer help and advice. Most academics in my field subscribe to a listserv called ISWorld; I participate because it provides me with useful information about events and opportunities and because I use it to post information to go to the group, for example, job descriptions when we are hiring new faculty. A person in a chat room on how to stop smoking is gaining from participation and then, if successful, has the opportunity to help others.

For many users, online communities provide a way to be recognized and to build their reputations. Most programmers who write code for open source software projects are not compensated with money; their payoff is in terms of reputation and appreciation by others for their programming talents. Social networking sites encourage participants to post their profiles so others can learn about them. The profiles give people the opportunity to write as much about themselves as they like and to write in a way that enhances their reputations. Most academics have personal home pages on the Internet for the same reason, to help build their reputations by sharing their work with others. Rating systems on eBay establish the reputations of buyers and sellers.

A sense of efficacy means that someone has had an effect on the world, that the person has some influence. One of the ideas behind the concept of democracy is that individuals have an influence on government. In democratic countries, people expect to have a say on outcomes. There are many examples of online communities exerting significant influence on individuals and organizations, as we shall see later in this chapter.

People like to feel connected; man is a social animal and online communities provide a sense of community. Most of the communities involve two-way interaction. If you post a comment to a discussion group, it is likely that someone will remark on your comment and you will become part of the discussion thread. The vast majority of bloggers open their blogs for comments from readers. When you rate a product on Amazon.com, readers have a chance to indicate whether or not your rating was helpful, providing feedback to raters.

Online communities have proven to be surprisingly influential. eBay claims that its policies are guided by its user communities. News articles suggested that Senator Joseph Lieberman's defeat in the Connecticut Democratic senatorial primary in 2006 was due to a campaign against him that was fueled by blogs. Many Democrats in the state were unhappy with Lieberman's support for the Iraq war and his closeness to President Bush. Liberal and anti-war blogs from around the country, but especially in Connecticut, attacked Lieberman daily and rallied support for Ned Lamont, his opponent in the primary.

The bloggers were heavily involved in the "kiss float." It appeared in a picture that President Bush kissed Senator Lieberman. Opponents of the senator made

Figure 4.1
The Kiss Float

Courtesy of Tim Tagaris.

a float (see Figure 4.1) showing the supposed kiss and drove it to all of Lieberman's campaign stops. We will never know if the bloggers were responsible for Lieberman's defeat in the primary, but they certainly must have played a role. Despite their efforts, Lieberman came back and won the general election as an independent.

THE EBAY COMMUNITY

eBay is an Internet phenomenon; it is an organization that exists only because of the Net. The business model is outstanding: eBay never owns anything; it provides a marketplace for buyers and sellers. eBay has no inventory expense, no cost of goods sold, and does not have to worry about accounts receivable. Of course, eBay does have concerns that many brick and mortar firms do not. For an electronic marketplace to work, buyers have to trust sellers and their representations as to what they are selling. Both buyers and sellers have to trust each other to exchange funds and to deliver a product. eBay has to be constantly vigilant for fraud and cheating in the market. eBay is optimistic and has adopted the motto that "We believe people are basically good."

One way that eBay helped to solve the trust problem was to create a community of buyers and sellers who rate each other. Before making a purchase a buyer can review the seller's feedback scores (see Figure 4.2).

Beyond feedback for buyers and sellers, eBay's CEO, Meg Whitman, claims that the best ideas for the market come from users (Frei and Rodriguez-Farrar, 2002). As an example, she cites eBay Motors. The company saw that users were listing cars under "miscellaneous" so it set up a separate site for cars. Soon after, eBay became the largest auto site on the Internet. Who would have thought there could be a national market for used cars? Used cars are inherently local; the buyer wants to see the car. The trust created by feedback and the eBay community create conditions that make a buyer feel comfortable bidding on and buying a car located hundreds or thousands of miles away.

eBay's founder, Pierre Omidyar, asked for feedback from buyers and sellers while he was building the site, making software changes in the evenings based on that day's comments. Once a manager at eBay tried to change the color of feedback stars and received angry email, hundreds of messages, for two weeks. She had to change her approach to soliciting feedback from users before making any changes (Frei and Rodriguez-Farrar, 2002).

To foster community-building, eBay offers discussion boards, groups, blogs and chat rooms. The groups page is shown in Figure 4.3. Its introduction states:

> eBay Groups connects you to eBay members who share common interests. You can create and grow your own community, and participate in discussions, newsletters, polls, calendars, and photo albums.

Here users can join or create a new community, one that is a part of eBay, which is great for the company! Chat rooms are more informal and are not necessarily grouped around a particular topic. Its first chat room, which is still running, is the eBay Café. In keeping with eBay's philosophy of being guided by its members, there is a chat room to discuss changes in the site. And of course there are category specific chat rooms including collectibles, antiques, Beanie Babies, cars, clothing, computers, sports, and trading cards among others. It is interesting to note that eBay claims 203 *million* users and close to 100 million items for sale on its site at any time, with seven million new items added every day (*Wall Street Journal*, 10/25/2006).

eBay is not alone in trying to build a community; Amazon and other sites feature buyer feedback and reviews of products. However, the notion of online communities pervades eBay and is central to all aspects of the company's operations. Community members feel a part of the marketplace; they influence design and policy decisions. Their ratings help community members feel comfortable buying and selling on the site. If an organization tries to create a community of any type, the eBay example shows that it needs to be ready to be influenced by the community. It is clear that online communities are not the equivalent of fan clubs; members expect to have an influence on events.

Figure 4.2
Feedback at eBay

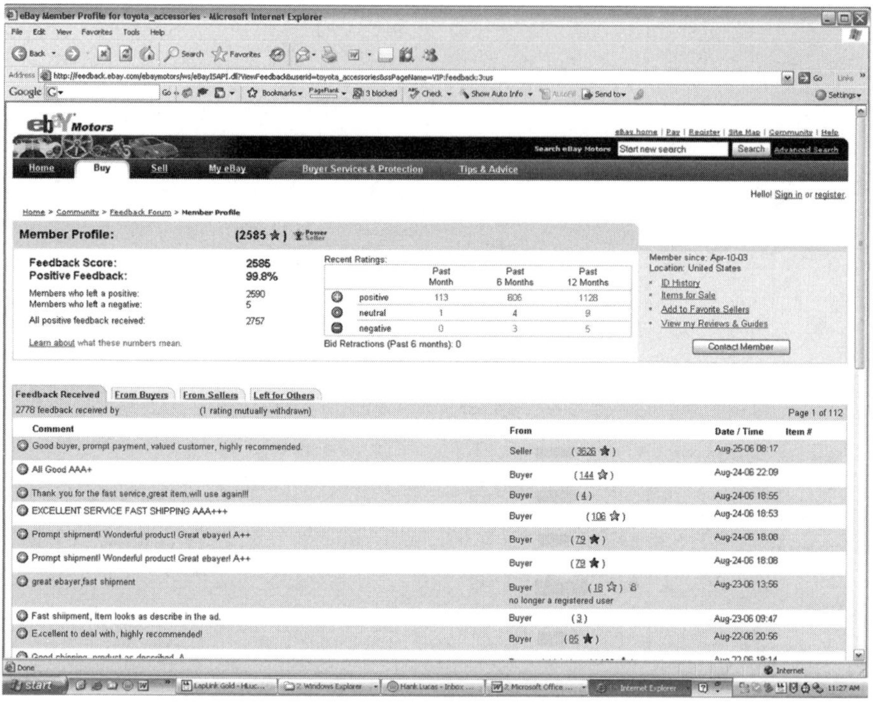

THE MYSPACE PHENOMENON

MySpace is about creating one's own network of friends. Unlike other sites where anyone who joins a chat group becomes a member, with MySpace you choose whom to include in your network. People write rather amazing profiles of themselves on the site, and anyone who wishes can browse these profiles and search for a class of people, like females between 25 and 40 who are interested in dating. For some on the site, the number of connections is a sign of high status. There are also a large number of discussion groups on the site. For example, there are 3,000 different groups on automotive topics.

The growth of MySpace has been exponential, making it a good investment for NewsCorp, which bought the site from its founders. By May of 2006 it was the second most visited site on the Internet after Yahoo. MySpace is estimated to have over 80 million visitors and some 250,000 new members sign up daily

Figure 4.3
eBay Groups

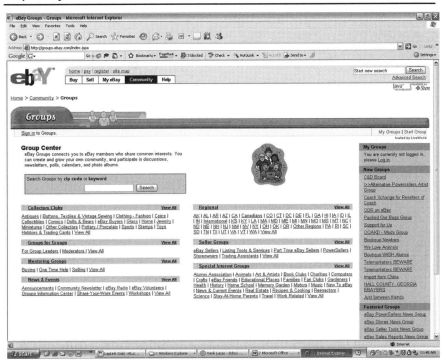

(*FinancialWire*, 5/22/2006). As a result of the success of social networking sites, services like Yahoo are seeking more feedback from their users.

A JUNIOR MYSPACE

If MySpace works for teens, how about creating something for the younger child? One answer is Club Penguin, which is aimed at 8- to 12-year-olds. Other similar sites include Imbee, Neopets, Whyville, Toontown, and Twinland.com, which allow children to create their own personal Web pages with videos, photos, and blogs. A few of these sites offer educational games. These sites have strict parental controls, safety features, and little or no advertising. Some of the sites have word filters and live people who monitor discussions as they take place. Users have to supply a parent's credit card and email address to be sure that an adult approves their use of the site (*Business Week*, 10/2/2006). Sites such as these are pulling children away from television and putting them in a more interactive environment.

THE COLLEGE NETWORK: FACEBOOK

A Harvard student named Mark Zuckerberg founded Facebook in 2004 to replace the paper directories that students find on campus with bad photos and basic information. The idea was to put more, better quality information on the Internet. Within three weeks, 6,000 Harvard students had signed up, and Zuckerberg figured out it would make sense to open the site to other schools. Soon Facebook had grown to 1,500 colleges in the United States. With venture capital backing, Zuckerberg launched a high-school version of Facebook. The introduction to Facebook states:

> Facebook is a social directory that enables people to share information. Launched in February 2004, Facebook helps people better understand their world by giving them access to the information that is most relevant to them.
>
> Facebook's Website has grown to over 8 million people and, according to ComScore, ranks as the seventh-most trafficked site in the United States. People with a valid email address from a supported college, high school or company can register for Facebook and create a profile to share information, photos, and interests with their friends.
>
> Source: Facebook.com.

Facebook has opened up its site to technology companies and programmers who want to contribute features to its services. The idea is to provide more value for the site's 24 million active users. One new feature allows members to recommend and listen to music, place Amazon book reviews on their pages, play games, and join a charity drive all while staying on the Facebook site (*New York Times*, 5/25/2007).

Because participants can post any information about themselves, there have been problems with students who put too much in their profiles. Several students were denied jobs after recruiters read what they had said about their drinking and partying preferences in Facebook. It appears that this site has become an integral part of the college scene, helping to create a community of students.

AN ONLINE INTELLIGENCE COMMUNITY

Since 9/11 there has been much attention focused on the 16 U.S. intelligence agencies. As recently as 2003, a new employee in the Defense Intelligence Agency was disappointed to find that the state of search technology was up-to-date for 1995, but that search programs were not even close to the power of Google. Chat groups were impossible to form among different agencies because their software could not interconnect. Much of intelligence revolves around information sharing, and the technology just was not there to share. The 9/11 report concluded that information about the plot was known, in bits and pieces, to different intelligence and law-enforcement agencies, but the lack of sharing made it impossible to anticipate the disastrous attack.

In the fall of 2005 two CIA analysts began testing whether a "wiki" could help analysts share and assess intelligence; they named their system Intellipedia. (A "wiki" is based on the technology in www.wikipedia.com where experts collaborate to write articles similar to an encyclopedia; the key here is shared content creation.) By the fall of 2006, some 36,000 intelligence community members had contributed 28,000 pages to the wiki. The effort includes blogs and chat rooms for intelligence analysts. For example, the CIA set up a test blog to capture information from around the world about avian flu; in a few months the site amassed 38,000 participants.

In the intelligence community there are two big issues with this technology. First there is a concern with errors. Will the posting of incorrect information lead to inappropriate decisions? Those who back these Internet tools say no because there are so many people involved. Wikipedia succeeds because everyone checks the work, and an expert will find an error. The second concern is secrecy, which is pervasive in intelligence work. How do you keep sensitive information from people who are not authorized to view it? Unfortunately, there is no answer here, and the debate is still raging in the intelligence community. The upside is that blogs, wikis, and chat groups are easy to create with proven software. You do not need a huge budget, nor do you risk the kind of failure that the FBI had when it scrapped its $170 million case file system (*New York Times Magazine*, 12/3/2006).

THE POWER OF ONLINE COMMUNITIES

We have seen the power of the community at eBay in providing reviews and feedback on how to design the marketplace. Companies with products and services to sell are increasingly looking to advertise on social networking sites and to generate positive reviews of their wares. The downside is that negative reactions to a product will be communicated across a social group very quickly. One survey suggested that people who participate in an online community (if it is done well) return to a site nine times as often and spend five times as long as on other sites (*Wall Street Journal*, 9/26/2006). As a result, organizations are trying to build branded online communities; examples include Campbell Soup, Tulane University, and TV Guide. If people in the community are talking about a company there, they are also talking about it and its products/services offline. All of this makes for a very powerful way to promote and market to customers.

Some companies use online communities as a super focus group. GlaxoSmithKline, the pharmaceuticals firm, sponsors an online community devoted to weight loss and dieting. Glaxo is getting advice from members of the community on how to package and market a new weight loss pill it is planning to release. In addition, the company has the benefits of learning from members of the community about their battles with the bathroom scale (*Business Week*, 9/4/2006).

Some of the smaller online stock brokers are promoting social networking as one of their main attractions. For one of these brokers, customers create profiles that describe their investing strategies, stocks they follow, and even their recent trades. Another broker lets users publish blogs to share their investments and insights on the markets. The brokers do background checks on customers so one can feel more confident about the advice than general information on the Web. TradeKing reports that about 2,500 of its customers are active as bloggers or in publishing their trades. This number is 5 percent of the firm's clients, but this group generates over 10 percent of the firm's revenue. The founder feels that this evidence suggests those who trade more also network more (*BusinessWeek*, 9/10/2007).

The National Hockey League has established a social-networking site called NHL Connect. Fans create personal profiles, add friends, upload photos, post videos from YouTube, make comments, and participate in chat groups. There are links to blogs from hockey team members. Nike has a social-networking site, Joga.com, which is designed for soccer fans. Local soccer groups can sign up and create profile pages while fans are able to blog and form communities around teams and players and organize local games. By the end of the World Cup in 2006 the site had attracted a million users. A gym equipment manufacturer, Life-Fitness, encourages individual gyms to set up a LifeFitness site to build a community of gym users. These users in turn create a demand for the company's treadmills and weight machines. Air France-KLM started a social networking site for business travelers to China, Club China. The site helps members do business in China by providing information on finding a translator or car service. Members gain admission to a country club that has locations in three Chinese cities. A user provides a profile and can search for business contacts. The club has 3,000 members and 40 percent log on every month (*Wall Street Journal*, 1/29/2007).

Firms working with online communities must integrate them into their other activities as eBay has done. A company has to be willing to listen to community members, accept their feedback, and change policies and procedures if so requested. Starwood Hotel & Resorts has an employee who spends six to eight hours a week monitoring and participating in Web sites that exchange information about hotels. The participants in these sites tend to be more frequent travelers and potentially loyal customers. William Sanders, a Starwood customer service representative, is known as the "Starwood Lurker" on FlyerTalk. Sanders speaks as himself rather than a corporate representative and is not afraid to admit a mistake (*Hotel and Motel Management*, 9/17/2005).

A recent experience at Facebook demonstrates the power of community members. In the summer of 2006, Facebook implemented two new features that recorded users' actions on the site and notified all of their friends about what happened. As an example, a news feed might say that six of your friends had changed their profile pictures, Jane Doe had left a group, and John Doe went from being "married" into a "relationship" (*Wall Street Journal,* 9/7/2006). The reaction from members was fast and furious. By the next day, Facebook added privacy options that let users decide how much personal information should be shared with the two new newsfeeds (*Wall Street Journal,* 9/8/2006).

How good are online communities in their reactions to products and predictions of success? A recent academic study predicted the box office success of Hollywood movies both with and without online ratings. The forecast used opening weekend box office receipts and online ratings to predict future revenue for the movie. This model with online ratings performed better than the more traditional forecast that used the movie's marketing budget and professional critics' reviews. In fact, the model performed as well as forecasts that used two weekends' worth of box office data (Dellarocas, Awad and Zhang, 2006).

An unusual application of blogs involves people's efforts to get out of debt. Those heavily in debt are creating anonymous blogs that reveal to strangers the details of their finances that normally are kept a deep secret. In 2006 the average American household carried about $7,200 in revolving debt (usually credit cards) and $21,000 in total debt. One woman owing $22,000 on her credit cards posted the information on her blog, but she won't talk to family or friends about her debts. Others post the results of shopping trips where they only bought groceries that were on their list and ate at Subway for $8. Why publish this information for the world to see? One blogger said that keeping the blog made her conscious of her spending. She does not want to let her readers down, even though they are all strangers. If she uses her credit card, she has to confess on her blog, and this is keeping her from buying a new LCD TV on credit. Does the public act of blogging help people with problems discipline themselves (*New York Times,* 2/18/2007)?

Who is the typical blogger? A report by the Pew Internet & American Life Project answers the question (Lenhart and Fox, 2006). First, 12 million people keep blogs, and 57 million Internet users read blogs. While we have emphasized the influence of blogs on politics, most bloggers talk about their life and experiences. Only 11 percent say they focus on government or politics. Blogging is a phenomenon of the young: 54 percent of bloggers are under 30. Most bloggers treat it as a hobby, and half spend just one or two hours a week on their blogs. The survey found that 87 percent of bloggers allow others to post comments on their blogs. Figure 4.4 in an example of a colleague's blog.

The Pew survey statistics do not quite mesh with the influence ascribed to blogging in the Connecticut primary. It is possible that when confronted with a highly emotional issue like the Iraq War, more people turn to politics. It may also be that the 11 percent of bloggers who focus on politics are very energetic and are political activists. Regardless, the blog is changing the face of American politics in ways that are not entirely clear at this point. Figure 4.5 is the home page of the DailyKos, a leading liberal political blog site.

Figure 4.4
A Colleague's Blog on Google Blogs

Courtesy of Galit Shmueli.

In addition to blogging, Web videos are influencing political races. John Tester, the Democratic opponent of the U.S. senator from Montana, Conrad Burns, posted videos of embarrassing statements and gaffes from his opponent on YouTube in campaigning for the seat in 2006. The video clips attracted

Figure 4.5
The DailyKos

Courtesy of The DailyKos.

attention in the press and they appeared to be help Tester in the Senate race (*Wall Street Journal*, 10/9/2006). The Internet is all about transparency, and politicians now face the prospect of every off-hand comment ending up on a popular Web site.

Politicians are also discovering social network sites as a way to reach voters under 30. A number of politicians have joined MySpace to attract both voters and donations. One politician reported that the number of online donations to his campaign jumped more than 50 percent after he joined MySpace. A volunteer said he joined a campaign because of the endorsements he saw for a candidate on MySpace as well as the visitors he found on the site. This candidate has a full biography, trivia about himself, and an ongoing slideshow from the campaign (*Wall Street Journal*, 10/14–15/2006).

Barack Obama was very successful during the 2007–2008 primary season in using the Web to foster an online community; more than 65,000 people have registered on his site. Five thousand of his supporters use online tools to create their own events and fundraisers around the United States. The Obama, Edwards, and McCain campaigns have seen social networking help broaden their contributor base. These fans may only donate $50–$100, but the campaigns can contact them later for more. About a quarter of Obama's $25 million first-quarter fundraising in 2007 came from 50,000 donors on the Internet. His site provides a "groups" section where supporters can create or join online groups that share ideas, blogs, and organize events. Groups exist by geographic area and interests, such as a group of educators who support Obama (*Wall Street Journal,* 5/26–27/2007).

YouTube, Yahoo, and MySpace are encouraging campaign discussions on their sites. MySpace plans to have a virtual election for its 168 million members to vote on presidential candidates. YouTube has a channel for candidates' videos that allows voters to post their own videos and comments in response. Yahoo has an election portal with links to the candidates and the ability to undertake discussions between candidates and voters. Hillary Clinton asked about what should be done to improve health care in the United States and received over 38,000 responses. This kind of response creates problems for the candidates who do not have enough staff members or time to answer all of the contributions (*Wall Street Journal,* 4/4/2007).

Combined with Internet fund-raising, online advertising, podcasts, emails, and listservs and social networking sites, blogs make it possible to refine a candidate's message and target specific groups and individuals. The Internet is much more efficient than older forms of advertising, and we expect to see a decline in TV political ads in coming elections. It all began only a few years ago when Howard Dean raised significant campaign funds through small contributions on the Internet; now the power of the Net combined with online communities is reshaping the face of politics. Could it also change the face of democracy by encouraging greater participation in the election process?

REFERENCES

Dellarocas, C., N. Awad and K. Zhang. "Exploring the Value of Online Product Ratings in Revenue Forecasting: The Case of Motion Pictures." College Park, MD: Smith School of Business, working paper, 2006.

Frei, F., and H. Rodriguez-Farrar. "eBay (A): The Customer Marketplace." Boston: Harvard Business School, 2002.

Kollock, P. "The Economies of Online Cooperation: Gifts and Public Goods in Cyberspace." In *Communities in Cyberspace.* Marc Smith and Peter Kollock (eds.). London: Routledge, 1999.

Lenhart, A., and S. Fox. "Bloggers: A Portrait of the Internet's New Storytellers." Washington, DC: Pugh Internet & American Life Project, 2006.

Surviving

Internet technology provides a great infrastructure for offering different kinds of services to customers. The services we see demonstrate how innovative individuals can be given the opportunity.

Customers clearly benefit as Internet services force firms to unbundle and as they lower costs while increasing convenience. For people working in the services industry, the level of competition is fierce, and the "switching" costs for customers are very low, as is loyalty to a site or company.

Technology is the engine that leverages the work of knowledge workers. It is creating unparalleled opportunities for efficiency and productivity. The individual or the business that eschews the use of technology will fall behind competitors that are rapidly adopting it. It is very likely that getting behind here will mean that your business will be acquired by another or that it will fail as more efficient firms undercut your prices and offer better quality service at the same time. If you are working in services, you need to be a competitive innovator, and you can never stop thinking about the next innovation.

---

the data for exceptions. The key to success for a retailer like this is to have exactly the right amount of inventory available for its shoppers. Wal-Mart uses the data for daily operations and for negotiations with suppliers; it helps set sales goals for vendors. On a longer-term basis, the data provide insights for locating new stores. In the future, Wal-Mart has technology in place that will allow it to go to "scan-based selling" in which the supplier owns the item until a Wal-Mart cashier scans it for a customer. These goods would never appear in Wal-Mart's inventory or on its books, but they would go into its sales figures (*Wall Street Journal*, 6/6/2006).

While some worry about the amount of data Wal-Mart maintains, the company argues that it has little use for using information at the level of the individual shopper. Rather, it is interested in aggregated data to answer questions like, "What high-demand products are in short supply at stores in Florida after a hurricane?" The answer to this particular question recently turned out to be Pop Tarts and beer, and so, for the next hurricane, Wal-Mart sent trailers full of these products to Florida.

Wal-Mart represents a quiet transformation; most of us just see the results and can only guess at the technology that lies behind this company's success. It is an example of technology speeding up processes and reducing cycle times. This retailer also illustrates gains in productivity from economies of scale and from relentlessly applying IT to improve efficiency and customer service. In this process, Wal-Mart has become a fierce competitor contributing to the creation of a hyper-competitive economy.

——— 5 ———

Transforming Services

P ost-industrial economies are service economies. The largest numl
employees in the United States works in services, and the retailer
Mart is the country's largest employer (see Figure 5.1). Manufact
requires capital investment for plant and equipment; a fabrication plant for
puter chips costs well over $1 billion. The major capital investment for a se
firm goes to information technology. Consider a stock brokerage firm: it l
take orders, send those orders to a market, report the trade, update the cu
er's account, send or receive payment, and keep customer records. The b
uses information technology to execute the entire process. Technology has
formed this and other service industries.

A VISIT TO WAL-MART

Wal-Mart has 3,600 stores in the United States and serves about 100 n
customers a week. While noted for its low prices and large number of s
behind the scenes Wal-Mart has a highly sophisticated computer and com
cations infrastructure. The store obtains detailed information about the pr
it sells, and some information about customers, from its checkout scar
Clerks and managers have wireless hand-held computers for gathering
inventory data. Wal-Mart also uses computer models to help answer que
like how many cashiers are needed during particular hours at a store. The
pany has 460 terabytes (10^9) of data stored on NCR Teradata mainframe
puters that are designed for data warehousing and data mining.

In technology circles, Wal-Mart is famous for its supply chain and log
systems. It shares much of its data with suppliers. For example, Kraft can a
Wal-Mart data to see how its products are selling. Wal-Mart uses its huge
of data to look for opportunities to improve efficiency, especially by moni

Figure 5.1
U.S. Employment by Sector

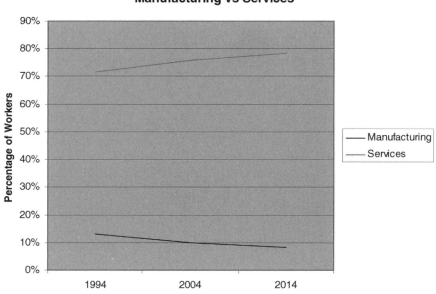

Manufacturing vs Services

Source: U.S. Bureau of Labor Statistics.

THE TECHNOLOGY BEHIND THE BIG BROWN TRUCKS

Rule: *Technology will speed up every process, reducing cycle times and driving inefficiencies out of the economy.*

UPS is one of America's best known companies. It is hard to go through a day without seeing one of its 66,000 drivers in a brown truck. The carrier moves an average of 15 million packages a day worldwide. Twenty years ago, UPS's technology consisted of stop watches and clipboards as industrial engineers studied every aspect of the delivery of a package to reduce the time required to an absolute minimum. UPS trained drivers to fasten their seat belts with their left hand while starting the truck with the right hand. Drivers' instructions included honking the horn when arriving at a residence so the person inside would start for the door before the driver rang the bell.

The success and rapid growth of FedEx, UPS's biggest rival, led Big Brown to revise its thinking about information technology. FedEx was the first to introduce package tracking by computer. Managers at UPS said, "Why should we bother? UPS tells the customer when it will deliver, and it delivers at that time." But it turns out that customers do like to track their packages, and UPS began spending nearly $1 billion a year on technology in the late 1980s.

Today its four-million-square-foot hub in Louisville processes more than a million packages from 100 planes and 160 trucks in four hours. Its airline operations center schedules some 600 UPS and chartered planes and crews around the world each day. This group also sets up 11 spare planes, which can pick up packages trucked from, say, an airport that is fogged in (*New York Times*, 7/12/2007).

The IT budget at UPS supports 4,700 IT employees; an Internet site that gets 18.5 million visitors a day; 3,700 servers; 15 mainframe computers; and a vast telecommunications network. UPS began an initiative in 2004 to squeeze more efficiency out of the system that picks up, transports, and delivers all those packages. Customers create their own address labels on the Web or using UPS-supplied software. Data from these labels goes to the distribution center nearest the package's final destination. Dispatchers at these sites download addresses and use custom software to build a delivery route for each driver that takes into consideration weather conditions, traffic, and, of course, the location of each stop.

The distribution center generates a separate label containing instructions on where to load the box in the delivery truck so that the driver can work from the front to the back of the vehicle. Packages that are "Next-Day Air" and "Early A.M." shipments are placed near the driver so they can be dropped off by 8:30 a.m. The $600 million route optimization system maps out the next day's schedule for each driver in the evening. The software designs each route to minimize the number of left turns to reduce time at stop lights and fuel costs. The system captures institutional knowledge that used to reside with the truck loaders and drivers so that it does not leave with them if they go to another job (*BusinessWeek*, 3/5/2007).

The system is in place for about two-thirds of the drivers, and in February of 2006 it helped reduce total miles driven by 1.9 million compared to February of 2005, a 3 percent reduction. That first quarter UPS spent $578 million on fuel, so the reduction in miles translates into major fuel and maintenance savings. The Louisville division manager claims that his drivers have gained enough time from the system to pick up seven to nine more packages beyond their 100-pickup daily average. UPS is projecting a $600 million savings in operating costs when the system is completed by the end of 2007.

The next generation of hand-held computers for the drivers will have GPS capabilities. UPS expects to be able to pinpoint within minutes when a driver will arrive at a destination. Someday in the future, UPS might be able to schedule deliveries by appointment! The new handhelds also sound an alarm if the driver forgets a package or is about to deliver a package to the wrong address (*Wall Street Journal*, 7/24/2006). One analyst estimated that as much as 10 percent of UPS' revenue comes from charges it can levy on customers that are enabled by technology—for example, using data about package size to charge more for an oversize package (*New York Times*, 7/12/2007).

ONLINE STOCK BROKERS CHANGE THE GAME

Charles Schwab was one of the early discount brokers. It paid its brokers a salary rather than a commission and provided very few services beyond trade execution. When the Internet became available for commercial use in 1995, it was natural for Schwab to become an online broker using its compatible business model and the IT skills it had already developed for its current business processes. At first, Schwab offered Internet trades at $29.95 each. In addition to Schwab, entrepreneurs with IT and brokerage knowledge developed new business models based entirely on the Net, exemplified by companies like eTrade. These brokers today charge from $6.95 to $25 to trade 100 shares of stock. E-brokers have lower average costs than their full-service competitors. There are no expensive research divisions or physical branch offices. In another example of customer self-service, investors enter their orders themselves, reducing the need for a broker or order taker.

What happened to the full-service brokerage model? For years, before the electronic traders came along, full service brokers like Merrill Lynch offered customers a bundle of services that included trade execution. An investor at Merrill might pay $100 to trade 100 shares of a stock. In addition to the trade, the investor received advice from a broker (financial consultant), research on companies and industries, and other services like estate and financial planning.

The full-service brokers were not happy with competition that was charging considerably less for a trade. A Merrill official even called online trading bad for investors and bad for America because he said it encouraged people to make frequent trades rather than invest. Full-service brokers accused online brokers of doing a poor job of executing trades so that it cost the customer more in total than the full-service broker.

What is the quality of execution? It is possible for a broker to obtain what is called a price improvement. Suppose that a share of stock is quoted as $50 bid and $50.05 asked. This spread means that a market maker will pay $50 for a share and will sell a share at $50.05. If an investor wants to buy 100 shares, he or she would expect to pay $50.05 per share. What if his or her broker is able to get a price of $50.03? This investor has had a price improvement of $.02 per share or $2 on his or her 100-share order. The full service broker argued that it obtained more price improvements than online traders who sent their orders to electronic markets or Electronic Communications Networks (ECNs).

We undertook an experiment to test this contention and to assess the impact of online trading on the brokerage industry. We opened accounts at six brokerage firms, four of which were electronic and two of which were full-service firms. We designed an experiment in which we purchased or sold shares of the same stock at exactly the same time with three brokers on each trial. After all the trials, there were a number of interesting results. First, the online brokers routed shares of New York Stock Exchange (NYSE) listed stocks to online ECNs, while the full-service brokers sent most of these orders to the NYSE itself. As a result, the full-service brokers obtained more price improvements for NYSE stocks than the online brokers. However, we traded a mix of NYSE and NASDAQ stocks, and when we aggregated all of the trades, the price improvements at the NYSE were not enough to overcome the large differences in commissions between on-line and full-service brokers. The total, all-in trading costs for 100 shares of stocks at the market price were lower for the online brokers (Bakos et al., 2005).

Online brokers therefore managed to pierce the bundle offered by full-service brokers. It could offer only the trade execution for far less money. The customer, at least at first, had to find his or her own research, though it was often available for free on the Internet. Online brokerage is a good illustration of our rule that *Some services are better bundled, some are better unbundled and the market will choose the winners.* In this case, a number of customers decided they did not want to purchase the bundle.

Online brokers began to attract a significant number of customers, creating new competition for the full-service broker. Merrill Lynch launched a review of the accounts it offered to customers and the impact of online trading. Some Merrill brokers were telling management that it needed to get into online trading. When senior officials had focus groups with customers, they found a lot of interest in online trading. One customer admitted that he had an account with Merrill which he used to trade once a year, but that account gave him access to Merrill research. The rest of the year he did multiple trades with his online broker. The final consideration was that Merrill feared it would lose the coming generation of investors now in college; today's students live on the Internet and were unlikely to trade with a broker that did not offer online accounts.

Merrill undertook an extensive analysis of its accounts using data from its present customers. The company developed an elaborate simulation to estimate how many customers would switch to an online account, how many new customers it might attract, and the net impact on revenue. The worst case scenario was that Merrill would lose $1 billion in income by customers switching online. Feeling it had no choice, Merrill developed a cafeteria of accounts to offer clients. The most interesting new account was called Merrill Lynch Unlimited Advantage. This account allowed virtually unlimited trading for a fixed annual fee based on a percentage of assets with a $1,500 minimum per year. This account changes the relation between the broker and the client. In a commission-based account, the broker makes money if the client trades regardless of whether or not the client makes money. With an asset-based account, the broker makes more money when the client's wealth increases (Altshuler et al., 2002).

The addition of online trading options to its existing account structure turned out to be a winner for Merrill—it is stronger than ever today. Online trading has transformed the brokerage industry, and in the process, Merrill-Lynch transformed itself with a new business model to respond to this innovation. The extent of the transformation is illustrated by an announcement by the Bank of America that it is starting to offer up to 30 free trades a month to customers with at least

$25,000 in deposits. The new program started in the Northeast in the fall of 2006 and was scheduled to be extended to the rest of the country in early 2007. According to an analysis, the bank is dropping its $5 to $10 fees for trading to try and use its 5,700 branches in 29 states to improve the ranking of its lagging brokerage unit (*Wall Street Journal,* 10/11/2006). As of late 2006, brokerage fees at the low end of the market ranged from free to $12.99 per trade. At some point, will brokers begin paying you to execute a trade?

YOU CAN RESIST ONLY SO LONG

Rule: *Individuals, organizations, and countries who resist technological change and fail to adapt will be left behind.*

The New York Stock Exchange (NYSE) is a not-for-profit corporation and self-regulatory organization whose origin lies in the 1792 Buttonwood Agreement signed by 24 brokers in lower Manhattan. Since the 1934 Securities Exchange Act, the NYSE's rule book and self-regulatory activities are overseen by the Securities and Exchange Commission (SEC). Success in these NYSE roles encourages liquidity and attracts companies to list their stock on the NYSE and become a "Big Board" or "NYSE listed" company.

The U.S. securities industry's back-office crisis in 1969 forced the NYSE to close for trading on Wednesdays for six months ending in mid-1970. Manual, paper-based procedures, including the physical movement of share certificates, were unable to keep up with the growing trading activity. The opening of the National Securities Clearing Corp. and the Depository Trust Co. in 1972 and 1973 led to better back-office efficiencies and greater clearing and settlement capacity. The continuing growth of trading volumes and additional listings in the 1970s led the NYSE to consider its alternatives for expanding its trading capacity. Rather than undertake costly expansion of its physical floor, the NYSE chose to invest in IT to increase the capacity of the market.

The exchange was controlled by its member firms which are the broker-dealer and specialist firms that own the NYSE's 1,366 "seats." Access to the floor and participation in the NYSE market requires a seat to be owned or leased. A seat provides trading privileges and access to the trading floor. The NYSE's auction market structure ensures fair and competitive prices by matching buyers and sellers. Every NYSE stock is assigned to a single specialist who works from one of the NYSE's 20 posts. A specialist is usually responsible for 5 to 10 individual stocks. The rest of the NYSE's floor population are brokers handling orders for clients on a commission basis, clerks, or exchange officials.

The NYSE faces two forms of competition: competition for order flow and competition for listings. Order flow competition comes from established markets and new entrants. Through a provision known as unlisted trading privileges (UTP) provided in the 1934 Securities Exchange Act, securities listed on any national securities exchange may be traded by other such exchanges. The other established venues for trading NYSE-listed stocks include the five regional stock exchanges, which include the Boston Stock Exchange, the Chicago Stock Exchange, the Cincinnati Stock Exchange, the Philadelphia Stock Exchange, and the Pacific Exchange. In addition, NYSE listings can trade in the "third market" in which a broker routes an order to a market-making firm registered with the National Association of Securities Dealers (NASD). The dealer firm is obligated by SEC rules to provide "best execution," and may sell to a customer at the displayed offer quote, and may buy at the bid price, or may improve on the quotes and trade at a price more advantageous to the customer.

Since the early 1990s, a number of new entrants have competed for NYSE trading volume. The operations of these entrants rely on advances in information technology. Specifically, the NYSE has faced increasing competition from electronic trading systems at the Chicago Stock Exchange, from Alternative Trading Systems (ATSs) such as the now-defunct Optimark and from Electronic Communication Networks (ECNs) such as Instinet, which are based on network technology and online computer systems to match buyers and sellers.

The experience of stock exchanges in Europe demonstrate the intense competitive pressures on the industry. According to the *Wall Street Journal* (1/20/2005):

> Just before the Euro was launched in 1999, there were still 32 stock exchanges dotted around Europe. Since then, three exchange operators have come to dominate the business. And soon it may be two, Deutsche Borse AG . . . has held informal talks to purchase the London Stock Exchange PC, which operates Europe's largest exchange. . . . Behind this action and other consolidation that has swept Europe in the past few years is the same factor that has driven U.S. exchanges to consider mergers: fierce competition to offer the lowest cost of trading.

The NYSE faces competition for company listings from a variety of sources. The other markets for companies to list their stock are the NASDAQ Stock Market and the American Stock Exchange (AMEX). The listing requirements for NASDAQ and AMEX are less onerous in terms of firm size and market capitalization. NASDAQ was launched by the National Association of Securities Dealers (NASD) in 1971 as a way of replacing the daily "pink sheets" of prior day prices with real-time price quotes of small capitalization firms in the over-the-counter (OTC) marketplace. Although NASDAQ was shown to lower trading costs in the OTC market, firms that grew large enough continued to migrate from over-the-counter NASDAQ trading to list on the American Stock Exchange, and subsequently the NYSE. In the mid-1980s, however, the NASDAQ began retaining firms as they grew, with one example being Microsoft, which was eligible for a NYSE listing shortly after its 1986 IPO. Nevertheless, many NASDAQ listings would easily qualify for an NYSE listing (e.g., Microsoft, Cisco, Dell, Intel, etc.), but the firms choose to remain on NASDAQ.

To what extent has the NYSE been confronted with transformational technology? Electronic markets of all types, from the NASDAQ to ECNs, represent new entrants that are transformational in nature. Electronic markets fundamentally alter traditional ways of doing business. Investors interact through computers and a network, and there is no physical floor in which traders and other personnel meet. Electronic markets use technology to dramatically change how tasks are carried out, enabling firms to operate in different markets, serve different customers, and gain considerable competitive advantage by doing things differently. Electronic markets do not require a physical floor, nor do they need the labor content of a physical market. Trade execution is instantaneous.

For over twenty years, the NYSE invested heavily in information technology to process transactions and to support the trading process. In the early period (to 1987), the objective was to provide sufficient processing capacity to function properly with volumes three times those of an average day. This capacity "multiplier" was later increased to five times daily volumes. The major IT projects at this time were to develop market systems capabilities focused on the NYSE's "point-of-sale" (POS), which is how the Exchange refers to its specialists' posts. These included: (1) the Designated Order Turnaround system (DOT, 1976), which became SuperDot in November 1984; (2) the Common Message Switch (CMS, 1977); (3) the Intermarket Trading System (ITS, 1978); and (4) the Specialists' Display Book (1983). These systems supported the specialist by increasing his or her capacity to process trades. For example, SuperDot routes orders electronically to the specialist who can review and execute them on a screen.

From 1987 until 1995, investments in IT showed little increase, matching a weak economy and market volumes that were growing slowly. The Exchange improved capacity somewhat with its major initiative being broker booth support through the Broker Booth Support System in 1993.

Beginning in 1995, the NYSE invested more heavily in IT as trading volume accelerated and as competition from the NASDAQ became more heated. NASDAQ's active IPO calendar of popular, new technology listings, its rising volumes, and the growing use of ECNs for NASDAQ trading were causing the NYSE to look vulnerable. It lost ground to NASDAQ in the late 1990s "bubble." The NYSE's share of market value of all U.S. listings fell to 68 percent in 1999 from 87 percent in 1990. In this period, continuing to the present, the NYSE's IT strategy has been to use technology aggressively to meet competition from a number of sources as well as to satisfy demands for trading capacity. The focus has been on faster turnaround time for orders being reported back as completed trades, converting the market price increment from eighths (12.5 cents) to sixteenths (June 24, 1997), and then to decimal pricing (January 29, 2001), and achieving greater levels of market transparency for participants off the floor. The Direct+ system is a direct response to the threat from ECNs; it features automatic execution for limit orders up to 5,000 shares, with execution times averaging 0.8 seconds. This system bypasses the floor broker and the specialist and makes the NYSE look like an ECN to users of the system.

In 2005, with its market share dropping below 80 percent, the NYSE announced plans to merge with the ECN archipelago and to become a public company, a merger it completed in 2006. This move followed the ouster of its long-time chairman in a scandal over the size of his compensation and retirement funds. The Exchange's reasons for the proposed merger and change in ownership included:

- Creating the world's largest equities market.
- Combining an auction market with all-electronic trading functionality.
- Providing the ability to compete with other global markets.
- Providing greater liquidity in each market, lower transactions costs, and better prices.
- Creating diversification by trading NASDAQ and NYSE securities.
- Providing cost savings of $100 million dollars in each of the next three years.
- Gaining greater access to capital as a listed company.
- Letting the NYSE become a one-stop marketplace for investors, traders, and securities issuers (NYSE S4 Filing with the SEC, 2005).

The Exchange noted that some customers wanted greater speed and choice in order execution, and that, in particular, institutional investors wanted to purchase stocks instantaneously and anonymously, something hard to do with the physical floor business model.

The change in ownership structure effectively removes much of the resistance to change at the NYSE from specialists and other members of the exchange who have done extremely well financially through its physical market. Instead of being run by its members, the Exchange becomes a public corporation with an elected board of directors who represent the shareholders.

While there are many reasons for the major changes at the NYSE, technology played a major role in this transformation. Innovators developed a new market structure that was all online. High-speed or "fast" markets are very important for institutions like mutual funds. These traders have strategies that involve purchasing or selling stock at the NYSE and simultaneously buying or selling products like futures, options, and other derivatives on another exchange. The traders do not want to wait for a specialist to match orders. Their whole strategy depends on trading before any of the prices currently in effect change. The NYSE with its specialist system and physical floor could not compete.

Direct+ was a move in this direction, but it was not enough. The Exchange needed something more dramatic, and a merger with an online exchange and public ownership demonstrated a serious change in strategy. The Exchange is expanding the Direct+ system to create a "hybrid market" which combines an auction market with electronic trading. In the fall of 2006, the NYSE changed its rules to allow investors to trade electronically as often as they desire, ending previous restrictions that limited trades to twice a minute and to orders that included price limits. The time to execute a typical order dropped from nine seconds to one second with the changes (Lucas, Oh, and Weber, 2007).

Why such need for speed? As mentioned, investors today execute complex trading strategies that involve buying and selling instruments on two different exchanges simultaneously. Their strategies are based on taking advantage of prices of different securities very quickly before the prices change. The margins on these trades are very small, but the "statistical arbitragers" make a large number of trades to generate quite respectable profits. How fast is fast? BATS Trading moved its computers from Kansas City to New York and New Jersey and co-located them with exchange computers. A typical trade now takes one-thousandth of a second rather than twenty thousands of a second because data does not have to make the trip from Kansas City to New York (Byrne, 2007).

The SEC has announced new rules that will in effect require markets to offer electronic trading in 2007 (*Wall Street Journal,* 10/5/2006). By January 2007, the NYSE market share was down to 55 percent, and so the challenge is clear: it must use the electronic market to recover its lost market share. It is interesting to note the current estimates for the percentage of trades done electronically on different exchanges: Almost every major exchange is at least 70 percent electronic.[1] Physical processes will become digital, dramatically reducing cycle times.

The NYSE used technology for many years to stave off competition, but eventually it had to capitulate. And what of the physical space constraints that were historically a concern at the exchange? Since 2005 the number of people on the NYSE floor has dwindled to 1,700, down from 3,000. The Exchange is in the process of reducing its physical trading space (*New York Times,* 9/23/2007). This story is another example of our rule about the futility of resisting a technological transformation. The answer is to embrace change and figure out how to move forward in a different world.

GOING GLOBAL

Rule: *Local markets will become national and international.*

Rule: *Technology will continue to accelerate globalization.*

Rule: *Technology will speed up every process, reducing cycle times and driving inefficiencies out of the economy.*

New management at the NYSE saw the need to create a viable electronic market alternative to the Exchange's physical floor trading system. The move to merge with Archipelago immediately provided this electronic market and the ability to think about a dramatic increase in business and scope for the exchange. Electronic markets scale beautifully; such systems are always designed with extra capacity to meet peak demands. As volume increases, you can add hardware and software capacity in advance of the peaks while current extra capacity handles a steady increase in volume. If an exchange buys or partners with another exchange, it is easy to increase share volume, and it provides a larger and more liquid market for investors.

The mergers of markets continue; in the fall of 2006 the Chicago Mercantile Exchange bought its rival for a century, the Chicago Board of Trade, for about $8 billion. Both the popularity of futures and other derivates and the imperatives of electronic trading drove the merger:

> The proposed combination represents another triumph for electronic trading over pit trading. The Chicago Board of Trade started so-called open-outcry trading in 1848, and three years later traded its first corn-futures contract, for delivery of 3,000 bushels. . . . The Merc's value has surged, driven by the growth of its electronic trading system, called Globex. By 2001 the CME had passed the CBOT to become the largest U.S. futures exchange by number of contracts traded. . . . As a part of the deal, the CME will close its trading floor and move the remaining trading in its pits to the CBOT . . . . That will cut the number of major exchange trading floors in the U.S. to two: the CBOT's and the New York Stock Exchange's. (*Wall Street Journal,* 10/18/2006)

As a result of the availability of technology, exchanges are also going global. NASDAQ has purchased stock in the London Stock Exchange and has made no secret of its desire to take over that exchange. The NYSE group merged with Euronext, which has exchanges in Amsterdam, Brussels, Lisbon, and Paris. The combined exchanges could reduce expenses by moving to one electronic trading system.

HIGH-SPEED TRADING

Much of the pressure for fast trading has come from investors, especially institutions and those who trade using computer algorithms. The Lime group of companies, particularly Lime Brokerage and Tower Research Capital, are examples of firms that rely on extremely fast markets. Mark Gorton, the founder of the group talks about his businesses:

> Tower is a quantitative hedge fund manager. We do a lot of automated trading. We currently trade about 100–150 million shares every day in the U.S. and a percent or two in the major exchanges around the world in terms of volume. So we have computers that are processing data from all around the world in real time and spitting out buy and sell signals and trading like crazy, and we have people working here to program those computers. . . . The trading that we do now would have been impossible to do 10 or 15 years ago just because the markets weren't that electronic, and there was no way to process the information. Because of technology, markets have gotten a lot more efficient—the speed at which they move and the tightness of the spread and things like that. Markets are noticeably different than even five years ago.

Have markets become more efficient as a result of electronic trading? Mark comments:

> It's difficult to explicitly measure that, but one simplistic measure is the bid/ask spread. The bid is the price at which people are will to buy a stock, and the offer is the price at which people are willing to sell it. Historically, a lot of stocks were priced in terms of an eighth or a quarter . . . so people might be willing to buy a stock at fifty and sell it at fifty and a quarter. If you were going to go buy and sell a share very quickly, it would cost you 25 cents to do it in that example. Now . . . that spread is narrowed to frequently a penny or less than a penny in a lot of cases, and so . . . we actually have the effect of lowering the costs. For average people at home and institutions, the competition is so intense that it creates these very, very efficient markets.

Tower is an algorithmic trading company, a strategy enabled by technology. Mark describes what they do:

> There's been this shift from markets involving humans touching every order to just computers doing this, and again the New York Stock Exchange is moving there . . . . It used to be that every single time you put in an order it was literally written on a piece of paper and handed to a person. Computers are really good at that sort of order-matching functionality. Markets are a lot faster, and it's a lot cheaper to trade. When it was actually people doing the trading, then someone standing on the floor of the exchange had superior information and there was a type of trading that someone on the floor of the exchange could do that no one else could. . . . It is a very complicated thing to do to have a computer decide when to buy and sell and not have it lose money; it's a very difficult thing to do. . . . The trading is very probabilistic. If you take enough bets that are in your favor a little bit at the end of the day, your chances of making money are reasonably good. What we really like is volatility. The things that we don't like are quiet markets; when there are things moving around and there's action, that's when there's opportunities, but when things quiet down that's when there's less opportunities.

Alistair Brown from Lime expands on algorithmic trading:

> Your competitors, meaning all the other algorithms builders, all the other hedge funds, are mining . . . this data historically, and they're running statistics. So, people learn from the market data that's already out there so they begin to get familiar with what your algorithm is doing. . . . If you leave it that way, the chances are the performance and the money it makes will decay until eventually it will start to lose money. Most of our customers are continually tweaking their algorithms just because everyone else is. It's kind of an arms race for these guys who are trading, and the smarter guys are working really hard at always being a step ahead of the rest.

The motivation for founding Lime Brokerage:

Lime Brokerage has been set up specifically to cater to very high frequency customers like Tower Research Capital. From a technical point of view, it's a surprisingly difficult challenge to process the amount of messages we do in a short period of time and not have them back up at all. What Lime Brokerage prides itself on doing is being super fast even when the markets are going crazy and there's a lot of activity; so we have been re-engineering our system time and time again to be really fast . . . .

Will open outcry markets continue to exist? Alistair comments:

That's a good question; I don't know the answer. My gut feeling is that yes it will eventually go away altogether. I don't really see the reason for it. It will probably take some time. It went away in Europe, Paris, and London. As they moved electronically, they ran the two side by side. It was actually remarkable—I think it was a matter of weeks, and they just shut down the open outcry. Obviously the people in the open outcry business don't want that to happen so they're protecting it as much as possible. . . . There's definitely less job opportunities in that space. Whether it will go away totally, we'll see. My feeling is that eventually it will.

And just how fast is Lime's software?

We're really on the third iteration of our software. We thought we were getting close to the limits of it, . . . our market data is down to delivery times of a microsecond versus milliseconds, so now you're sub 1000ths of a second for market delivery.

For the individual trader, the technology provides tremendous productivity, but at the cost of excessive work. One Chicago trader works 12 to 16 hours a day trading U.S. government securities, European bank instruments, wheat, gold, and metals. The opening of the Eurodollar market overseas determines his start time of 5 p.m. on Sundays. During normal working hours, he is at his firm's offices in Chicago, and then he returns home to continue trading there. A lot has changed since this trader worked 6.5 hours a day shouting orders in a pit at the Chicago Board of Trade. He had to write tickets for each trade, and the speed of this process was the limiting factor in his productivity. Today with technology he averages 50,000 trades a day, ten times his volume under the manual system. On heavy days he has approached 100,000 trades a day on a number of exchanges (*BusinessWeek*, 8/20 & 27/2007). One challenge for knowledge workers is to balance work and family time and avoid the temptation to work 24/7.

CONCLUSIONS

How much of a transformation do electronic securities markets represent? A quotation from the *Wall Street Journal* (5/27/2006) provides the answer:

All of this is a vast change from the way trades used to be processed, with messages passed from a customer to a dealer to a pit trader and back again. "Now you look on the screen, you hit a button, and 40 milliseconds later you trade at the price you saw," says Arman Falsafi, head of the Chicago Merc's European operations.

What's the downside of huge improvements in trading speed? It is hard to understand the reason for price changes. Before all-electronic trading, the physical floor provided information on what was behind price movements.

[O]n the floor traders can get a sense of whether it is actual oil users, like refineries or airlines, or financial speculators that are doing the buying or selling. "Now, if people ask what's going on, you can say, Well, I see numbers flashing on the computer, but unless it is my customers driving it, I can't tell." (*Wall Street Journal*, 4/10/2007)

But the information that is missing was available only to a small number of people. Electronic trading has eliminated their advantage and made the markets more transparent.

The question is not if physical markets for trading securities of different types will disappear, it is when they will disappear.

NOTE

1. These estimates came from participants in the 2007 Smith School of Business, University of Maryland Netcentricity Conference on the Transformation of Securities Markets.

REFERENCES

Altshuler, S., D. Batavia, J. Bennett, R. Labe, B. Liao, R Nigam, and J. Oh. "Pricing Analysis for Merrill Lynch Integrated Choices." *Interfaces* 32, no. 1 (January–February 2002): 5–19.

Bakos, Y., H. Lucas, W. Oh, G. Simon, V. Viswanathan, and B. Weber. "The Impact of E-Commerce on Competition in the Retail Brokerage Industry." *Information Systems Research* 16, no. 4 (December 2005): 352–371.

Byrne, J. A. "Hooked on Speed." *Institutional Investor's Alpha,* January 2007.

Lucas, H., W. Oh, and B. Weber. "Information Technology and the Transformation of the New York Stock Exchange." Robert H. Smith School of Business, working paper, 2007.

E-Government

E-government is about providing information and delivering services to citizens, businesses, and other government agencies via information technology. The primary vehicle for providing e-government is the Internet and World Wide Web, and the reasons for investing in e-government initiatives include:

- Providing better service to citizens and businesses.
- Reducing the costs of providing service thereby making government more efficient.
- Bringing the government and citizens closer together to encourage greater participation in our democratic system.
- Increasing the transparency of government agencies.

E-government efforts follow our rules:

Rule: *Organizations are shifting as much work to consumers as possible: the age of customer self-service is here.*

Rule: *People want freedom to set their own schedules, to work and engage in leisure activities from a location of their choosing.*

Rule: *Technology enables powerful online communities: power to the people.*

Rule: *Technology will speed up every process, reducing cycle times and driving inefficiencies out of the economy.*

Nothing illustrates the move to customer self-service as well as the IRS. This agency experiences a huge peak in volume around April 15, and it is faced with a mammoth task of converting paper tax returns into machine readable data.

Surviving

We all suffer if governments fall behind in the technology revolution. First, they fail to provide the kind of online services discussed in this chapter. Second, they miss out on the tremendous efficiency improvements that come from automating services, especially applications that let citizens answer queries and input transactions online.

Voter turnout is very low in the United States, which is a threat to our democracy. Wikipedia estimates that about 70 percent of eligible voters in the United States are registered, and slightly over 50 percent vote in presidential elections. If governments lag the rest of the country in providing services, and if they operate at low levels of efficiency, taxpayers will stop supporting them. And if cynicism about government grows, fewer and fewer people will vote and provide input in the political process.

Technology will not solve all the problems of citizen participation in government, but the failure to adopt technology will most certainly exacerbate them.

What is the impact on cost and cycle time if the IRS makes it possible for a million people to file taxes electronically? How about 30 or 40 million people? One motivation for e-government initiatives has been budget pressures on government entities. E-government can have a dramatic impact on efficiency and costs, especially for transactions between the government and other parties.

E-government via the Internet provides access to government information and services 24 hours a day, seven days a week. Some experts believe that providing services and information to citizens makes people feel government is helping them more. As a result, it is hoped that citizens will participate more in our system and that e-government will strengthen democracies.

E-government also helps increase transparency, especially in developing countries. Consider the Open system in Seoul, Korea, where citizens apply for various permits online. If one does business online and pays electronically, there is very little opportunity for a government official to ask for a "tip" or transaction fee that goes into his pocket.

The Taubman Center for Public Policy at Brown University has a research program on e-government; its 2006 survey of over 1,500 state and federal sites has some interesting findings. These include:

- 77 percent of the sites have executable services online. In other words, one can conduct transactions.
- 1 percent of the sites are accessible via personal digital assistants and/or cell phones.
- 30 percent of the sites have some form of foreign language translation.
- 64 percent of the sites are written at the 12th grade reading level, which is higher than the average American reading level.

- The highest-ranking states are Texas, New Jersey, Oregon, Michigan, Utah, Montana, New York, Illinois, Indiana, and Pennsylvania.
- Top-rated federal sites include the portal firstgov.gov; sites at the Departments of Agriculture, Housing and Urban Development, Commerce, Treasury, Education and State; and the IRS, Postal Service, and Social Security Administration.

The report also features novel services including:

- Some states have tourism sites with online planners for mapping out a trip including accommodations and dining. Some systems recommend businesses in the state.
- Citizens in Iowa and Massachusetts can pay traffic tickets online.
- Indiana, Montana, and Utah feature live chat for help.
- Alaska has a Web cam at its Department of Motor Vehicle Offices so you can see how busy the office is at any time.
- In Minnesota and Idaho you can pay child support online.
- Pennsylvania has a video guide on how to use different voting machines.
- Ohio has online shopping for products from correctional industries. (West, 2006)

The Pew Internet and American Life Project has conducted several surveys of how Americans use the Internet to interact with government agencies (Horrigan, 2004). The findings of one study suggest that Americans with Internet access are more likely to contact the government than non-Internet users, and these Internet users say that e-government improves their relationship with government. Some 54 percent of all Americans, regardless of the Internet, contact government in a typical year (beyond the act of filing taxes):

- 30 percent contact government to conduct a transaction like renewing auto registrations.
- 25 percent contact the government with a specific question such as the hours of a park.
- 19 percent express an opinion to a government agency on a policy question.
- 11 percent seek help for a specific problem.

The Pew survey showed that Internet users are more likely to contact the government. Some 72 percent of Internet users contacted the government in 2003 while only 23 percent of non-Internet users made contact. Some 30 percent of the Internet users employed email or the Internet to try and change a government policy or influence a politician on how to vote on pending legislation.

SOME EXAMPLES

Where do you start to access e-government? One answer is with a portal, a "super" Web site that organizes information and refers you to other Web sites where you can find out more about a particular topic. The federal government's

Figure 6.1
The Firstgov Portal

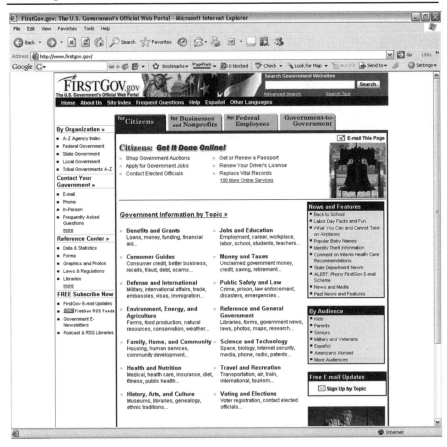

portal, www.firstgov.gov, is a well-regarded site (see Figure 6.1). This site provides government information organized by agency or by topic. It includes links
to the Web sites for states as well as federal agencies. The site has a section on
how to contact government officials by phone, email, or through regular mail.
The information begins with the president and includes members of Congress
and state governors. There is an address for the firstgov response team for
directing any question about government; the team will respond within two
business days. You do not complete transactions on the portal. Instead, the
portal helps you find the Web sites that will answer questions and process your
transactions.

   The federal government is interested in e-government to reduce costs and provide better service. The E-Government Act of 2002 created and provided funds
for a federal department to expand web-public services. The vehicle for managing

this program is an Office of Electronic Government and Technology in the General Services Administration. As a result of this and other legislation, the United States has developed a significant e-government infrastructure.

While it is nobody's favorite agency, the IRS has moved into e-government with enthusiasm. The IRS considers us to be "customers" and has experimented with technology for years to reduce the tremendous volume of paper it deals with each year. In the 1990s, the IRS spent $10 billion on technology, particularly on systems to scan tax returns sent in by the public. The commissioner of the agency in the Clinton administration was forced to admit that this huge sum had produced systems that "do not work in the real world."

Enter the Internet and the age of customer self-service. Instead of trying to scan taxpayer documents, why not have the taxpayer enter the data in machine-readable format in the first place? The major problem to be overcome is security and fraud, and there have been problems with thieves filing false returns and collecting refunds. But overall, the program has been a tremendous success with over 72 million electronic tax returns filed in 2006. There are several ways to file electronically; a simple approach is to turn the process over to a tax professional authorized to file electronically. For the do-it-yourself taxpayer, there are a number of personal computer programs that are available commercially. You buy the program from a retailer or download it from a Web site, prepare your return, and file it electronically. According to the IRS, 37 states and the District of Columbia allow the taxpayer to simultaneously file federal and state returns electronically.

Another way to file online is to take advantage of "free file," an alliance between the IRS and tax preparation companies for taxpayers with adjusted gross income of $50,000 or less. The IRS Web site lists the advantages of free-file (see Figure 6.2):

- Reduced tax return preparation time;
- Faster refunds;
- Accuracy of return;
- Paperless process using electronic signatures;
- Acknowledgement of return receipt;
- Variety of free services to choose from;
- Reduced fears about transmitting tax data to third parties;
- Use of free tax preparation software is comparable to the Alliance Company's paid product.

One problem with technology in the public sector is measuring the return on investment. Many of the benefits of IT are found in providing better service to citizens, but it is hard to place a dollar value on better service. The IRS is a clear example of how the technology provides dramatic increases in efficiency and faster cycle times. How much does it cost to key 72 million tax returns into computers? The IRS avoids this cost through its e-filing programs. In addition, the taxpayer who is due a refund does not have to wait to receive it until someone

Figure 6.2
The IRS Free-File Program

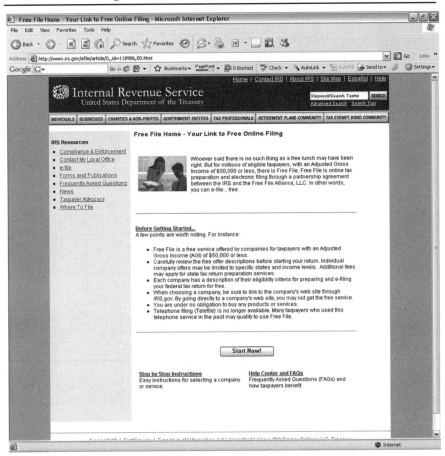

gets around to entering her return, so refunds go out more quickly. It is always encouraging to find a "win-win" situation.

In addition to numerous federal sites, citizens have the opportunity to interact with State Web sites. The Montana site is particularly informative and useful (see Figures 6.3 and 6.4). As you can see, Montana provides a number of online services for its citizens. A business can pay a variety of taxes online with a credit card or through electronic funds transfers. These taxes include liquor and cigarettes, corporate licenses, lodging facilities, oil and gas, and rental vehicle taxes. A company can file its annual report online with the secretary of state. You can also search a database of convicted felons. Individuals can pay their estimated taxes and final tax bills with a credit card or eCheck.

Figure 6.3
The Montana Home Page

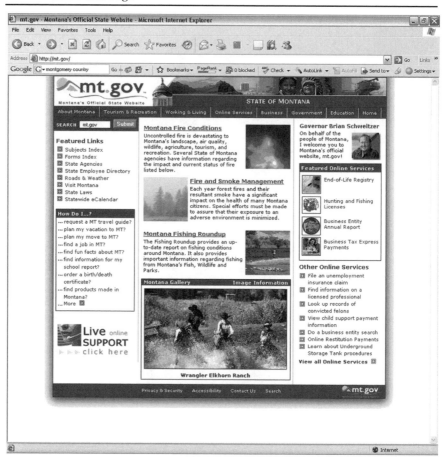

You can also buy hunting, fishing and conservation licenses in minutes, and you can "print your temporary license and go fishing right away." An end-of-life registry provides forms to be filled out and submitted to a database that contains your instructions for health care providers on how you want to be treated under different medical conditions near the end of life.

All levels of government can provide electronic access for citizens. Montgomery County, Maryland, for example, is often cited as one of the leading Web sites for counties (see Figure 6.5). This site contains a wealth of information about the country including its budget, upcoming elections, recreation programs, flu emergencies, and traffic reports. It allows a citizen to view and pay property taxes online. You might visit this site or the one for your own county to see the myriad of information and services available (http://www.montgomerycountymd.gov/).

Figure 6.4
Montana's Online Services

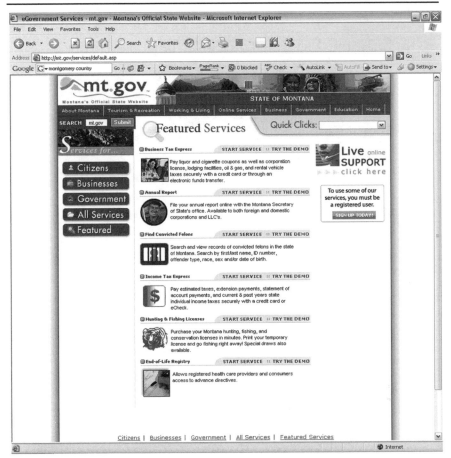

The applications we have seen so far are concerned with providing better services to citizens and increasing the efficiency of different government offices. A novel e-government system in Seoul, Korea, has another purpose: to promote openness and transparency in government (see Figure 6.6). The OPEN system (Online Procedures Enhancement for civil applications) promotes transparency in city administration by reducing delays and eliminating the unfair handling of civil petitions and applications. According to the Web site, the system has three objectives:

1. Ensure transparency in administrative procedures.
2. Provide citizens with easy access to submit civil applications through the Internet without having to make phone calls or visit government offices.
3. Increase the credibility of city administration.

Figure 6.5
The Montgomery County Home Page

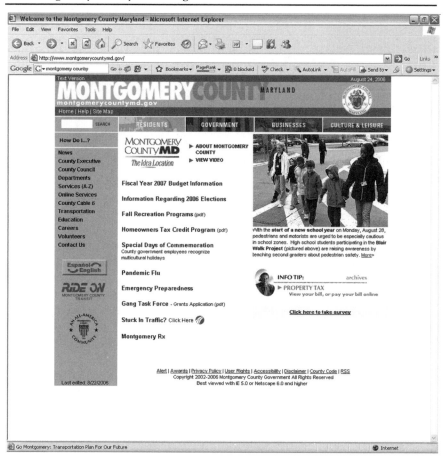

Courtesy of the Montgomery County Office of Public Information.

While not explicitly mentioned in the objectives, one benefit of this system is the fact that a transactions system run through the Internet makes it harder for city employees to demand side payments or bribes for approving petitions. Given the damage that public corruptions does, we might recommend systems like OPEN for the countries perceived as being highly corrupt in the Transparency International Corruption Perception Survey (http://www.infoplease.com/ipa/A0781359.html).[1]

VIRTUAL GOVERNMENT

Rule: *Every process is becoming digital, mobile, and virtual.*

Figure 6.6
Seoul OPEN System

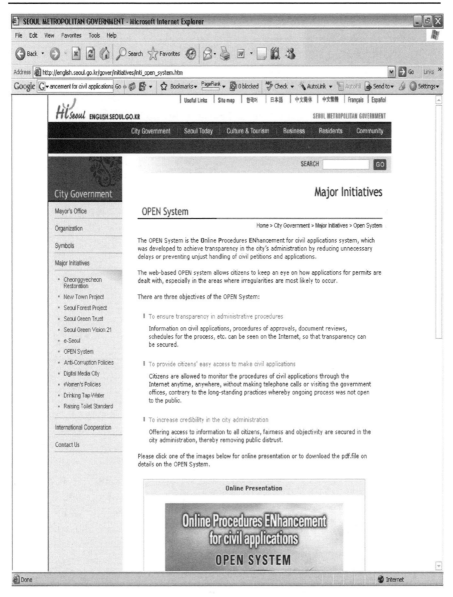

Courtesy of the Seoul Metropolitan Government.

Is having information and some transactions services online a real transformation in government? There are a number of trends that have emerged from efforts to build e-government at all levels, from cities to the federal government:

1. A new focus on the citizen as a customer who needs to be served.
2. Customer self-service to increase governmental efficiency and reduce cycle times for service.
3. A growing belief that electronic connections increase citizen participation and confidence in government at all levels.
4. The creation of a virtual government that is relatively flat in structure and that greatly facilitates citizen interactions.

Government organizations are the topics of thousands if not millions of stories and jokes. Supposedly someone asked Napoleon how it felt to run France, and he replied, "Sir, I do not run France, 10,000 civil servants run France." Most people think of any government as a giant bureaucracy with many layers of supervision. Bureaucracy has a number of features, including departmentalization and routinization of services. Add to this political concerns of public officials who are interested in being re-elected and the environment becomes even more treacherous. This form of organization can be criticized for rigid procedures and a lack of focus on individual clients. Rather, the focus is on the organization and following rules (Tat-Kei Ho, 2002). Bureaucracies are associated with employees who have high needs for job security, and they satisfy these needs by "following the book." As a result, when citizens appear in person at a government office, they often feel that they are being mistreated by a civil servant whose salary they pay.

When we moved to Maryland, I applied for a driver's license only to find out that in Maryland one had to have his middle name spelled out on a driver's license. That had never happened before, so I looked at all my forms of ID to find that they just had my middle initial. The supervisor at DMV said I would need to get a birth certificate to document my middle name. Of course, the state where I was born quoted a 6-8 week lead time for a copy of a birth certificate, much longer than I was supposed to be driving in Maryland with my out-of-state license. My passport only had a middle initial, and I frantically searched the house for an official-looking document that spelled out my middle name. I spotted it on the wall and took a canvas bag of college degrees to the DMV. Each included my middle name. Problem solved.

E-government creates a new governmental structure electronically. If you look back at firstgov.gov, you see that there is a listing of departments and agencies. However, there is also a list of services. Many times a citizen knows what he or she wants, but has no idea where to go for it. You could phone different agencies and look for a referral to the one offering the service you need. Alternatively, you can look on a web site and find the service directly. The virtual government looks as if it is organized by services for its constituents rather than arbitrarily designed departments. On the web, the government is no longer a nameless, faceless bureaucracy where one could be passed endlessly from person to person to find the answer to a question. A virtual government is far more *transparent* than a physical government. If the government agency responds with useful information in a timely manner, the virtual government is going to appear more responsive to citizens. If people have a positive experience, they will be more inclined to participate in government and will be less cynical about it. So we can see the potential for a virtuous circle, where success breeds more success, and quite possibly we will achieve the dream of government "of the people, by the people and for the people."[2]

NOTES

1. In the 2005 survey the most corrupt countries are perceived to be Chad, Bangladesh, Turkmenistan, Myanmar, Haiti, Nigeria, Equatorial Guinea, Cote D'Ivoire, Angola, and Tajikistan. In case you are wondering, the least corrupt are Iceland, Finland, New Zealand, Denmark, Singapore, Sweden, Switzerland, Norway, Australia, and Austria; the United States is number 17.

2. In case you've forgotten, these words are from Abraham Lincoln's Gettysburg Address.

REFERENCES

Horrigan, J. B. "How Americans Get in Touch with Government." Washington: Pew Foundation, 2004 (www.pewinternet.org).

Tat-Kei Ho, A. "Re-inventing Local Governments and the E-Government Initiative." *Public Administration Review* 62, no. 4 (July/August 2002): 434–444.

West, D. "State and Federal E-Government Sites in the United States, 2006." Providence, RI: Taubman Center for Public Policy, 2006 (http://www.insidepolitics.org/egovt06us.pdf).

——— 7 ———

Transformations in Manufacturing

According to the National Association of Manufacturers, over 14 million people in the United States were employed in manufacturing in May of 2006, down from 17 million in 2000. The output of 378,000 manufacturing businesses constitutes 12 percent of the U.S. Gross Domestic Product, and two-thirds of our exports are manufactured goods. Manufacturers export each month about what American farmers export in a year. The United States is by far the world's largest manufacturer by raw value of the goods it produces, some $1.79 trillion in 2005, which is nearly twice the value of the nearest competitor, Japan. China makes a lot of consumer products, but the United States tends to make goods that are complex, difficult to transport, and time-sensitive (*Wall Street Journal*, 10/25/2006). The top manufacturing industries in terms of sales are in order:

- Food
- Computers and electronics
- Motor vehicles and parts
- Fabricated Metals
- Chemicals
- Machinery
- Pharmaceuticals
- Plastics and rubber products
  (Source: www.nam.org).

How does technology transform manufacturing? Let's revisit some of the rules:

Rule: *Technology will speed up every process, reducing cycle times and driving inefficiencies out of the economy.*

Rule: *Physical products will be marketed with information components.*

Surviving

Technology is an imperative for manufacturing firms. The economy is global, not just local, and the revolution in communications technologies means that a firm can source raw materials, assemblies, and finished products from a variety of locations. The first revolution from technology in manufacturing has been ongoing automation of production; the second one in progress is using communications technologies to provide flexible and efficient production.

What happens to those who fail to innovate? The commercial printing story in Chapter 2 provides a good example of the failure to keep up. The printing technology adopted by the industry leaders is expensive, so they needed to increase the scale of their operations, which led to overcapacity and cost-cutting in the industry. The small printer who ignored the technology or who could not afford to invest in it was at a distinct disadvantage. The number of print firms employing 100 or fewer people has shrunk dramatically in the last decade.

In manufacturing, those who are left behind like the small printers will be bought out by others, or they will be forced to lay off their workforce and close their doors. Survival requires innovation and adoption of technology in this global economy.

Rule: *Products and services that can become digital will, and their physical representations will disappear.*

Rule: *Local markets will become national and international.*

Rule: *Technology will continue to accelerate globalization.*

Rule: *The spoils go to innovators and those who can execute.*

Rule: *The rapid development of new technology-based business models is responsible for a hyper-competitive economy.*

Rule: *Individuals, organizations, and countries who resist technological change and fail to adapt will be left behind.*

Almost all of our rules of the revolution in technology apply to manufacturing. The technology is reducing cycle times dramatically and creating greater efficiencies. Consider the case of Harry Lee, the owner of TAL, a closely held shirt manufacturer with headquarters in Hong Kong. In the early 1990s TAL began to supply J. C. Penney's with house-brand shirts. Lee saw that Penney's was holding up to nine months of inventory, twice the level of its competitors. Mr. Lee thought of a solution. Why not let his company send shirts directly to Penney's stores rather than in bulk to the retailer's warehouse? Such a move would cut handling costs in half, and Penney's could respond more quickly to customer tastes. As things stood, this time the retailer missed the sale of hot items because it took so long to restock, and the stores had to discount shirts that were not popular.

Mr. Lee found that Penney's sales forecasts often were off. He offered to write a program that would let TAL forecast shirt sales and respond quickly to actual sales from the stores. Lee hired programmers to build a model that forecasts shirt inventories in 1,040 Penney's stores by style, color, and size. In some stores, inventories fell by half.

Suppose that a customer at a J. C. Penney store in Atlanta buys a white Stafford dress shirt, size 17 neck, sleeve length 34/35, on Saturday. Monday morning, TAL downloads the record of the sale, and by Wednesday afternoon, a factory worker in Taiwan packs an identical replacement shirt in a package to be sent to the Atlanta store. That same weekend, the Atlanta store sold its last two sage-colored shirts in one size of another house brand. The TAL computer model recommended an ideal inventory size of two shirts of this style, color, and brand. The Taiwan factory made the replacement shirts and sent one by ship and one by air to replenish inventory with TAL paying for the air freight.

It is interesting that TAL tells Penney's what to buy rather than the other way around (*Wall Street Journal*, 9/11/2003). This example says it all about the impact of technology on manufacturing. Technology accelerates globalization, and work shifts easily to the country with the best price/performance ratio for the company. Penney's can send its sales data any place in the world instantaneously thanks to the Internet and communications technologies. The downside of this capability is the steadily declining manufacturing workforce in the United States. The upside is that consumers are able to purchase products for less money. It is clear from this and many other examples that technology is speeding up processes and reducing cycle times. The flow of information is so good that Penney's can eliminate most of its inventory of dress shirts because the retailer has substituted information and technology for physical products in inventory. TAL has been an innovator that is able to execute in technology, manufacturing, and logistics.

THE VIRTUAL MANUFACTURING COMPANY

Cisco is the prototypical Internet company, a fitting description for a firm that owes its existence to the Net. Cisco began business in 1984 and has developed into one of the premier suppliers of the components that make the Internet work—routers and switches, among other products. Routers and switches connect the different "pipes" that comprise the Internet and they intelligently send data over the Net. But Cisco's products are not just for Internet service providers; all types of organizations use Cisco's network components in their own networks and connections to the Internet. For example, Cisco bought Linksys, a major supplier of wireless home networking gear, and it is an active player in the market for IP telephony. Cisco is an international company with 47,000 employees worldwide. Its Web pages talk about how it is a participant in the technological revolution:

The Network is the Platform

The emergence of the network as a platform is changing the entire value chain of technology and placing the network squarely at the center of innovation: as many as 14 billion devices will be connected to the Internet by 2010. The explosion of devices will be fueled by more and more services and tasks being handled online, from phone calls to personalized searches to downloading videos, games and other forms of entertainment.

The role of the network is evolving beyond that of infrastructure. It is emerging as a secure platform for delivering the customized and personalized experience that 21st century users expect—whether that means delivering new services as a carrier, boosting productivity for businesses of any size or consumers looking for real-time, personalized entertainment and services.

As an increasingly intelligent network evolves into a platform, users will be able to communicate from any device and in whatever mode they choose.

Cisco is leading the transition to a network-centric technology environment. By combining its core strength (IP) with intelligence, the company is creating a powerful communications platform that will serve as the basis for the convergence of data, voice, video and mobile communications in a secure, integrated architecture.

Source: http://newsroom.cisco.com/dlls/company_overview.html.

Cisco is a virtual company. What does it mean to be virtual when you are a manufacturing firm? For Cisco, it means that the company does little or no manufacturing. Just as for Penney's and TAL, Cisco outsources its manufacturing to a group of contract electronic manufacturers (CEMs). These companies have manufacturing plants around the world that specialize in making electronic devices from cell phones to computers. A roster of names for CEMs includes Solectron, Flextronics, Celestica, Sanmina, and Jabil. Hon Hai is a Taiwan-based CEM with a factory complex in Shenzhen, China that employees 270,000 people building electronics products including Apple iPods and iPhones, HP personal computers, Motorola cell phones, and Nintendo videogame consoles (*Wall Street Journal*, 8/11 & 12/2007).

Figure 7.1 shows the Cisco business model, one that is based on the communications capabilities of the Internet. Somewhere around 90 percent of Cisco's orders come from customers using the Internet. What a great advantage for Cisco; it does not need a large staff of order takers because the customers do the work of order entry.

Rule: *Organizations are shifting as much work to consumers as possible; the age of customer self-service is here.*

In addition to entering their own orders, when customers have questions or problems with Cisco equipment, the vast majority of them consult an extensive

Figure 7.1
Cisco's Business Model

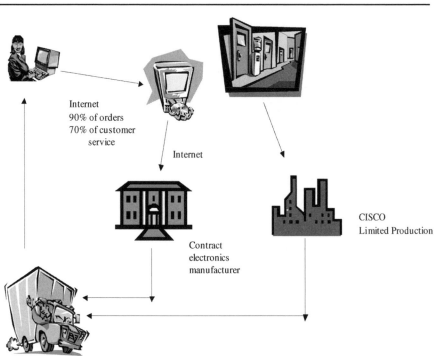

Internet
90% of orders
70% of customer
service

Internet

Contract
electronics
manufacturer

CISCO
Limited Production

Reproduced with the permission of John Wiley & Sons from *Informational Technology Strategic Decision Making for Managers* (Lucas 2004).

online knowledge base about Cisco's products, both hardware and software. How has Cisco managed to accomplish this major feat in customer self-service? Cisco's approach began with the Internet. It predated all other online firms, including Amazon and eBay. Cisco's model has spread to online retailing and e-commerce sites around the world. One of the reasons Cisco was so successful with its approach in the beginning is because many of its customers were engineers designing and maintaining networks. Using the Internet came naturally to them, both for ordering and for solving problems.

Is Cisco any less of a competitor because it is virtual? The results speak for themselves: Cisco is one of the leading firms in each market where it chooses to compete. The company designs and markets products even though a Cisco employee may never touch the physical device delivered to a customer. It invested over $3 billion in 2005 in R&D and introduced 50 new products that year.

Rule: *The spoils go to innovators and those who can execute.*

HIGHLY EFFICIENT MANUFACTURING

Dell Computer has a corporate strategy of being the low cost producer of personal computers. Efficiency is the mantra of all of its operations, from its direct order model for sales over the Internet and through toll-free numbers to a highly efficient manufacturing operation. Manufacturing efficiency contributes to Dell's strategy of being the price leader for PCs.

Its newest factory in Winston-Salem, N.C., is an example. This new factory covers some 750,000 square feet and is twice as large as Dell's next largest plant in Austin. The company expects 40 percent faster production at this new plant and a reduction of downtime by 30 percent. The assembly process has been designed so that equipment is handled 25 percent less than at other factories. The ultimate speed should be for computers to come off the line at a rate of one every five seconds.

Dell's manufacturing approach requires suppliers to keep two weeks of supplies in Dell's plants; Dell draws on these suppliers to take two hours worth of parts for the PC assembly line. Ten years of manufacturing research went into the development of the Winston-Salem plant, which is an effort to go to the next level of manufacturing efficiency. The features of the new plant include:

- Robots that put computer chassis on conveyers while other robots put completed machines into boxes to reduce worker injuries from lifting.
- All lines are equipped with the tools to build any of the company's 40 machine designs any time. Management says its focus is "how do we get it to the customer in the shortest amount of time?" Older plants can produce up to four models of one type of computer; changes in type require the line to shut down for retooling.
- There is a small stock of common parts at each assembly line so that workers do not have to visit the nearby supermarket storage area for each computer. Complex models require "kitting," but standard models are often built from common parts. Dell locates stocks in exactly the same place on every line so a quick glance shows if a particular part is running low.
- Three workers on a team, each with a specific set of tasks, build a computer.
- The plant implemented a quick-test procedure with a tester working with each three-person assembly team. The tester checks the wiring of each computer and sees that it will boot. If there is a problem, the assembly team finds out right away.

Dell builds information technology products, and it uses the technology to achieve its strategy of offering low-cost, high-quality computers to its customers (*Business 2.0,* December 2005).

AN IN-DEPTH EXAMPLE

Many of our examples describe IT-enabled transformations in broad strokes. This section presents a detailed study of one manufacturing firm to illustrate how very specific technologies can make a revolutionary change in a business's operations. We discuss how IT is responsible for the changing rules of competition in this industry as well as the transformation of a company from a craft-based profession to a digital business, from a traditional manufacturing "production" industry to digital information management.

The setting for this example is the commercial printing industry in the United States. This industry is comprised of 32,000 mostly small companies distributed throughout the country. Commercial printing includes all custom printing other than newspapers, magazines, and books. In 2000, total industry revenues were $89.7 billion, and with 570,000 employees, it was the fourth largest manufacturing employer in the United States. Most commercial printers operate in a single location with fewer than 100 employees and have annual sales of $2 to $10 million. Although commercial printing is categorized in government statistics as a manufacturing industry, at some companies the bulk of the workforce spends their days operating computer equipment in settings more akin to offices populated by white-collar professionals.

Figures 7.2 and 7.3 present graphs of Census Bureau data on the commercial print industry. The figures show that total industry revenues peaked in 2000 and have been in decline since. Shipments per employee display a more favorable trend, suggesting that the industry is becoming slightly more productive. For the period from 1997 to 2002, many traditional printing firms exited the business, especially in lithography. Based on data from the National Association for Printing Leadership, major industry changes are occurring; the number of firms with fewer than 100 employees shrunk dramatically between 1998 and 2003 and is estimated to decrease further. Larger firms, those with more than 100 employees, remained at about the same number during this period.

The significance of technological change in this industry is vividly illustrated in the public statements of senior executives in the printing business. For example, R. R. Donnelly's 2000 annual report talks about its technology initiatives:

> eWeek currently ranks us #19 of the top 100 innovators in e-business networking. We are a pioneer in managing digitized images and text, and hold more than 25 issued and pending patents for emerging technologies. For more than 23 years we have been first with every significant technological advancement in the printing industry. Our digitally networked plants ensure identical high-quality standards worldwide while improving our reliability and reducing cycle time. And, we continue to look to the Internet to make procurement, internal operations and customer transactions even more efficient. Every day, more and more customers transfer files to us over secure Internet connections to speed production, while giving them more time to create their content, hone their pricing or sell more ads. (p. 9)

There are two main reasons commercial printers have been experiencing an increase in costs and a reduction in margins. First, print customers have greatly reduced the number of suppliers with whom they do business as a result of a

Figure 7.2
Commercial Print Industry Shipments

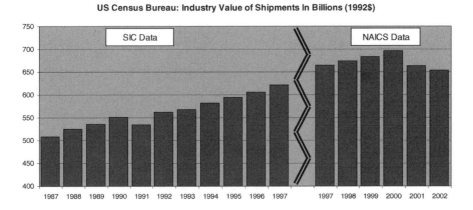

US Census Bureau: Industry Value of Shipments In Billions (1992$)

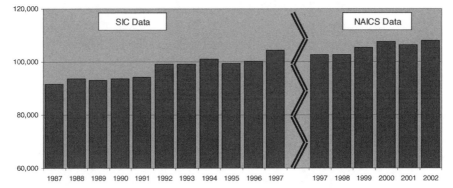

US Census Bureau: Industry Shipments per Employee (1992$)

focus on simplifying and streamlining the print supply chain. This trend means that a printer must offer a wide range of services, essentially all that the client may need, to participate in the customer's simplified supply chain. Second, the need to offer a full line of services requires the commercial printer to acquire equipment and recruit a workforce capable of supporting the printer's larger scope and scale. As a result of adding equipment, the printer is forced to find additional business in order to obtain a return on its investment, leading to price cutting in order to keep equipment busy.

It is interesting to note that increasing capital costs for equipment have occurred at the same time as decreases in variable costs. A printing process that is heavily digital uses significantly fewer consumables (for example, film), particularly during pre-press compared to older, craft-based operations. Quality improvements result in less spoilage and rework during the print process as well. Also, printing equipment that is digital can easily handle volume increases, which

Figure 7.3
Number of Printing Firms by Specialty

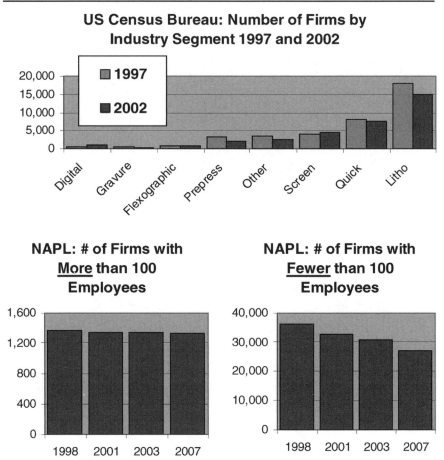

Source: Adapted from information from the National Association for Printing Leadership.

reduces the expense of adding capacity once sufficient printing infrastructure is in place. These trends strengthen the advantages of companies that have a large base of operations, access to capital, and are knowledgeable about technology.

Rosen (2003) argues that these trends are not an isolated experience, but that the industry is going through a structural change characterized by:

1. Substantial underutilized capacity
2. Heavy price competition
3. Unpredictable sales volumes
4. A continuing evolution in technology

5. Increasing capital requirements
6. Customer demands for service
7. Uncertainty over continuing investments.

Rosen (2003) attributes a number of the structural changes to information technology. As described above, customers and competition force printers to invest in new equipment to improve their offerings, quality, and productivity, and the end result is underutilized capacity. The need to acquire expensive new equipment raises the capital requirements for the firm while over-capacity leads to price-cutting, with the end result of both trends being pressure on margins.

Not surprisingly, the early days of commercial printing were characterized by intensive use of heavy machinery and a preponderance of blue-collar workers. With the advent of digital technologies and the growth of commercial software market, the ability to manipulate soft copies of images fundamentally changed the nature of the commercial printing business. Correspondingly, the work itself became more knowledge-intensive and required a higher skill level for employees. There are three major technological milestones in this transformation:

1. The introduction of the Macintosh computer and page makeup software which dramatically impacted workflows, skill requirements, cycle times, and costs in pre-press operations. This technology turned printing from a film-based to a digital medium.
2. The introduction of digital to plate equipment, enabling an operator at a Mac to produce a printing plate by issuing commands to the plate-maker.
3. The use of a network to link different offices and plants, making it possible to send digital print jobs to any location.

Digitization represented a completely new paradigm and work process for printers and, to the extent that it was new to the adopting organizations, it exemplified a radical innovation (Rogers, 1995).

Digital technologies have a profound influence on all parts of the printing supply chain. Not only is the competitive balance between buyers and suppliers changing as customers do more of their own prepress preparation of materials for printing using desktop publishing systems (Porter and Millar, 1985), the nature of product itself is changing as customers expect increasing capabilities for the management of digital images as opposed to simply their creation. The requirements for workers in the print sector have changed from a skilled craft union worker to an IT worker who uses a computer rather than film and razor blades to prepare a print job. Finally, the need for increased investments in IT to stay competitive has created strong entry barriers into printing.

An information technology-intensive approach to printing increases quality and capacity, contributing to overcapacity in the industry. Demands by customers combined with overcapacity result in price reductions and pressure on margins, making it harder for the small printer to justify an investment in digital printing equipment that is needed to stay competitive. How do firms survive in this turbulent economic climate where their core business is threatened?

EarthColor (EC), founded in 1983, has grown to become the New York metropolitan area's largest commercial printing company. Through a combination of both mergers and acquisitions as well as organic growth, EC grew sales by 246 percent between 1998 and 2000, earning the number three ranking in American Printer's Top 50 Fastest Growing Printers. EC was ranked number 44 in the 2002 Printing Impressions 500 and ranked number 46 on the 2001 list. In 2002, it was one of 28 companies with revenues between $100 and $150 million.

In 2004, EC had eight U.S. locations providing a wide range of commercial printing services including web inline printing, sheet-fed printing with aqueous and UV coating, digital prepress, computer-to-plate production, digital asset management, full bindery capabilities, fulfillment, national publication ad work, and outdoor advertising. All of EC's locations are connected by a virtual private network (VPN) which makes the Internet appear to be a private network for the company.

In order to appreciate the impact of digitization on commercial printing, it is helpful to examine the business process that existed prior to the application of IT. First, the client or the client's agency sent copy to the printer. The printer processed the copy in a prepress operation, and the amount of effort involved depended heavily on the condition of the copy. Usually, this included manual typesetting and laying out the copy. (Today, more often than not, the printer receives copy that is closer to final because the client's agency is using a desktop publishing and art system to prepare it.)

When the copy was regarded as complete, the next step was to make a printing plate. Then proof copies were produced and checked carefully for errors, colors, and overall quality. The proofing step may have resulted in the need for corrections and the production of a new plate. Once an acceptable plate had been produced, the operator prepared the print run by loading the plate and setting up the press. The press operator had to be sure that the ink colors were correct before starting a run. When the proof copies from the press were acceptable, the operator ran the job. The final step involved packaging the printed copies and shipping them to the customer.

The process was predominantly manual, error-prone, and, by today's standards, terribly inefficient. Plates were not reusable, and to the extent that errors were not caught early in the process, there could be significant wastage of resources as multiple proofs were created. Furthermore, the production of a new plate not only represented depletion of raw materials, it also introduced delays into the process. Proofing errors that were detected after the press had been set up consumed operator time in readjusting the press settings and increased overall cycle time.

Information technology has had a major impact on three aspects of EarthColor's production process including prepress, plate-making, and the flow of work among locations. The first technology transformation at EarthColor was the introduction of Macintosh and page make-up software in prepress. Prepress refers to the operations a printer performs on customer's submissions for printing before creating a printing plate. The amount of work in prepress depends on the degree to which the material from a customer is finished. Prepress might involve setting type and making up pages, creating images and editing them, or only touching up colors. The following steps describe the prepress process for an image:

- Scanning—When artwork arrives from a client in a non-digital format it is fed through a drum scanner. Today, the drum scanner creates a high-resolution digital image.
- Color separation—In sheet printing, multiple plates are created for each color. During the prepress process, the desired colors are separated into individual components. In the pre-digital era, the color separation process was a fine craft, requiring a detailed understanding of how to combine colors for maximum effect. Today, this process is completely digitized and automated.
- Stripping—a film stripper lays down the individual film layers, carefully lining them to prepare for plate-making. Each layer of film needs to be precisely aligned so that printed image that is generated from multiple plates is also aligned. This process no longer exists in a digital prepress operation.
- Imposition—Most print jobs are a fraction of the size of the printing plate. Therefore, individual pieces are combined to fill up the entire printing size (and are then cut to individual piece size). Today, a graphics program handles the imposition of individual images.
- Proofing—Before a printing plate is created, a customer is provided with proofs to review and approve. Originally, a proof was created in a custom printing process. Today, the proof comes from special high-resolution printers which require comparatively minimal labor. For certain (lower quality) printing jobs, proofing is moving to a completely digital process.
- Platemaking—By exposing a metal plate to light, the film image is transferred onto the plate surface. Just as the film processing industry has moved from the hand-crafted tasks of a dark room to self-contained automated equipment, so has the plate-making process.

Individually, the technological advances in each sub-process have reduced prepress labor. Collectively, they have changed the fundamental nature of prepress from physical materials to bits and bytes. The process input, customer artwork, process outputs, customer proofs, and, ultimately, printing plates may remain physical items, but the intervening steps are performed entirely on computers. As a result, the work environment for employees has experienced a significant transformation as well.

As craft-based industrial positions are replaced by computer-based prepress activities, the improved efficiency is responsible for a significant portion of the overall reduction in EC employees. The small increase in pay for the new positions is more than offset by the reduction in overall headcount, resulting in much lower labor expenses. For the workers who could not adapt to the Macs, the technology has been competence-destroying. Likewise, advances in printing press technology have increased production capacity without increasing associated personnel requirements. Indeed, one source of overall productivity increases is that higher quality outputs from the prepress process reduce the need for expensive production re-work.

The second major technological transformation at EarthColor involved digital-to-plate processes. After the introduction of the Mac, complementary developments occurred in the equipment manufacturing sector. The companies that manufacture plate-making equipment moved to accept digital input when the preprint process became computerized. As a result, it is a matter of a few keystrokes for a prepress employee to generate a new printing plate. The digital-to-plate process has both reduced customer cycle times and improved quality as it is easy to produce a plate, fix errors, and generate a new plate. Following the lead of the plate makers, press manufacturers developed interfaces so that the initial color settings for ink can be downloaded from a computer. A press operator still has to fine-tune the colors on the press, but by providing the starting point for the mixtures, the computerized process saves considerable time. The digital-to-plate machines are remotely monitored by the equipment supplier, providing a further reduction in labor compared to having a staff of mechanics to service plate making equipment.

EarthColor's third technology transformation is its network that ties all operations and plants together. The transition from film to digital print production enables "location transparency" and makes it possible to transfer jobs from one location to another over a network, thereby building a virtual pool of resources that EC can use to service its customers. EarthColor has established such a network among its different locations so that a prepress employee at one location can control a plate-maker at another location. EC uses this capability to balance plant costs and transportation costs with service levels. Each of its plants has a different cost of production, primarily due to regional wage differences. Customers are located around the United States, so the network allows managers to minimize the combination of production and transportation costs or to meet a looming deadline by processing a job at a plant with extra capacity.

The smooth flow of business between multiple EC locations has encouraged the movement of production equipment from higher cost locations to lower cost locations. For instance, labor costs in NYC can be as much as three times that of lower cost locations such as Florida or Texas. Network capabilities allow those plants to directly transfer plate definition and printing color specifications created by NYC prepress workers.

Taken together, the three innovations have not merely allowed EC to survive in an industry whose strategic logic was forced to evolve towards low-cost production and to thrive by expanding internal capabilities. Over the course of EarthColor's history, the customer buying process has evolved first from marketing personnel purchasing services to centralized procurement and then from those purchasing agents to supply chain managers. Customers have seen a

Table 7.1
The Impact of IT on EarthColor

Business Process	Enabling Technology	Before	After	Impact(s)
Pre-Press	Network	Jobs came through local account representative with pre-press and production completed in same location.	Jobs may arrive from any EC location and may be produced in any location.	Improved profit margins by moving work to low-cost locations and balancing work-loads during peak time periods such as earnings reports season.
Pre-Press	PC Hardware (Macs) and Software	Pre-press operations involved multiple labor-intensive processes with specific craft skills and expensive consumables (e.g., film and inks).	Fully digital process for retouching of customer art work, color definition, and other plate definition steps.	Pre-press operations require 80% fewer employees, have 66% lower labor costs, with a 200% increase in manufacturing contribution. Some nonrevenue-generating tasks, such as production of multiple proofs, have been eliminated.
Plates	Digital to Plate	Plates created manually in a labor-intensive multi-step process.	A single machine takes digital input from standard desktop graphics software to create plate.	Reduced labor costs. Increased consistency in production output. Reduced cycle times.
Production	Remote Cameras	All production management performed on-site.	Additional oversight of FL and TX production work performed from NY location.	Cost reductions by minimizing production downtime. Increased ability to meet tight customer delivery timeframes.
Production	Network	Production limited to jobs provided by local pre-press.	Production of jobs created in other EC location.	Cost reductions by moving work to low cost location. Improved efficiencies through workload balancing.
Production	CIP3	Color levels for print job manually set by production staff based on estimated color levels.	Exact color levels set digitally.	Reduced labor costs. Higher quality output with increased consistency.
Account Management	Network	Salespeople sold only products offered by the production location they worked at.	Salespeople offer printing services provided by any other EC location.	In 2003 over 17% of work was sold in one location and produced in another.

dramatic reduction in production lead times, prices, and quality increases especially related to product consistency. The more recent changes to supply chain management have further decreased the number of vendors that customers do business with and increased the value placed on integrating the finished commercial printing good with other business processes.

The grid in Table 7.1 summarizes technology-enabled changes to core EC business processes. The digitization process started at EC's NYC offices in the 1990s and has been replicated at new locations beginning with Barton Press and continuing through multiple locations added during a merger with IGI.

The technology at EarthColor has had a striking impact on major aspects of the firm. At an aggregate level:

- During the four full years spanning 2000–2003, the number of EC employees has dropped by a cumulative 42.6 percent.
- During this same time period, revenue per employee has increased 268 percent.

The overall impact of information technology on EarthColor, and on commercial printing, is profound. Table 7.1 shows the significant changes in EarthColor's workflows and processes. Moving from film to digital printing is an extraordinary change in terms of quality, response and cycle times, and economics. Digital printing means that images can be received from clients and sent to printing plants literally with the click of a mouse. Technology changes the nature of work in prepress, reduces labor costs, and reduces costs in production through quality enhancements and workload balancing. The sales force can sell work in one location that is produced someplace else. Revenue per employee is up significantly for EarthColor at a time when the economic situation for printers is poor, with declining prices and pressure on margins.

EC illustrates how the spoils go to the innovators and those who can execute and how technology helps lead to a hyper-competitive economy. It shows how physical processes are becoming digital and how those resisting change or unable to change are being left behind. For EarthColor as a company, the technology revolution has been competence-enhancing. However, for small printers with fewer than 100 employees and for the employees of EC who lost their jobs, the technology has clearly been competence-destroying. Many did not survive the technology revolution. Manufacturing has been shrinking in the United States due to competition from lower-wage countries. Maintaining a technological edge is an important strategy for keeping a viable manufacturing sector in the United States (Argarwal, Johnson, Lucas and Kashan, 2007).

REFERENCES

Abrahamson, E., and Rosenkopf, L. "Social Network Effects on the Extent of Innovation Diffusion: A Computer Simulation." *Organization Science* 8 (3) (1997): 289–309.

Agarwal, R., and Lucas, H. C., Jr. "The IS Identity Crisis: Focusing on High-Visibility and High-Impact Research." *MIS Quarterly* 29 (3) (2005): 381–398.

Agarwal, R., S. Johnson, H. Lucas, and R. Kashan. "Technological Discontinuities: The Transformation of EarthColor." Smith School of Business, working paper, 2007.

Anderson, P., and Tushman, M. "Technological Discontinuities and Dominant Designs: A Cyclical Model of Technological Change." *Administrative Science Quarterly* 35(4) (1990): 604–633.

Bakos, Y., Lucas Jr., H. C., Oh, W., Simon, G., Viswanathan, S., and Weber, B. "The Impact of E-Commerce on Competition in the Retail Brokerage Industry." *Information Systems Research* 16(4) (2005): 352–371.

Bradley, S. P., and Nolan, R. L. *Sense & Respond: Capturing Value in the Network Era.* Boston, MA: Harvard Business School Press (1998).

Chiasson, M., and Davidson, E. "Taking Industry Seriously in Information Systems Research." *MIS Quarterly* 29(4) (2005): 591–605.

Copeland, D. J., and McKenney, D. L. "Airlines Reservations Systems: Lessons from History." *MIS Quarterly* 12(3) (1988): 352–370.

Crowston, K., and Myers, M. D. "Information Technology and the Transformation of Industries: Three Research Perspectives." *Journal of Strategic Information Systems* 13 (2004): 5–28.

Dehning, B., Richardson, V., and Zmud, R. W. "The Value Relevance of Announcements of Transformational Information Technology Investments." *MIS Quarterly* 27(4) (2003): 637–656.

Eisenhardt, K. M. "Building Theories from Case Study Research." *Academy of Management Review* 14(4) (1989): 532–550.

Eisenhardt, K. M. and Sull, D. M. "Strategy as Simple Rules." *Harvard Business Review* (January 2001): 106–119.

Garud, R., and Kumaraswamy, A. "Vicious and Virtuous Circles in the Management of Knowledge: The Case of Infosys Technologies."*MIS Quarterly* 29(1) (2005): 9–33.

Kohli, R., and Kettiner, W. J. "Informating the Clan: Controlling Physicians' Costs and Outcomes." *MIS Quarterly* 28(3) (2004): 363–394.

Markus, L., and Robey, D. "Information Technology and Organizational Change: Causal Structure in Theory and Research." *Management Science* 34(5) (1988): 583–598.

Mason, R. O., McKenney, D. L., and Copeland, D. J. "Bank of America: The Crest and Trough of Technological Leadership." *MIS Quarterly* 21(3) (1997): 321–353.

NAPL, Printing Industry Information; http://www.napl.org/newsroom/industry_info.htm (accessed November 6, 2003).

Porter, M. E., and Millar, V. W. "How Information Gives you Competitive Advantage." *Harvard Business Review* 79(3) (1985): 63–78.

Rogers, E. M. *Diffusion of Innovation* (Fourth ed.). New York: The Free Press (1995).

Romanelli, E., and Tushman, M. "Organizational Transformation as Punctuated Equilibrium: An Empirical Test." *Academy of Management Journal* 37(5) (1994) : 1141–1166.

Rosen, Robert H. *The Graphic Arts CEO.* Honesdale, PA: CEO Roundtable Press (2003).

Tushman, M., and Anderson, P. "Technological Discontinuities and Organizational Environments." *Administrative Science Quarterly* 31(3) (1986): 439–465.

Venkatraman, N., "IT Induced Business Reconfiguration." In Scott Morton, M.S. (Ed.), *The Corporation of the 1990s* New York: Oxford University Press (1991): 122–158.

Yin. R. *Case Study Research.* Beverly Hills, CA: Sage (1984).

8

The Digital Pipeline

The Internet is a transformational technology; it has changed the way business operates and the way we live. Over 60 percent of U.S. households have an Internet connection, and three-quarters of those have broadband or high-speed Internet access. However, the United States ranks 25th in broadband penetration behind countries like South Korea where it is 89 percent and Canada at 63 percent (*Wall Street Journal,* 8/9/2007). It is estimated that one billion people in the world have Internet access with 250 million having broadband connections. Asia-Pacific is the largest broadband center, and Latin America is the fastest growing broadband region in the world. Europe has 233 million people online, with 55 million having broadband (eMarketer, 2006). The world's population is about 6.6 billion people, so 15 percent of the world's population can access the Internet.

The U.S. Defense Department funded the development of the Internet with the first nodes brought online in 1969. The Internet developed new ways to transmit data over communications lines; its protocols are known as "packet switching" and are totally different from conventional circuit-switching technology. When a person made a phone call in 1969, the phone company set up a dedicated circuit between the caller and the person being called. If the conversation was interrupted, or if someone put the phone down and left the circuit open, the call still consumed the same capacity from the carrier. Packet switching involves breaking a message into small packets, each with the address of its destination, and sending the packets over different routes to that destination. The receiving end has to reassemble the packets in the proper sequence. Since the network is only sending data when packets are ready, it uses bandwidth much more efficiently than a circuit-switched network.

In the United States, telecommunications companies, including phone and cable companies, are converting their networks to packet switching. At the same time, new entrants are coming into the communications business with products

> ## Surviving
>
> The digital pipeline to our homes provides us with many benefits including access to the Internet and a huge amount of content. It is the path for music and increasingly for videos. For children, it is a necessary part of a modern education. An educated person today has to know how to conduct research and make use of the Internet to do their job.
>
> There has been great national and international concern about being left behind in the digital revolution. National policy in the United States has been to provide Internet connectivity for schools and libraries. The first "digital divide" between well-off children and children living near or in poverty has largely been erased by this access. While children of relatively wealthy parents have their own computers, poor children are able to access the Internet at school or in a library, reducing the impact of the divide.
>
> The outlook is not as promising at the country level. There are huge disparities among developed and developing countries in Internet learning and access for children. If you believe in the technology revolution, then it is clear that developing countries have to join in or they will fall further behind in a world economy that is increasingly digital, mobile, and virtual. Yet how does a development agency trade off Internet access against providing potable water to a village? The One Laptop per Child initiative is an effort to answer the huge technology needs of children in less developed countries, but it has to be supplemented with teachers and tutors who can get the machines running and provide basic instructions on how to use them. If developing countries fall behind in the technology revolution as they have in so many other aspects of the economy, then there is little hope for them.

and services that are digital. The intense competition and rampant confusion in telecommunications is an illustration of:

Rule: *Products and services that can become digital will, and their physical representations will disappear.*

A CONFUSING COMPETITIVE LANDSCAPE

If one assumes that having Internet access is a good idea, there are several questions that arise:

1. What provider and what technology will provide Internet connectivity to your home?
2. What provider and what technology will provide Internet access when you are away from home?

3. How can the United States and other countries expand Internet access to their population and reduce the so-called "digital divide"?

In the United States, the first question involves a confusing and rapidly changing scene as new technologies and new players appear with innovative offerings. Table 8.1 describes the competitive environment in the United States at the time of this writing. Why is this story important? Many of the transformations discussed in this book depend on the Internet. The Internet enables electronic commerce, online communities, communications, email, and much else. Both fixed and mobile connections to the Internet are key to maintaining current transformational aspects of the technology, and for the development of future features,

Table 8.1
The Telecommunications Landscape in the United States

Technologies	Incumbents who are threatened	Challengers with new technology	Responses by incumbent
Fiber optics	Cable operators	The four regional phone companies	Digital cable, Phone→VOIP
Voice over Internet protocol (VOIP)	RBOCS (The old Bell operating companies, like Verizon) with fixed lines and dedicated circuits for each call	Cable, wireless, Vonage	DSL, fiber to curb, video alliances DSB, acquire wireless capabilities
Direct Satellite Broadcast (DSB)	Cable companies	The four regional phone companies, Cable	Form alliances to provide Internet access
Wireless	Regional phone companies, but they have wireless subsidiaries and alliances	Advancing cellular generations	Build new wireless networks
DSL	Phone companies	Cable operators	Faster DSL
Digital Cable	Regional phone companies	Cable companies	Verizon fiber network, DSL
IPTV	Cable, networks	AOL, Yahoo, iTunes, YouTube	?
WiMax (urban areas)	Telephone companies and cell phone companies	Google, Cisco, alliances	Seek legislative protection

businesses, and services. Expanded access to the Internet is also important for developing nations and for individuals who do not have access now.

When commercial television arrived in the 1950s, signals traveled through the air. Everyone had a pair of "rabbit ears" (inside antenna) or an external antenna on the roof. At this time the only way to have telephone service was with a physical line to your house or apartment. Today, most people in the United States receive their television via cable or direct broadcast satellite, a $56 billion market. An estimated 9 percent of Americans have dropped their land lines and rely exclusively on cell phones for voice communications. At first users connected to the Internet through high speed lines at work (if they were lucky) and from dial-up connections at home. Broadband or high-speed Internet access makes it possible to use many web sites where response time is just too long with a dial-up line. So today much TV content comes via a wire (cable) instead of through the air, and a huge number of phone calls involve at least one party connected without a wire on a cell phone. How quickly things change.

Who are the players in the Internet access business today?

- Cable companies offering broadband access over their networks.
- Verizon with fiber optics lines to the curb; AT&T with fiber to the neighborhood.
- Telephone companies offering Digital Subscriber Line (DSL) connections.
- Cellular operators with medium-speed connections to the Internet.
- Companies offering wireless "hot spots," in airports, coffee shops, and other locations.
- Companies proposing wide-area wireless using technologies like WiMax.

The most competitive battle today is between the phone and cable companies. Both of these industries are near saturation in terms of signing up customers; growth will come from new services and stealing customers from other service providers. Each side is trying to convert customers from its competition. Cable companies offer phone service over their digital cable lines. The cable companies charge less for phone service than the phone companies, and the customer receives cable TV, Internet access, and phone charges on the same bill. Cable has a big advantage because a cable is a fat pipe for data into the home compared with a phone line, which consists of two twisted wires.

While phone lines connect most dwellings in the United States, as originally configured they are a low-bandwidth medium. Through continued research and development, engineers have been able to send more data at higher speeds over the twisted pair lines that run from the curb to the subscriber's house. The phone companies offer DSL service to many households though there can be limitations due to the subscriber's distance from a telephone central office. Some of the regional phone companies have alliances with direct view satellite TV providers to sell their television services to the phone company's customers.

Verizon is a special case among the four remaining regional telephone operating companies. It is investing at least $18 billion through 2010 to run fiber to the curb and cable from the curb to the dwelling unit. Verizon management is convinced that a telephone company needs to replace its low-speed communications with high-speed fiber. It is installing fiber across its service area and simultaneously applying for permission to offer television services to compete with those from cable TV companies. Verizon is able to provide the customer with a single bill for voice (fixed and cellular), Internet, and television. Verizon's costs for hooking up a new customer had dropped to $933 by August of 2006, down from $1,220 in January (*Wall Street Journal,* 9/28/2006).

The cable companies began their competition with the phone companies by offering phone service along with cable television. Sending voice as data packets using Internet protocols fits nicely with the private broadband cable network; video and voice travel easily over the same network. Cable firms have been successful in signing up customers for phone service, and the phone companies find themselves losing subscribers for their landline phone service, contributing to the fierce competition between phone and cable.

VOIP (voice over Internet protocol) technology has also led to more competition for the phone companies. Taking advantage of the existence of the Internet, businesses like Vonage offer VOIP telephone services to homes with a high-speed Internet connection. Because VOIP carriers have little invested in plant and equipment, they offer calling at very low rates.

If it is possible to send voice over the Internet, why not transmit video the same way? As content providers figure out how viewers will want to see their product, they are experimenting with making content available on the Internet after it has appeared on a TV network. TV shows and excerpts from shows are available on some Internet service provider Web sites and iTunes. CBS is developing an online service as an alternative to the evening news, something the network says will allow it to bypass the cable networks. In the fall of 2006, Apple began to sell movie downloads from Walt Disney on iTunes. It takes a minimum of half an hour to download a movie from iTunes, but the viewer can start to watch it a minute after the download starts. What is the threat from these services for the cable companies? The Internet can store an unlimited amount of content, giving TV watchers access to many more films than on-demand cable services provide, and it can do so more efficiently.

Another Internet service, Skype, provides free calling. The developers of Skype previously produced successful file-sharing software. eBay bought Skype to provide the opportunity for free voice communications during auctions. But Skype offers a lot more. A user at a computer can make a free call to any other computer on the Internet. "Skype out" lets the user call a conventional phone from his or her computer for a small charge. It is also easy to add a video camera on a PC and have a videophone conversation as well as a conference call.

Who else connects to the home? Power companies have been investing in technology that allows them to send Internet traffic over the power line to your house. Because every room is wired for power, Broadband over Power Line (BPL) requires no special wiring and Internet access becomes available in every room in a house. There are two experiments underway now, and many power companies are watching to see if they should begin to offer this service.

Comcast has responded to all of these threats by rebuilding its cable network using Internet technology, which will allow phone, broadband, and TV content to use the same cable wires. To accomplish this feat, the company is developing a national fiber-optic network connecting 45 major cities. It has leased 19,000 miles of cable from Level 3 Communications for $100 million. This network will let Comcast store content centrally instead of at the 4,500 head-end transmission centers where it is stored now. The central storage will be virtually unlimited in contrast with the limited storage at the head-ends (*Wall Street Journal*, 10/13/2005).

MOBILE INTERNET ACCESS

The regional phone companies also have interests in wireless, cellular systems and are competing with themselves to offer Internet connectivity over these networks. While faster than dial-up, the cellular Internet connection speed is about a third of the speed of a cable Internet modem and 10 percent of the speed of Verizon's least costly fiber connection. The cellular carriers are currently expanding their data networks, but as of now, a subscriber does not have medium-speed connectivity all across the United States from one carrier.

Starbucks began a trend by offering wireless Internet access in its stores. Another place where people with a desire to access the Internet wait is airport lounges and gates, and many airports have wireless access available. Most locations with these wireless "hot spots" charge a fee for access, and as of now, they do not interoperate. So if you pay a fee to use Starbucks' network, that does not let you access the network at the local airport. For now the answer is to pay by the hour for Internet access in many hotels, airports and other locations, or look for a free wireless network "hotspot."

COMMUNITY ACCESS

Has the Internet reached the point of being an essential public utility? Should cities provide Internet access for all of their residents at a reasonable price? In some cities, especially in the Midwest, a municipal authority provides electrical power. Should Internet access follow that path and be available to all, subsidized, if necessary, by the city? According to the website http://www.muniwireless.com, there are 300 municipal or country wireless projects that are working, being installed, or at the planning stage.

The city of Philadelphia thinks the answer to the questions above is "yes." It is turning the 135 square mile city into a wireless hotspot for its 1.6 million residents. The city wants to make broadband available in neighborhoods which are not reached by broadband phone lines or cable and those that cannot afford to pay commercial rates for high-speed service. The city will offer access for up to

25,000 low-income homes for $9.95 a month and plans to distribute 10,000 PCs as a part of the effort to bring technology to those who do not have access now. The technology is similar to the WiFi networks many consumers have in their homes to share a high-speed connection among different computers. EarthLink is building the system for the city, and it is being financed by taxable bonds (*InformationWeek*, 5/21/2007). As one might expect, the phone companies oppose this plan and have lobbied heavily against it. They have tried to get different state legislatures to pass laws making it illegal for a municipality to offer Internet services to its residents.

On August 28, 2007, EarthLink restructured itself and appears to have exited the municipal WiFi business. The networks of thousands of WiFi nodes proved more costly to build than predicted, and the company did not see a way to earn profits. EarthLink will stop investing in municipal WiFi projects unless cities are committed to investing in the network (*InformationWeek*, 8/27 and 9/3/ 2007). This action by EarthLink is not the end of municipal access; small cities will continue to invest in WiFi, while larger cities will move to WiMax. The technology of WiMax is similar to WiFi, but the nodes have much greater range, up to 30 miles, drastically reducing the number of nodes needed to cover a city. Plus, it will provide faster speeds than WiFi.

Cisco, IBM, Seakay, and Azulstar Networks are collaborating to build and operate a regional wireless network in Silicon Valley that will serve 2.4 million residents. The system will offer an open wireless network to all residents and visitors in the 42 municipalities that cover 1,500 square miles. One megabit access will be free, and there will be a number of additional services for businesses and individuals for which the company will charge fees. The network will be privately owned and operated (*Market Wire*, 9/5/2006).

Google and EarthLink have proposed a plan to offer free wireless connectivity in San Francisco in an attempt to take business away from the telephone companies. What is in this for Google? It makes most of its money from advertising; by offering free wireless services it will bring more people to its Web site, increasing the opportunities to sell ads and generate click-throughs to advertisers' Web sites. Google's large advertising revenue will pay for the free wireless access. At the time of this writing, the project has proven very controversial and the outcome is in doubt. However, the phone companies have something else to worry about with this new business model from Google. The phone companies do not have Google's large advertising base to support free service, and they may be forced to cut their access rates because of the competition from free wireless.

By mid-2007 more than 90 cities had launched WiFi services with nationwide spending estimated at $236 million in 2006; that number is expected to double in the next few years. As with any new business, there have been problems resulting in delays and cost overruns. At the same time, phone companies have reduced the price of their Internet connections so that the vendors building WiMax networks in cities are asking for local governments to guarantee that they will be customers and asking them to put up capital for the projects (*Wall Street Journal*, 8/16/2007).

The danger to the phone companies is that everyone will abandon their services when less expensive wireless becomes available. For a company like Verizon, which has bet billions on the appeal of a fiber network to the dwelling, the threat is very real. City-wide networks would let a subscriber use the Internet at home and have the same connection when traveling or located at any other part of the city that is included in the wireless network. There would be no need to subscribe to multiple service providers, one for home and one for mobile access.

TRANSFORMING THE TELECOMMUNICATIONS BUSINESS

At this point, it is pretty clear that the old line phone companies are facing a huge challenge and are likely to have their business models transformed. Competitors on all sides are attacking the traditional franchise of the local telephone company:

- Cable companies are offering phone services.
- Wireless carriers are offering voice and data services.
- Start-ups like Vonage and Skype are offering VOIP calling.
- Municipalities are interested in providing Internet connectivity as a utility.
- Google wants to capture people for its Web site by giving free wireless access to the Net.

What's a phone company to do? What strategy should the phone companies follow? The answers to these questions are not clear, and each phone company has a different strategic response. Some are pushing their DSL connections, while Verizon is making the bold and risky move of building a fiber optic network to the customer's curb. The companies are consolidating to the point that there are only four regional phone companies remaining. SBC and Verizon have purchased the major long distance carriers, AT&T and MCI, respectively. The phone companies have come face-to-face with three of our rules:

Rule: *The spoils go to innovators and those who can execute.*

Rule: *The rapid development of new technology-based business models is responsible for a hyper-competitive economy.*

Rule: *Individuals, organizations, and countries who resist technological change and fail to adapt will be left behind.*

The results of this highly competitive scene are hard to predict. It seems likely that there will be a variety of ways in the United States to access the Internet and charges for doing so should drop due to the competition. There will be demand for different mobile solutions to interoperate so that a subscriber can pay a fixed monthly amount and have access in urban hot spots, Starbucks, and airports around the country for this one fee.

WHO WILL BE LEFT OUT?

As the Internet grew dramatically in the 1990s, there was great concern in the United States that we faced a "digital divide." Users of the Internet were largely white and affluent. Children that were in low-income groups who also tended to be minorities did not have Internet access. With the impetus provided by the Clinton administration, the United States connected schools and libraries to the Internet. A recent study found that much of the digital divide has been reduced in the United States, at least for children. While the affluent white student has a computer in the home or in his or her room for doing schoolwork and communicating with friends, the low-income minority child accesses the Internet at school or in a library, but the low income student has access to and is using the Internet.

What about the rest of the world? People in many other countries, especially developing nations in Africa, Latin America, and parts of Asia, do not have access to the Internet. There are many barriers to connecting with the Internet including:

- Lack of a device to make the connection.
- Lack of a communications infrastructure.
- Lack of electrical power.
- Insufficient funds to pay for Internet access.
- Government censorship for religious or political reasons.
- Lack of education and training on how to use the technology.

Nicholas Negroponte, formerly head of the M.I.T. Media Laboratory, now heads the One Laptop per Child initiative. His idea was to create an inexpensive laptop computer that governments could buy to distribute to citizens or that low-income individuals could buy themselves. The inexpensive laptop runs open source software and is designed to access the Internet (see Figure 8.1). The computer is designed to require minimal power.

While originally created for the developing world, there is interest in the United States in this machine as well. When he was governor of Massachusetts, Mitt Romney proposed a $54 million program to equip each of 500,000 middle and high schoolers with laptops which the students could keep (*Seattle Times,* 11/17/2005). In the fall of 2006, One Laptop per Child announced an agreement with the government of Libya to supply computers to all 1.2 million Libyan schoolchildren by the summer of 2008. Libya will invest $250 million in the project to receive 1.2 million computers, one server per school, and a team of advisers to set up the service, satellite Internet access, and the rest of the necessary infrastructure. It is possible that Libya will be the first country where all school-age children have Internet connections for educational purposes. So far,

Figure 8.1
One Laptop per Child Prototype

Photo by Mike McGregor. Courtesy OLPC.

this nonprofit has announced tentative purchase agreements with Brazil, Argentina, Nigeria, and Thailand. A Taiwanese company, Quanta Computer Inc., will manufacture the laptops (*New York Times,* 10/11/2006). There are trials underway in ten countries with a total of 25 planned by the end of 2007. The current price of the machines is about $175, which should drop as production ramps up (*BusinessWeek,* 7/9 & 16/2007). There is great optimism that this project will dramatically expand access to modern technology and reduce the digital divide.

We should note that the inexpensive laptop is not the only solution being offered to bring technology to the developing countries of the world. Microsoft argues that a cell phone device like a super personal digital assistant is the answer since many countries have cell networks and people who already are familiar with the phones. Another Microsoft initiative is a pay-as-you-go computer where people would pay just for their use of a shared machine. Advanced Micro Devices is working on a PC in India that will sell for about $200.

Intel has several low-cost systems including a ClassMate $320 notebook computer for students. It has launched a "community PC" for $350 that can run on a car battery and has a one-button "recover" feature when the machine crashes (*Business Week,* 6/12/2006). Intel is working on price reductions to below $300 for the ClassMate and a price of $200 for another version of the machine. A chemistry teacher in Mexico reported that her students with the Intel laptops participate more in class and are more interested in reading and searching for information online. Intel recently started trials in the United States of a more powerful version of the ClassMate for children in the developed world (*Business-Week*, 7/9 & 16/2007).

With a little work, a laptop for every child has the potential to make a real difference in education. Despite rhetoric and laws on standards and testing, schools in the United States reflect the communities in which they are located. A failed school is a sign of a failed community that has taken the school along with it. One of the many differences between successful, affluent suburban schools, and poor, inner city schools is the extent of parental involvement. The suburban school has a highly involved group of parents, many of whom volunteer at the school. Parents are in touch with school officials about their children and interact with the teachers. What if every child in the inner-city school had a laptop computer and Internet access? What if the teachers had Web sites for each class that talked about what was going on in class and showcased the work of students? It is possible that students could teach their parents how to use email to communicate with teachers and to access and respond to teacher and administrator blogs. It is not clear what we need to dramatically improve education, but I am convinced that technology of the kind discussed here has an important role to play.

But the computer is only one part of the equation; there is a need to attack other parts of the challenge, especially in developing countries. Less than 4 percent of Africa's population is connected to the Web, the lowest of any part of the world. Most of these connections are in northern Africa or in the country of South Africa. The most significant problem is lack of infrastructure; in many African countries communications networks were destroyed during wars. These countries have concentrated on mobile phones rather than Internet access as there is far more demand for voice communications than for the Web. Africa also lacks high-speed connectivity to the rest of the world. Email and phone calls from some African countries have to be routed through Britain or the United States, increasing expense and delivery times. It is estimated that 75 percent of African Internet traffic is routed through these other countries (*New York Times*, 7/22/2007).

The lack of a communications infrastructure in many developing countries can be addressed in two ways: the government and international bodies. The government solution will take some time as building a communications infrastructure is not easy or fast. Today it is likely that structure would be wireless as it is much less expensive to build a wireless network than bury cable in the ground. Internationally, agencies have made available satellite channels so that remote locations can access the Internet when no other option is available.

Electrical power can be provided by solar panels, generators, a crank on the computer, or, as in one village, by a child riding a stationary bicycle connected to a generator. For many in developing countries, the government or aid groups will have to provide free or subsidized access to the Internet. In the United States, municipalities will have to overcome the tactics of the phone companies to prevent them from offering low-cost Internet access to residents.

There are other barriers to Internet usage in other countries. For example, there is little we can do about government censorship of the Internet in some countries. Conservative religious groups and governments want to block Web sites and content. It is estimated that China has between 30,000 and 50,000 people attempting to censor the Web so that material objectionable to the government is not available. Our rule about countries falling behind that resist the technology may, in the end, force wider access to the Net.

Ability to use computers is another barrier. If one watches children online, it seems that using many of the features of the Internet are intuitive. However, for many people in the world, the technology presents a formidable barrier to use. One drawback of programs to distribute technology that are focused on hardware and telecommunications is the failure to provide education and training. There are stories of computers being placed in public locations that remain unused or children that use the machines only for playing games. In addition to hardware and software, any effort to expand the availability and use of the technology will require a massive training and educational effort. One solution is to create an "international technology corps" to educate new users and to train selected local users to train others. Such a corps could be formed under the auspices of the United Nations or a group of developed countries as a way to help developing countries advance to keep them from being left further behind.

SUMMARY

There is an old Chinese curse: "May you live in interesting times," which applies to the telecommunications landscape in the United States. The bottom line is that digital technology is transforming voice communications, video, and Internet access. There is a large cast of players, all of whom are fiercely competitive. Each uses slightly different approaches to create products and services based on its history, past investments in technology, and available infrastructure. It is too early to tell which firm and technology will dominate for each type of service. It may be hard to forecast how you will be connected, but you will be connected at home, the office, in your car, and wherever you are. As Carly Fiorina's rule says: *Every process will become digital, virtual, and mobile.*

9

U.S. Healthcare: A Desperate Need for a Transformation

Most of the cost and quality issues in healthcare are about wrong information at the wrong place at the wrong time in the wrong hands. That's what information technology does. Now, of course, the hard part about that is information technology is only one part of the solution. The other part is that people actually have to change what they do; that's the hard part. . . . It's easy to devise a new email system. It's harder to get people to change their habits. So one of the things that I would say is it is not technology that will slow its advance, it's people. Technology moves faster than people change their habits.
—Carly Fiorina interview, 2007

The U.S. healthcare system is broken. The medical profession has made extensive progress in curing and preventing illness and in incredible feats of surgery. The United States invests heavily in medical research to find cures for diseases that have plagued mankind for centuries. The bad news is that this huge system is failing on two counts: quality of care and administrative efficiency. Figure 9.1 shows past and projected health care expenditures in the United States; they are approaching $2 trillion and show no signs of a decrease. This amount is about 16 percent of the U.S. GDP, and the curve is moving upward with no inflection point in sight. The United States spends far more per capita than any other country on health care, almost 60 percent more than European countries, yet its population is not the healthiest in the world based on outcome measures like infant mortality. Worse, there are an estimated 45 million uninsured people in the United States.

A recent study by the Kaiser Family Foundation found that the cost of employee health care coverage rose 7.7 percent between the spring of 2005 and 2006, over twice the rate of inflation. Individuals paid an average of $2,973 out of a total family coverage bill of $11,481. Since 2000, the cost of family coverage has risen 87 percent while the consumer price index is up 18 percent and worker

> ## Surviving
>
> The health care industry is behind the rest of the economy in adapting to the revolution in technology. The question is how to keep from falling further behind and how to keep the system from falling apart completely.
>
> The objective of health information technology (HIT) is to dramatically improve the quality of care and produce large gains in efficiency, thereby reducing costs. Electronic health records improve the quality of care in several ways—for example, by providing the physician with a complete medical record where care is being delivered and by creating a huge database of medical outcomes that can be used to show which treatments work best. Electronic health records can also provide substantial gains in productivity by reducing duplicate tests and treatments and cutting back on the need to handle physical records.
>
> Transforming health care is going to require an alliance of a large number of parties including doctors; hospitals; insurance firms; federal, state, and local governments; and consumers of health care. To date, these entities barely cooperate as each tries to shift costs to the other. The technology to help is available; HIT is a huge implementation challenge that the United States has not yet tried to meet. The national effort is under-funded and not particularly well-coordinated. As a result, we may have a case of "the faster we run, the farther behind we get."

pay has increased 20 percent (*New York Times*, 9/27/2006). The premiums are rising faster for small firms than large, and one fear is that companies will be forced to drop health care coverage for their employees.

A small group of economists have argued that health care can become the engine that drives the economy since by 2030 it will likely consume 25 percent of the GDP. Since 2001, the health-care industry has added 1.7 million jobs while the private sector has added none (*Business Week*, 9/25/2006). These experts say that because the United States is so wealthy, and it requires so little household income to satisfy needs for food, clothing, and shelter, we will be glad to spend money on better health outcomes. Two members of this school ask a pointed question: As people age and become more wealthy, which is more valuable, an extra car or home theater, or an extra year of life (*New York Times*, 8/22/2006)? They point out that a baby born today will live to an average age of 78, a decade longer than the average for a baby born in 1950. If you have made it to your 40s, you can expect to reach 80. Proponents of this view argue that our large expenditures on health care have produced these kinds of positive outcomes (*New York Times*, 9/27/2006).

This argument helps to justify some of the large cost increases in health care; patients receive better care and more positive outcomes today than years ago. However, the logic of this explanation runs into two problems: the first is

Figure 9.1
U.S. Health Care Expenditures

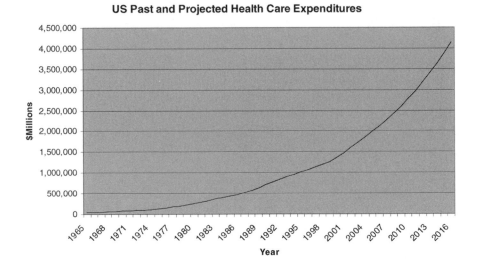

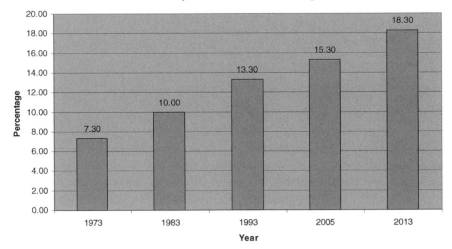

efficiency, and the second is quality of care on a broader scale. The current system is hugely inefficient which means that a great deal of money that could be invested in new medical treatment goes for wasteful processes. More serious is the fact that the current system is also highly error-prone because of the structure of health care delivery in the United States and a perverse incentive scheme.

A 2000 report by the National Institute of Medicine estimates that medical errors cause 44,000 to 98,000 deaths a year, about two times the number who die in auto accidents. A recent report by the Institute of Medicine concluded that medical errors harm 1.5 million people each year and kill several thousand, costing at least $3.5 billion annually (*New York Times*, 7/21/2006). The report concluded that drug errors are so widespread that a patient should expect to suffer one each day he or she is in the hospital, though many of these errors do not lead to injury. Errors often involve administering the wrong drug or the wrong dosage of a drug to a hospital patient. Technology can solve this problem.

It has also been estimated that 10 percent to 30 percent of health care costs are devoted to administration. From an administrative standpoint, in 2004 more than 90 percent of health care transactions occurred via phone, fax, or an exchange of paper (Burgleman, Pearl, and Meza, 2004). A visit to a typical doctor's office or hospital involves filling out forms and signing papers. After the visit, more forms are exchanged between the provider and insurance companies or the government. The former National Coordinator for Health Information Technology said in a newspaper article, "I'm the president's senior adviser on health information technology, and when I get an E.O.B. [explanation of benefits from an insurance company] for my 4-year-old's care, I can't figure out what happened, or what I'm supposed to do" (*New York Times*, 10/14/2005).

The article goes on to describe the huge piles of papers patients find waiting for them after receiving medical services, and estimates that close to 30 cents of every dollar spent on health care is for administration. Much of this amount goes to generating bills and explanations of benefits. After an office visit, a doctor sends a diagnostic code to the patient's insurer, which determines the level of payment. The codes, of course, differ from the codes the insurer prints on the E.O.B.s sent to the patient. And the billing codes in hospitals are entirely different as well. Technology cannot eliminate all paper in health care just as it has not eliminated paper in business, but it can go a long way toward reengineering the processes involved.

THE ROLE OF TECHNOLOGY

The technology exists today to make major improvements in the quality and efficiency of health care, but there are many barriers to implementation. How can technology help? It can be used to:

- Create an electronic medical record for patients, including a portable record (only 3 percent of hospitals have electronic patient records) (*New York Times*, 7/21/2006).
- Provide for electronic prescription writing and fulfillment (only 6 percent of the nation's hospitals have electronic drug order entry systems) (*New York Times*, 7/21/2006).
- Automate many hospital procedures to reduce errors.
- Automate many of the procedures in doctors' offices.
- Create automated payments systems encompassing providers and payers.

- Create databases of patient illnesses and treatments for research purposes and to enable "evidence-based" medicine.

Consider the following scenarios of patients, doctors, and hospitals and how a technology-based, rational system could improve things. Our hypothetical patient, Mary, has a cut on her leg that is not healing; it is red and sore. She goes to the Web site of her internist, Dr. Anne Young, and looks at the doctor's online appointment calendar. She finds an opening the next afternoon for unscheduled "walk-ins," patients who have a problem that has occurred suddenly and need immediate attention.

Mary arrives at the time of her appointment and presents the "thumb drive" memory stick on her car key ring to the receptionist. The receptionist inserts the drive in her USB drive and updates Mary's insurance record in the doctor's office computer system. Simultaneously, the system brings up Mary's medical record on the PC in the examining room where Mary will be treated. Dr. Young looks at Mary's wound and agrees that it is infected. She writes up the visit on the PC and the information is stored in Mary's electronic medical record. The doctor keys in a prescription for an antibiotic to treat the infected wound, and the system sends the prescription to the pharmacy where Mary buys her medicine. This information also updates Mary's personal health record on her thumb drive. The doctor tells Mary to call her in three days if the wound is still red and uncomfortable. Mary thanks the doctor and leaves to go to the pharmacy to pick up her prescription.

Dr. Young's updating of the medical record includes billing information to request payment from Mary's insurance company. The system automatically sends the information the company needs to process payment, and if there are no questions at the insurer, it will transfer an electronic payment that night to the medical group where Dr. Young practices.

At the pharmacy, a computer accesses Mary's electronic medical record to check the antibiotic the doctor prescribed for interactions with the list of any medications that Mary is taking. Fortunately, Mary does not use any medications on a regular basis, so the pharmacist prepares the bottle of antibiotics for her to pick up.

What is different in this scenario compared to the typical medical office visit? Notice that there was no paper involved; all processes and transactions took place electronically. The doctors, nurses, and pharmacist had access to complete information about the patient. Mary's electronic medical record, or EMR, provided common information that was both legible and up-to-date. The technology reduced the possibility of errors, and made the transactions involved much more efficient than today's paper-based systems.

This same approach is being applied slowly in hospital settings, and we will look at two systems which have made great progress. The idea is the same: reduce medical errors, improve the quality of care, and improve efficiency.

THE DEPARTMENT OF VETERANS AFFAIRS LEADS THE WAY

A decade or more ago, the U.S. veterans' health care system was considered to be in a state of disrepair. Today, the 154 Veterans Hospitals and 875 Department of Veterans Affairs (VA) clinics serve 5.4 million patients. The VA is ranked best-in-class by a number of independent groups using a broad range of measures including the percentage of members who receive flu shots, indicators of chronic care, and the treatment of heart disease according to a *Business Week* article (7/17/2006). Consider the following: Studies show that 3 percent to 8 percent of the prescriptions filled in the United States are in error, while the VA's prescription accuracy rate is better than 99.997 percent. As one might suspect, there is a lot of information technology that helps the VA achieve these rankings.

But technology is not the only factor involved. According to the article, the VA has adopted a culture of caring for its patients, for concern over patient safety, and for quality of services that "is pervasive." The technology in place is well within the state-of-the-art; in fact, most professionals can easily envision how IT can make a dramatic transformation of healthcare possible, but the implementation problems are daunting.

In the mid-1990s, a VA Health undersecretary, Dr. Kenneth W. Kizer, installed the most extensive electronic medical records system in the country while decentralizing decision-making. He also closed underutilized hospitals, which angered congressmen, so Kizer was never confirmed in his post and had to leave the VA! Kizer worked for a culture of accountability, saying, "Our motivation was to make the system work for the patient. . . . We did a top-to-bottom makeover with that goal always in mind" (*Business Week,* 7/17/2006, p. 51). What helped is that the VA is nationwide and that its funding comes from a single payer, which makes it much easier to implement major technological change.

The center of the technology is VistA, an electronic medical records system. The database records every office visit, prescription, and medical procedure, everything about a VA staff member's interaction with the patient. These records are available at any location 100 percent of the time. The VA estimates that 96 percent of its prescriptions and medical orders are entered electronically. The national total for comparison is closer to 8 percent. A VA official indicated that one out of five tests in non-VA hospitals has to be repeated because the results on paper have been lost. That does not happen in a VA hospital. VistA is the main reason the VA has been able to hold its costs per patient steady over the past ten years despite double-digit inflation for most health care prices. The VA spends an average of $5,000 per patient compared to a national average of $6,300.

An electronic medical record (EMR) database is a powerful tool for examining health care and its outcomes. There is a new emphasis in medicine on "evidence-based" treatment, which means that instead of guessing based on the doctor's past experience what treatment to prescribe, doctors should have access to the outcomes from different kinds of treatments. Treatment should be based on as much evidence as possible across a number of doctors and patients, not just on the experience or intuition of one doctor. The VA uses VistA to monitor treatment guidelines to see, for example, that doctors prescribe recommended shots. The VA has cut hospitalizations by 4,000 patients per year since it raised its vaccination rate for pneumonia from 20 percent to 94 percent.

Other automation includes robotic devices in hospital pharmacies to fill prescriptions, helping the VA to keep co-pays to $8. The bottles of medicine have a bar code which a computer scans. The system sounds an alarm if a patient is allergic and takes a drug that would cause a conflict. A VA nurse in Kansas suggested a bar code for patient ID bracelets after seeing rental cars being checked in using a barcode and scanner. The bar code helps insure that a patient gets the right procedure, something that has been a problem in some well-publicized cases of medical errors.

A PRIVATE HEALTH PLAN INNOVATES WITH IT

Kaiser Permanente is an integrated health system which includes the Kaiser Foundation Health Plan, Kaiser Hospitals, and Permanente medical groups. It serves over eight million people in the United States. The plan operates 30 hospitals, mostly in California. Its largest medical group is in northern California, with over 5,000 physicians and 20,000 support staff (Burgleman, Pearl, and Meza, 2004).

In the early 1990s the northern California region implemented a series of technology innovations starting with a common appointment and registration system for all facilities in the region, one that was able to handle 18 million office visits a year. The next application was a common database known as the Clinical Information Presentation Systems (CIPS) which contained every patient's laboratory data, radiology reports, EKG tracings, medication records, medical diagnoses, physician visits, hospital discharge summaries, and so on—a complete electronic medical record.

In 2003 Kaiser started KP HealthConnect, which is now available in most of the regions where the plan operates. The system has over 83,000 active users and offers a single database for patient information. Much of the implementation effort focused on training thousands of doctors and nurses, and this, plus lost productivity during start-up, has been more costly than the system (*Information-Week*, 5/28/2007).

Internet applications include the ability for the patient to make appointments, select a personal physician, and order medication refills. A subscriber can access the home pages for 5,000 physicians. There are also links to medical resources and information. Another application helps physicians by providing an electronic inbox for managing laboratory and radiology results. A doctor can schedule an appointment with a Kaiser specialist while the patient is in the examination room. Using the Internet, radiological studies like X-rays, CAT scans, and MRIs are available on the doctor's desk seconds after they are completed.

The system scans the database to look at each patient and prompt the doctor for preventive measures based on the patient's age and medical conditions. Because Kaiser is the insurer as well as the provider, there is no need for a doctor to obtain authorization before undertaking a procedure. The Kaiser database is also a rich source of information for learning the results of medical treatment and providing information for evidence-based medicine.

Kaiser can track the effect of different medicines on its patients. As an example, it has saved millions of dollars by using a generic cholesterol-lowering drug, lovastatin, instead of the more expensive drugs Zocor or Lipitor. The latter two drugs are more potent, but it turns out that many patients reach their target cholesterol level with lovastatin. Kaiser regularly monitors patients' cholesterol levels and enters the results in their electronic medical record. By examining the records of thousands of patients, Kaiser can determine whether lovastatin is sufficient for most patients, and it provide guidelines for doctors on when to use each drug (*New York Times*, 8/20/2006). Information really can make dramatic improvements in the quality of health care.

VIEW FROM THE MAYO CLINIC

We visited the famous Mayo Clinic in Rochester, Minnesota to see its electronic medical records system in action and to talk with two physicians and an IT specialist who have been instrumental in its development. The first efforts at the clinic to develop an electronic health record began in 1992, and the impetus came from the clinic's board of directors. When asked what would happen if Mayo had stayed with paper, Dr. David Mohr replied:

> Well, one humorous downside was this building was going to need significant structural re-enforcement. The records were getting so heavy; the volume of records were huge. You know, offices were stacked, secretary desks were stacked, records that used to be thin summaries were now turning into multi-volume encyclopedias, almost, of patient information.

During our visit we saw four rooms that contained six million file folders of patient records prior to the implementation of the electronic system.

The Mayo Clinic system actually consists of a number of different modules, each of which contributes to the electronic patient record. Dr. Mohr comments on the design:

> This electronic medical record is made up of many different modules that are visually integrated. Our log-on system allows us to bring up one application, which is the master list of patients that might be seen in an outpatient practice in a day or the master list of patients of a group of physicians that are taking care of patients in the hospital. And we can move the information—we can select a patient from that master list and then feed it to any of these other systems, like an imaging

viewing system, which allows us to easily pull in the radiology information. It feels like it's just one system.

The doctor guided me through the process of ordering a mammogram and some medication for a test patient in the system. The process was quick and easy, and the results of the mammogram would have been available on Dr. Mohr's PC if it had actually been completed.

Why did the Clinic undertake the massive investment of time, money, and effort to develop its system? According to Dr. Mohr:

> The major goal we had was to improve patient care through many sorts of devices. We wanted to make people more efficient. We wanted to remain financially viable. We wanted to bring the decision-making to the point of care, and we wanted to support the providers as the processes of care were becoming more complex. We wanted to bring that decision support to the provider. . . . We wanted to bring the ability to change work flows and respond to the changing environment to the electronic systems to make it easier for us to change in today's world. Lastly . . . we wanted to be able to use all this information and be able to capture the information in a way that we could improve patient care for future generations and support research and the way we were doing things.

It took a long time to develop the systems at Mayo according to Jessica Gosett of the IT group:

> Twenty-five years ago, probably the biggest focus was on turning manual process into electronic processes as long as it did not touch the physician, so [we automated] business workflows, registering the patients, and scheduling patients. We have a scheduling system that is as complicated as an airline scheduling system. . . . We started to build our non-clinical systems up first, and then things like the laboratories were next. And we thought how are we going to get people to use a computer? And we came up with the idea; we'll put workstations in their offices, but we'll tell them we'll give them email because email is very safe. And we gave them games; that's pretty safe too.
>
> And then we gave them test results so all they had to do was type in a clinic number for a patient, very little data entry. . . . Being able to look at results and then show the patient and say, "Here, let me give you a print out." In the past, they had pieces of paper that were transported throughout the environment through all of these buildings that would take at least a half of a day or more to get to if needed. . . . We've been totally chartless, not paperless; paper still floats around, but we don't create a paper chart anymore.

There are many positive results from the system according to Dr. Mohr:

> We have surveys in the hospital that show that over 93 percent of our patients feel that the computer helps their experience. The nurses working with the computer instead of the old chart has made it a better experience, they feel that the

information is available faster. We don't have the waits for a report of a CT scan or an MRI scan on a critically ill patient [any longer]. Now it's available almost within a few minutes of the person coming out of the radiology machine, MRI, or CT scan.

However, there are many changes that come from an electronic health records system:

We want to start gaining much more in the way of benefits from simply not having to manage charts. So there's a whole level of benefit that we expect to see, and those levels of benefits may be . . . in having analytical information available for research and prognostication. There's a whole other area of being able to improve processes. When you put in an electronic medical record, you just don't replace pieces of paper, replacing forms or replacing lab sheets that used to be in paper form. What you replace is actual processes, because that paper record used to move around [and] when it landed on a person's desk, it would have a little sheet on it telling him to do something . . . move something here, send something there, so all of our processes are part of this electronic patient record.

One can also use the system in a variety of ways to improve the quality of care by doing research on past interventions and their outcomes. According to Dr. Mohr, a data mining project should lead to many advances:

We can go into these paper records and see what happens to a person with a particular symptom or a particular diagnosis or disease and find out what happens over the course of decades. Data mining activities are very tedious, and they require a staff to painstakingly open up the paper record, go through the information, write it down on a form, and provide the information to the researchers and the statisticians who make the inferences and conclusions about these diseases. Our vision for the future is that we use these analytical warehouses . . . to understand much more detail about diseases then we could in the paper record.

From research it is possible to develop guidelines to help the physician. Dr. Mohr described some of Mayo's efforts:

You'd think [it would be easy to do] something like . . . recommending to a physician what to do if the potassium level was too low, or to remind physicians about what tests to order for a diabetic patient, and not to forget things, and to make modifications in the patient's program. But actually it gets extremely complicated with lots of "what ifs." Sure, the baby is supposed to get an immunization if the mother is hepatitis B positive, but what if the baby has immuno suppression, or what if the baby were premature? The goal was to create sharable electronic guidelines [like] a diagram that has a flow sheet with boxes and triangles and decision points so a caregiver could look at what the information and process flow should be.

Jessica Gosett described one major project at the clinic which addresses the next level:

The science of healthcare, individualized medicine, is taking all of that data, being able to build queries, being able to make that information immediately available across populations for that one patient at the time the physician sees that patient. So the patient comes in with certain diagnoses, certain symptoms, and the physician is wondering, "Should I use this medication or that medication? What has worked best for the last thousand patients that were in this situation?" And we also now have their DNA on file . . . [which will enable us] to say this one patient could be one of the three percent of the patients the medication would kill. And we've had examples already of that where we're able to help patients because we have that genomic data available.

What will medicine look like in five years? Dr. Nina Schwenk offers one view:

I think the biggest way that it will change is the fact that the patients won't have to come and see me. I think how we utilize the Web [for] home monitoring systems will help to simplify and hopefully make [care] more efficient, particularly patients with diseases like diabetes high blood pressure, lung disease. The second is clinical decision support. . . . Now I have to rely on what I remember, what I know, what I've read, what I keep up with, on going medical education. [For example], you've come in with diabetes. What's the newest drug? Should I use it in you? What are the contraindications? I have to either know that, or consult with someone, or pick up the phone and say, "What can you tell me as an expert to give to my patient?" So I think technology is getting to a point now where that information can be available to me at a click on the computer. Say the person that's sitting in front of me has this allergy. [The system says] better not use this drug, or they're also on this other drug, it may interact with what you're using; so it gives me alerts as well. What I think is probably the farthest away, and I'm not sure we'll realize this vision, is that here you are, you've got this disease. I know that Mayo Clinic has seen hundreds of patients if not thousands, depending on how rare the disease is over the last 5–20 years. How can I harness that information [and] . . . do an on-the-fly search to, say, this genomic profile, this clinical presentation, these lab results—[and then query] what were the outcomes of the individuals of the last 100 patients we saw with this disease with this drug versus another drug?

And is the doctor being removed from the process?

No, I actually think we're not. I actually think you're involving the doctor more; you're actually giving the doctor more tools. Right now you can say, "Blood sugar, high—you've got diabetes." Why do you need a doctor to tell you that? Because it depends where the sugar's from, what time it was taken, what the implications of that are, what is going to potentially work as an early treatment versus not. I think you actually give more powerful tools to the care providers as opposed to taking the care providers out. There's still a lot of judgment in medicine.

A RADICAL INNOVATION

One group of researchers is hard at work to find markers for various diseases, like different types of cancers. If doctors could screen patients and discover disease well before it manifests itself physically, it should be possible to destroy illnesses before they strike. It would be the ultimate in preventive medicine. The whole model for health care would change as there would be far less need to treat people who are sick; instead, doctors would treat patients to eliminate disease before it happens (Kessler, 2006). Even with this radical change, we still need to take the steps described in this chapter. An electronic record becomes even more important to show all of a patient's screenings and treatment by different physicians. There will still be traditional kinds of treatments for accidents, broken bones, and the like, and we will still have doctors, nurses, clericals, and insurance companies to deal with. Efficiency and quality of care will matter just as much if this vision becomes a reality.

WHY IS IT SO CHALLENGING IN HEALTH CARE?

Both of the examples in this chapter, the VA system and Kaiser Permanente, are in very favorable situations with respect to IT innovations because:

- They are one, centralized system.
- There is one insurer.
- The medical staff is on salary.

The vast majority of American health care is delivered by single or small group practices of physicians. These doctors have admitting privileges at one or more hospitals and participate in a network of referrals to different specialists. Each physician is an independent business person who has to worry about an office, malpractice insurance, billing, and relations with third-party payers. The physician also has a staff of at least one nurse and a receptionist, plus additional people to interface with insurance companies. Because each practice is an independent entity, there are no standards for the administrative side of the business. Some doctors have a staff that handles billing, others outsource it to a service provider. Competing vendors offer different solutions to manage the physician's office.

Except for the largest group practices, the scale of the business is small, too small to afford large investments in technology. Since the doctor's income is what is left over after accounting for all expenses, investing in IT really does come from his or her pocket. It has been estimated that implementing a commercial electronic medical record can cost up to $30,000 up-front per doctor for support and training. As a result, less than 5 percent of physicians in the United States have computerized systems (*New York Times*, 9/19/2005).

The situation in hospitals is not much better. Hospitals have implemented technology for various parts of their business, but there are no standards. The industry is beset with legacy systems—old systems—many of which were home grown, that do not operate well with newer technologies like the Internet. Hospitals also have funding problems, so the cost of technology is an issue. Because a hospital is a complex, high-reliability organization, any new technology that creates major changes in procedures is very risky.

The insurance companies and the government who provide the bulk of the payments for medical services should have an interest in better health care, but they focus on the short-term and could hardly be called innovators. Why did the insurance industry not organize and fund the development of electronic medical records years ago? They pay for the inefficiencies in the medical system, but they seem to be bogged down processing claims and trying to monitor doctors' decisions about patients. In fact, it seems that most of the players in health care spend their time trying to pass their costs on to someone else to pay.

And the technologists are not free from blame. There are many examples of systems developed for the medical industry that have been difficult or impossible to use. One study looked at three medical system implementations and found that only one of them was successful. This is a small sample, but one out of three is not a success rate to advertise to the next customer. There are other reports of hospital systems being removed after doctors objected to using them.

The benefits of investing in technology may also not accrue to the party making the investment. An individual practitioner is not greatly disadvantaged by not having an electronic medical record though a doctor seeing a patient on referral would certainly find it helpful. A physician in an emergency room would be much better prepared to help a patient if he or she had access to the patient's electronic medical record. On a national basis, one study estimated that a nationwide, interconnected EMR system could save $81 billion annually through improved patient care and efficiency. If providers used the system to actively pursue preventative medicine and treat chronic diseases, the savings would be doubled. But such a system would require major changes in the health system (Hillestad et al., 2005).

Staff members are also often unenthusiastic about new technology. It takes longer for a doctor to enter a prescription on a computer or PDA; scribbling something on a pad of paper is much faster, if not more legible. Time is definitely money for the independent physician, so why abandon manual techniques that are faster than automated ones? The only appeal here is to the quality of health care, and, to the physician being squeezed by insurance companies, that argument may seem completely theoretical.

The greatest interest today in health information technology is the EMR. The factors that impede the implementation of these systems include:

- Acquisition and implementation costs.
- Slow and uncertain financial payoffs.
- The fact that providers absorb the costs, while consumers benefit.
- The need for standards and interoperability.
- Privacy concerns among patients, and whether to allow patients to opt out.

(See Hillestad et al., 2005.) One small physicians' office in Philadelphia spent $140,0000 on personal computers and the installation of a system. The annual technology cost for the office is about $50,000, and the doctors are planning a $54,000 upgrade. The doctors have saved money in transcribing reports, and they handle 6,000 patients with three fewer office employees. One of the four doctors in the office says that the technology has improved the quality of care he provides, but that the savings have been less than the cost of the technology. It is estimated that only 5 percent of electronic health record systems are in offices with five or fewer doctors, which accounts for about half of the practices in the United States. Physicians get about 11 percent of the savings from electronic health records while the major benefit goes to insurance carriers who pay for fewer tests and enjoy automated record processing. Doctors bear the costs and others get the benefits (*New York Times*, 6/11/2007).

There are a number of vendors developing EMR systems. As an example, Microsoft has entered the field with its HealthVault initiative to better help people manage their health. HealthVault offers a personal health record that individual users populate with their medical treatments, insurance claims, and data from medical providers. The system is designed to interoperate with other electronic health systems so that they can update it automatically. Efforts such as this will help push the heath care field toward greater use of information technology, but the proliferation of different platforms and systems creates a major challenge for connectivity, that is, for having one system able to update the data in a different medical record system that a particular patient is using.

Looking beyond EMR systems, estimates of the impact of IT on health care run as high as a $120 billion a year savings in costs by eliminating duplicate tests, shortening hospital stays, and improving chronic care. Some estimates run as high as $600 billion a year, and there is speculation that savings from IT could help bail out Medicare; the hospital trust fund is expected to be broke by 2020 (*Business Week*, 10/31/2005).

So where do we go from here? The federal government is promoting electronic medical records and a national health information network consisting of a large number of independently managed regional networks. Dr. Robert Kolodner, the National Coordinator of Health Information Technology in the Department of Health and Human Services, has a vision for the future of medicine:

> I think we're on the verge of a quantum change in healthcare now and into the future. [We're moving towards] preventing illnesses . . . towards preventing the consequence of illness such as controlling blood pressure or keeping the cholesterol low if you're at risk. And even more, trying to predict who's at risk and making interventions so you never get hypertension or you never get elevated cholesterol or never develop diabetes. That's going to be the exciting part of the future. The electronic health record, the personal health record, the public health information systems are tools that, when properly used, can help to enable that transformation. By themselves, . . . health IT is not enough, but with the proper incentives to

improve the quality and the efficiency of care, these tools can help bring about a real transformation in the healthcare sector that we have today.

Dr. Kolodner also warns that the adoption of new technology will not be easy. It is not just a matter of setting up a new database to contain patient data:

> It's . . . a change in the workflow and so you have to think ahead, begin training people, bring them up to speed on the applications they'll be using. It's not like using a word processor or a spreadsheet. There are different parts to the electronic record [and] you need . . . to make sure you're going to [document] them properly, signing the notes. If you have an incomplete note, you have to remember to go back and sign that note for them to be available to the other providers. And so it's a different way of doing business than what people may have learned in the past. The opportunity is that it can be something where you can deliver much better quality care, but there is this learning process that the doctors and the system needs to go through . . . If it's not done well, then you don't fit into the clinical flow that will help providers deliver their care . . . so they will push back and not want to move onto the next stage of the use of . . . the electronic health record for doing decision support . . . .

The bad news is that health care expenditures are rising and look out of control. The good news is that these increases are unsustainable and that there is a renewed interest in the quality of care, and the only solution in sight is to try and transform health care as we know it in the United States with information technology.

REFERENCES

Burgleman, R. A., R. Pearl, and P. Meza. "Better Medicine Through Information Technology." Stanford, CA: Stanford Business School, 2004.

Hillestad, R., J. Bigelow, A. Bower, F. Girosi, R. Beili, R. Scoville, and R. Taylor. "Can Electronic Medical Record Systems Transform Health Care? Potential Health Benefits, Savings, and Costs." *Health Affairs* 24, no. 3 (September/October 2005): 1103–1117.

Kessler, A. *The End of Medicine: How Silicon Valley (and Naked Mice) Will Reboot Your Doctor.* New York: Collins, 2006.

10

Can Education Be Transformed?

E ducation is the key to the future of the United States. The largest segment of the population is knowledge workers, and the capital base that supports them is information technology. Employment in manufacturing and agriculture has been steadily shrinking and constitutes about 12 percent and 1 percent of GDP respectively.

One role of education is to teach people basic skills and facts. We believe that literacy is important, and the United States stresses universal education. Learning "reading, writing, and arithmetic" are important, but knowledge of these basics is not enough. Students need to learn how to think and solve problems. The revolution in technology described in this book has been powered by innovation, individuals coming up with new ideas that create significant changes in the world. The Internet, eBay, Amazon, YouTube, Digg.com, Facebook, and other inventions are innovations based on technology. Another crucial goal of education, then, is for students to develop their potential for creativity and innovation.

There are two questions about technology and education:

1. How will technology transform education at all levels?
2. How should the educational system prepare students to take advantage of the transformational aspects of IT?

The United States has about 77 million students in nursery through undergraduate institutions, and what is happening today in these institutions is determining the future of the country. Where do we stand? The good news is that approximately 85 percent of the U.S. population have graduated from high school, and 27 percent have bachelor's degrees. The bad news is that adults who do not finish high school earn 65 percent of what people who have a high school degree make, a gap greater than found in any other country. Some 44 percent of adults without high school degrees in the United States have very

---

Surviving

I have no doubt that anyone in school right now will see the impact of technology at some time in his or her career. Will this student be ready to adapt to the technology so that it is competence-enhancing for him or her? Or will the technology be competence-destroying and result in a demotion or the loss of a job? Are schools preparing students for the results of the technology revolution?

To take advantage of this revolution, the way we teach has to change. Teachers need to become more like guides, showing students the way to find information and synthesize it. There needs to be more exploration using the Internet and less lecturing. These kinds of changes are hard to bring about. Unfortunately, we have become obsessed with testing and grading students and their schools, and politicians like to focus on the school rather than the community in which the school is located.

Technology can help in another crucial area—encouraging parents in poor neighborhoods to get involved with their child's education and school. I am less optimistic that technology will help us solve the problem of the constantly increasing costs of college.

---

low incomes. They make half or less of the country's median income (OECD, 2006).

The United States leads the world in the proportion of 35 to 64 year-olds with college degrees, but it ranks seventh among developed nations for 25–34 year-olds. Our rate of college completion is in the lower half of developed nations. College is also becoming increasingly unaffordable for many American families. Pell Grants from the federal government for low-income students used to cover 70 percent of college costs at a four-year public university; today that number is less than half of the costs. College participation rates are flat and the chances of a U.S. 9th grader being enrolled in college in four years is less than 40 percent. In the best performing states, only about two-thirds of students in four-year colleges complete a bachelor's degree in six years (National Center for Public Policy and Higher Education, 2006).

Developing countries are increasing the number of their college graduates in the 25- to 34-year-old cohort, while the best educated U.S. cohort will soon be retiring. The preceding chapters have been about technology-enabled transformations. Who will develop the innovations to power future transformations? Who will use the technology that the innovators develop? We are a knowledge and service economy, and this kind of economy demands a highly educated workforce. The United States will be in trouble in coming years unless it undertakes some serious educational investment and reform.

K-12

The educational news in the United States is dominated by stories of failure, students who learn little and drop out of school. After the flooding in New Orleans from Hurricane Katrina, the state took control of most of the city's schools which had been problem-ridden for years. The reaction at the federal level to problems with our schools has been No Child Left Behind (NCLB), which involves extensive testing and punitive measures for schools that fail to improve on the tests.

In many urban schools, there appears to be an attitude that doing well in school is something to be avoided, while in more affluent, suburban schools, the most popular students are athletes. Friedman (2006) describes letters from teachers documenting immigrant parents asking teachers for more work and more rigor for their children, while native-born American parents ask for less work and more leisure for their children. In a diverse country with this large a student population, one can probably find examples of just about any point you want to make. Despite all of the conflicting evidence, a few things do seem clear:

- There are significant problems in many urban U.S. schools, a fact which does not bode well for helping low-income families improve their conditions through better employment opportunities. The manufacturing jobs that might have been available to the dropout or the high school graduate are disappearing, leaving low-wage service jobs in their place.
- U.S. school dropout rates are alarming. A report by *Education Week* (http://www.edweek.org/ew/articles/2007/06/12/40gradprofiles.h26.html) showed that ten of the nation's 50 largest school districts had dropout rates in excess of 50 percent:

City	Graduation Rate
Detroit	25%
Cleveland	34%
Baltimore	35%
Dallas	44%
New York	45%
Los Angeles	45%
Milwaukee	46%
Denver	46%
Miami-Dade County	49%
Philadelphia	50%

What jobs will a knowledge economy provide for these dropouts?

- Many schools are not challenging students, and students are not always interested in responding to a challenging curriculum.
- We will continue to be a knowledge economy, and the future depends on a highly educated workforce that is able to come up with new innovations to keep the U.S. economy competitive with other nations.

Many of the problems in education have nothing to do with technology, though there are certainly places where it can help. Poverty and the lack of parental guidance or even presence in the home is a huge negative for a child. One study found that 3-year-olds with professional parents have a vocabulary of 1,100 words on the average, while 3-year-olds with parents on welfare have a vocabulary of 525 words. Oklahoma has addressed this problem with a public pre-school system for 4-year-olds that enrolls 70 percent of eligible children. In this program, every teacher must have a bachelor's degree, and there is one teacher for every ten students (*New York Times*, 2/7/2007).

The most popular targets for school problems are teachers and administrators. My own experience outside of universities is limited. The teachers that I know are hard-working and dedicated to their students. Students may go home at 3:00, but the teacher's job is not over. These teachers have to work in the evenings, looking over that day's student work and preparing for the next day.

Given the level of innovation the workforce has exhibited already, it seems that the U.S. educational system, despite its problems, has been able to prepare some students to be creative and innovative. Our system stresses interaction between the student and the teacher and encourages students to ask questions. I have students from Asia and have taught there. The typical model is the teacher talking and students taking notes. These students score highly on standardized tests, but when they come to the United States, they have great difficulty coming up with an original research project for a dissertation. I am pretty sure that my lectures do not stimulate much creativity, nor do I believe it is possible to do so via a lecture.

A few years ago I was at dinner with friends in Singapore, a country that puts a lot of emphasis on education. My friend told me that the education ministry had decided that Singapore schools followed the lecture and listen model too closely; the children were not learning how to be creative. Now her daughter was being required to do group work with other students with the assignments being more unstructured than in the past, and she was struggling to meet this new challenge. When No Child Left Behind came along, I was struck that we were moving in the opposite direction, toward measuring rote learning with tests. I asked a middle school teacher about this phenomenon and she replied:

> One thing I think the country could do to make the school system better is create another way to measure student/school success besides standardized testing. I don't think that being able to answer multiple choice questions correctly shows how intelligent a student is. Also, it puts a lot of stress on teachers to "teach to the test."

This same teacher referred me to something called Bloom's taxonomy of learning, which includes:

Knowledge	Knowing facts, dates, events, ability to recall information
Comprehension	Understanding information and meaning, translating knowledge into a new context, predict consequences, infer causality
Application	Use information, methods, theories in new situations solve problems
Analysis	Observe patterns, see hidden meanings, identify components
Synthesis	Use old ideas to create new ones, generalize from facts predict, draw conclusions
Evaluation	Compare and contrast ideas, assess value of theory, make choices from arguments and data, recognize subjective arguments (Bloom 1984)

Those who design standardized tests are very skilled, and there are sophisticated tests available to measure a variety of skills. However, I cannot help feeling that some of the most important aspects of learning, at least from the standpoint of participating in the ongoing technology revolution, are not capable of being measured on a multiple-choice test.

So we have schools perceived to be failing, unmotivated students, and an incentive scheme that tells the teacher to teach to the test. How can we ameliorate some of these problems? First, a controversial statement: We have no failing schools. What we have is failing communities and failing parents. A child is in school for six to eight hours a day for 180 days a year. The school cannot raise a child. It can try to educate that person, but it cannot and should not replace the role of the parents. In many poor communities, for example, parents are failing to encourage their children to learn and are uninvolved in their schools. How quickly will a child learn to read in school if a parent has never read to that child?

Perhaps technology can help. We need to find out: Does technology allow the nature of the learning process to be changed? In what way should schools respond to the vast amount of information that is available online? Does this information mean that children should learn fewer facts and instead learn how to find facts when they need them? Many schools have replaced pencil-and-paper calculations with calculators; the same logic says that students will be relying more on finding information than remembering everything they have been taught. Moving in this direction requires major changes in the way teachers and students interact.

I spoke with a technology facilitator in a school system who had returned to school to earn an MBA. Her comments:

> Based on my experience, with the way teaching happens in elementary schools, there is no real room for technology. Teachers do a lot of lecturing or work with

manipulatives. Regardless of the technique, teachers are the clear leader in the classroom. They tell students what to do and how to do it.

Technology for most is a hassle to deal with. For technology to be truly effective,
teachers are going to have to become more of a guide instead of a leader. I think the
teaching profession will have to change completely.

In the future, I envision a more experiential learning educational process for
children. Children will get to figure out how things work or learn basic principals
on their own, which aligns with how they play. For example, most children have
to learn how to get through their video game on their own because their parents
have no idea how to operate it. Technology can facilitate experiential learning,
with instantaneous access to information and simulation capabilities. Children
will not have to wait for the teacher to tell them the information and they can
learn at their own pace. Teachers will be there to guide them in the right direction
or help those who are struggling.

One thing the teachers I talked with said they needed was much better communications with colleagues, administrators, and parents. There is a simple technological solution that can help here: email and Web pages. One policy objective
now that schools are almost all connected to the Internet should be to have email
capability for every parent of a child in school and, of course, for teachers. A class

Jimmy Margulies
The Record (Hackensack. N.J.)
King Features Syndicate

Courtesy of North American Syndicate.

Web page featuring student projects, pictures of students working, class assignments and objectives, and other information should help involve parents more in their children's education.

This technology is not expensive, but it does require labor to implement and to use on an ongoing basis. Someone has to create and update Web pages, and a teacher cannot be expected to send individual emails to 25 sets of parents every day. Schools will need to add Web masters, just as companies have individuals devoted to creating and maintaining Web pages. Communities will have to find the resources to provide email connectivity for families that do not have it already.

More challenging is the idea of providing all students with laptop computers. If schools are to bring out student creativity and prepare students for the kind of jobs that will exist when they graduate, then students will have to solve unstructured problems working in teams. Many of the resources the students need for their assignments are available on the Internet, and it is never too early for them to learn how to search, find and exploit the rich resources available on the Net.

Maine has launched a program to provide laptop computers to students and teachers in the 7th and 8th grades. An evaluation of that effort by the University of Southern Maine reported that:

- Teachers use the laptops for developing instructional material, conducting research on instruction and communicating with colleagues.
- Students use laptops most frequently for finding information (90 percent), organizing it (63 percent), and taking notes (57 percent).
- Over 70 percent of teachers surveyed reported that the laptops helped them better meet their curriculum goals and individualize their instruction to meet particular student needs.
- Over 80 percent of the teachers felt that students were more engaged in their learning and produce better quality work.
- There is considerable anecdotal evidence that the laptops have a positive impact on student attendance, behavior, and achievement (Silvernail and Lane, 2004).

A study of student and teacher views on technology and science in education came to the following conclusions (Project Tomorrow-Netday, 2005):

- Students are innovative users of technologies, adopting them to support learning and their lifestyles. Some 94 percent of students in grades 3–6 use computers in their free time. Many students have personal Websites.
- Communicating is a key motivator for students in using the technology; this interest becomes particularly strong by sixth grade. Over a third of students use email or instant messaging weekly by sixth grade.
- Younger students are adopting more sophisticated technologies, following their older siblings.
- Teachers are becoming more comfortable with technology, but are having a hard time keeping up with their students.

- "Students are strong believers in the power of technology to enrich their learning experiences."
- Over a third of 12th grade students say they access news Web sites for information.
- Teachers are using email extensively—97 percent use it, according to the report. They communicate with colleagues, administrators, support staff, and parents of their students. Over 80 percent of teachers use the Internet for research and lesson planning.
- Over 70 percent of students indicate that their school has a useful Web site, and 25 percent say that their schools provide laptops for school use.

With initiatives like One Laptop per Child, discussed in Chapter 8, a goal of giving every child a laptop computer to keep should be attainable in a country as wealthy as the United States. In addition, we should be able to provide instruction and training for teachers on how to incorporate the laptop into the curriculum, which appears to be a key factor in the success of these programs. One expert who has studied laptop use in K-12 education says that it takes time to train teachers how to integrate new technology into the classroom. Laptops are important for "innovation, creativity, autonomy, and independent research," according to Professor Mark Warschauer at the University of California, Riverside. As an example of success he points to middle school students in Yarmouth, Maine, who used laptops to create a Spanish book for poor children in Guatemala and to research and debate online Supreme Court cases. "If the goal is to get kids up to basic standard levels, then maybe laptops are not the tool. But if the goal is to create the George Lucas and Steve Jobs of the future, then laptops are extremely useful," according to Warschauer (*New York Times,* 5/4/2007).

There is a downside to student laptops; it is easy to visit inappropriate sites and to spend class time surfing the Web and sending instant messages. Some schools have reported that they see no progress or improvement in student performance with laptops, which contradicts some of the evidence above. Teachers report that the laptops are a distraction and get between them and the students. Schools are frustrated with having to repair the laptops which seem to break down frequently (*New York Times,* 5/4/2007). There have been reports of parents taking students out of laptop programs because their performance actually declined. Some schools are reducing the scope of their planned programs to give laptops to middle school students (*Wall Street Journal,* 8/31/2006).

Students can be very clever and figure out ways to use just about any educational innovation inappropriately. Schools can and do put filters on laptops to keep students from browsing sites that are off limits. Teachers can control the use of laptops in class; I have colleagues who do not allow them in their graduate classes because they feel the computers divert a student's attention. Parents can check on the sites students have visited by looking at browser logs. One good lesson is that you cannot just hand technology to a student; you have to develop an infrastructure and policies on how that technology is to be used. At the K-12 level, parents have to be involved with student laptops, and teachers will have to change a significant part of the curriculum to foster student creativity and innovation with the technology.

Our discussion rests on the assumption that there are parents available to take an interest in a child's education. In the most devastated communities, this assumption is not always correct. Solving educational problems for a family where parents are not functioning is beyond the scope of technology. If we want to attack this problem, it will require a large amount of funding to keep schools open as community centers in the afternoon and evenings, and to staff them with tutors to work with children. A new school superintendent in New Orleans is responsible for 12,000 students, 90 percent of whom are in poverty, and the majority have single parents. He is working to provide three meals a day at school, as well as dental and eye care. One of his ideas is to make schools into community centers and to keep them open at least through dinner and for 11 months of the year (*New York Times,* 9/24/2007). As of yet, society has not seen fit to widely adopt this or other solutions to this significant problem.

THE COLLEGE SCENE

U.S. colleges and universities have long been regarded as one of the bright spots in American education. From the standpoint of most indicators this view is correct. There are a few problems under the surface that are of concern, one of which is the economic model of higher education. Everyone is aware that college costs, tuition and room and board, have been rising faster than inflation for the past several decades, and there appears to be no end in sight. What is going on here?

It should be no surprise that the biggest expense for a college is salaries, and there has been a strong upturn in the salaries paid to college faculty since the 1960s. As a beneficiary of this trend, I am not complaining, but it does raise a serious question about sustainability. If an increase in pay is offset by an increase in productivity, there is no impact on inflation. But how can you increase the productivity of a college faculty member? One answer is to have the professor teach more classes, and the second answer is to teach larger classes.

These solutions by and large have not been implemented for several reasons. First, there is a feeling that small classes are better; the professor gets to know the student and there is more time for discussion. We see this belief in the progression of classes: introductory courses in the basics like economics and psychology tend to be very large lecture classes with hundreds of students, followed by smaller section meetings led by a graduate student. As a student progresses in his or her major, he or she takes more advanced classes and seminars with far fewer students in them.

At the top of the university hierarchy in the United States are the research universities; they attract the best faculty members who are interested in staying up in their profession, both by conducting leading-edge research and remaining abreast of the latest trends in the field. Several of my freshman economics professors were at the same time advising President Kennedy, and that made for an exciting class. If a faculty member increases the number of classes taught, or the number of students being taught, it takes away from time for research and publication. Research and publication enhance the faculty member's reputation, keeps his or her options open for moving to another institution some day, and builds the reputation of the university. For the research university, it is difficult to create conditions for faculty to be more productive by teaching more.

Technology can help here, but I am afraid that it will not create a turnaround in the economic model of the university. Two scenarios below describe what is possible with today's technology for a student and a faculty member. They focus on the environment each faces and their implications for productivity should be clear.

A Future Undergraduate Student Scenario

Kate Adams is an undergraduate major in business at the University of Maryland (UMD), class of 2014. Every morning Kate logs one of her devices onto the campus network using her name, password, and fingerprint. This single login allows her to access any campus system via her UMD passport without having to log in to that system. Every system that Kate accesses is Web-enabled, and she uses one of her browsers to interact with it.

In her junior year, Kate is taking a full set of courses in her major, attending most of her classes, which meet in person in Van Munching Hall. For today, she has chosen to carry her large PDA around campus; this device allows her to access each class's instructional system to download slides and other material the faculty has placed on the course site.

Today Kate notes that she has no classes that meet physically until later in the evening, but she is scheduled to participate in two exercises. The first in finance class requires her to work alone, retrieving data from several financial databases to test a hypothesis about insider information and its impact on efficient financial markets. She accesses the databases through her student university portal, which Testudo, the university online course system, configured for her at the beginning of the semester to reflect her courses and site preferences.

Kate's second project of the day is with her team in the supply chain class, which has to run a business simulation investigating the "bull whip" effect among second- and third-tier suppliers. Three members of her team meet in a conference room, but a fourth member is ill and joins them via a wireless connection that supports video conferencing. The students use one team member's tablet computer to download the simulation from a server and execute it with different input parameters. One teammate acts as moderator as they outline their report on an electronic whiteboard. When finished, the system scans the whiteboard and emails an image of the outline to each participant. Kate develops a graph of their results, while another team member writes a short summary of their findings. They merge their work, and file it in the course homework electronic mailbox for their instructor to review.

As Kate is walking to the dining hall for lunch, she receives a reminder that she set for herself to check her bursar's account to see if she has been credited for a course that she decided not to take at the last minute. Her personal portal includes access to the student-facing administrative systems at Maryland, and she quickly brings up her account on the screen, noting that the change is still pending. Kate clicks the "push to talk button," and is connected with a staff member in the bursar's office. The staff member checks the internal system and finds that the credit is scheduled to be applied that night. Kate sets her reminder to fire again in two days so she can check once more on the credit.

In her dorm room after dinner, Kate switches to a laptop computer to complete the assignments in her information systems class. The author converted the text for the class into a Web book, which students can easily search when looking for a specific topic, and students follow hyperlinks to explore concepts further. Today the instructor is in China, so the class is being held at 7 p.m. via the audio/video conferencing site the university subscribes to. Members of the class log on to the conferencing site and join the class. Each student is able to see the person talking in a video window while they share a white board and lecture notes on their screens.

The next morning, Kate decides to work on her research paper for the marketing class. It is a beautiful, warm spring day, so she selects her tablet PC with attached keyboard and works from a bench on the campus mall. Her single logon and passport allow Kate to access all of the resources in the library. Fortunately, the library converted all of its databases to a common format and built a search portal to make it easier to undertake research. The portal submits all of her search parameters to the relevant databases and generates a consistent report of the returned results. Kate retrieves the full text of several articles and uses her tablet to annotate them by writing her reactions in the margins with the tablet's stylus.

That afternoon, Kate decides she is ready to take a test in finance and downloads and completes the examination. Upon submitting the exam, she immediately receives her score on the objective questions. The instructor will look at her essays and grade them in the next few days. The feedback on objective questions includes links to passages explaining the answers to the questions Kate had wrong.

To relax after the exam, Kate runs several animations from the supply chain class which show the before and after impact on a vendor of implementing RFID tags for the products in its warehouses. She then joins her tennis team video chat group to catch up with what her teammates are doing. Later that day, she will have a video chat with her information systems professor in China and another one with her younger sister at home.

A Future Faculty Scenario

Brian Lee is a faculty member in the Smith School of Business at the University of Maryland specializing in operations management and supply chain. Today he has two classes to teach, one a full-time MBA class in College Park and the other an executive MBA class in Zurich. In setting up these classes, Brian developed links to a variety of relevant materials and posted them to the university's instructional support system. Students work independently following the links and completing assignments. His "in person" class meets once a week, and Brian has frequent video-office hours to meet one-on-one with his students.

In addition to live classes with students in Zurich, Brian has asynchronous class assignments for the students to complete, again using the school's instructional system. Brian also meets with students and student teams from Zurich using the video conferencing capabilities available through the university network and the Internet. Students in both classes complete a number of exercises, including case studies, simulations and animations of different aspects of the supply chain.

After class, Brian initiates a video conference from his office with colleagues at three different locations who are working together on a research project. They share results and run data analyses together. When they start drafting the paper, they will perform some of the editing online simultaneously, sharing the draft manuscript.

At 5:00 Brian connects to a class at the University of Virginia where he is to be a guest lecturer that day. A video of Brian appears in one window on a large screen in Virginia while his slides appear in another window. Brian's screen has an additional window which is an image of the remote class. After the class, Brian goes home to an evening of research, using the university's access to public and proprietary databases to collect and analyze data for his projects.

WHEN WILL WE GET THERE?

These scenarios are for the future, but the technology described is almost all available, though not yet at an affordable price. Many if not most college campuses have wireless networks and students can use portable devices all over the school. High-quality video conferencing now is too expensive for most universities, but the price will come down at some point. The biggest challenge, however, is not the technology, but it is re-orienting our teaching to take advantage of it. Class assignments have to change, and faculty and students must get used to working together remotely as easily as they do in person. And in a time of rising college costs and tuition, someone must find a way to fund new technology and the creation of new course content.

DISTANCE AND ONLINE EDUCATION: NOT QUITE READY FOR PRIME TIME

Brian in our scenario teaches and meets with students online. I have done a limited amount of online instruction, and the experience was not a total success. The big difference in the scenario for the future is that Brian has video links. The teaching in which I was involved occurred online via the Internet. My students were Executive MBA Candidates in China, and I was teaching them from my home in Annapolis, Maryland. The classes were either at 7 p.m. in the United States, which was 7 a.m. in China, or vice versa. The design of each class was interactive and involved a case discussion; students were supposed to answer a series of questions before the class to prepare them for discussion.

The Chinese students in this class were naturally reticent, a characteristic magnified by the medium. It was very difficult to get a discussion going and it was easy for both the students and the instructor to lose focus and become distracted. The technology, for the most part, worked. Students and I shared a white board, I could bring up Web sites on all their PCs to talk about, and the audio sounded as if they were next door. Students clicked on an icon to raise their hand, and I clicked to give that student a microphone to speak. Students could click on different symbols to applaud, laugh, and answer a question yes or no. My belief is that with Brian's system including video, the experience would be much more positive. The newest "telepresence" systems create the feeling that people located remotely are in the same room with you, but these systems are also the most costly. They require expensive equipment, and it is not clear if they will provide the same feeling of being there if you have an instructor in one place and 35 students in another.

Today we have a hierarchy of higher education in the United States. The first level is community colleges which offer terminal associate's degrees or preparation to transfer to a four-year college for a bachelor's degree. There is a wide variety of colleges in the United States, ranging from small liberal arts schools, to large state-supported universities with tens of thousands of students, to elite Ivy League-level colleges and universities. The majority of college students today do not live on the campus of a four-year institution, so there have to be alternatives to the residential college experience.

Students will have a range of options, and we will see the same hierarchy of institutions reflected in the means of instruction. The most basic level will be online instruction for students who cannot access learning in any other way. Technology will gradually make online learning more effective and exciting, but all of my students have said they prefer a physical class with everyone present to the online experience. We may finally achieve the promise of sharing the insights of leading scholars by using technology to have them instruct students at several schools at the same time. The middle of the instructional hierarchy will be remote and part-time education, where students come to a satellite campus to meet with an instructor either in person or electronically. The top of the instructional hierarchy will be a small class in which faculty and students interact face-to-face on campus.

What about proprietary colleges, especially those that deliver most of their instruction online? Their main advantage is convenience and affordability. For the online proprietary schools to provide the same quality of education as traditional universities, they will have to attract top-ranked faculty who are considered leaders in their fields. Because nonprofit schools view online, for-profit schools askance, it is going to be very difficult for them to attract top academics. Until that happens, these schools will remain at the bottom of the hierarchy.

THE THREAT TO ACADEMIA

Can technology solve all the problems of the university? The application of technology can create major changes in the education system, but there will have to be other reforms if the United States is going to remain competitive in a global economy. If you asked most faculty members what the mission of the university is, they (hopefully) would say "education and research." The teaching mission of the university produces graduates whom we hope will benefit greatly from their years of study. The average wages and living conditions of college graduates still exceed those of high school graduates, and most economic analyses show that a college degree is a very good investment. University researchers are responsible for major advances in medicine, electronics, computer science, and our understanding of society, politics, and history, to name a few.

However, if you read the newspapers, or go near a university on a game day, you get an entirely different impression of why universities exist. To TV broadcasters, higher education is around for two reasons: football and basketball. Unfortunately, many alums and school administrators agree with the TV networks! As long as athletic departments dominate academics, our universities will never achieve their full potential. The NFL and NBA are not going to participate in the technology revolution; they will never make the United States more competitive in the world economy.

Athletics are great, and everyone should be active physically, for one's physical and mental health. Intramural athletics and competition among schools in minor sports (everything but football and basketball) are an integral part of the experience of going to college. I am fully in favor of these programs and am happy to see them subsidized from other revenues as intramurals will never pay for themselves.

The problem with big sports in college is that they corrupt the institution and send a message to the world about the primacy of athletics. Do we want the young children we are trying to motivate to study harder to believe that the major focus in college is football and basketball? Should this student concentrate on basketball with the hopes of making it to the NBA? Only a handful of players each year become successful professionals, and we are sending the wrong message to young people when we put an emphasis on these sports.

The media reflects what its readers and viewers want, and the world is enamored with sports. This point was driven home in the *Wall Street Journal* on August 18, 2006. The title of the article was "The Real No. 1," and it described the results of a new ranking scheme that ordered schools by who trained the best NFL players. The top 10 of the 30 are listed in Table 10.1.

Table 10.1
Top NFL Schools and Graduation Rates

School	Football Graduation Rate 1996–1999	Basketball Graduation Rate 1996–1999
Florida State	42%	40%
Florida	42%	67%
Georgia	39%	11%
Tennessee	40%	8%
Ohio State	49%	10%
Michigan	65%	67%
Miami	67%	75%
Auburn	56%	60%
LSU	37%	23%
North Carolina	61%	64%

Source: *Wall Street Journal.*

The data comes from the NCAA Web site and are the federal graduation rates; they do not count students who transfer to another school and graduate there. A state university might have an overall graduation rate of 75 to 80 percent while a private school will have a higher rate, into the 90s. With a few exceptions, the graduation rates for football and basketball appear well below average; in some cases the numbers are shocking. What is going on when the basketball team's graduation rate is 11 percent? You may say that some players are leaving school to become professionals, but did the NBA really draft 77 percent of LSU's and 89 percent of Georgia's basketball players from 1996 to 1999?

This focus on sports corrupts the university both educationally and financially. In 2006 it came out that the interim chairman of the Sociology department at Auburn taught more than 150 directed-study students at one time in 2004–2005. Directed studies is an independent readings course where the instructor provides assignments, but does not hold classes. About 20 percent of the students in these courses were athletes, according to the *New York Times* (7/13/2006). Eighteen members of the 2004 Auburn football team (undefeated and ranked second in the country) took a combined total of 97 hours of these directed-studies courses in sociology and criminology. Universities have tutoring programs for their athletes and point them to undemanding majors. One professor reported an athlete who read on the fourth grade level (http://insidehighered.com/news/2006/07/20/sports 7/20/2006). Favoritism, tutors, easy grades, and high drop-out rates are a corrupting influence on the educational mission of the university.

One of the reasons schools promote these two big sports is financial. Basketball and football often bring in enough revenue to fund all the other sports that do not make any money. In addition, alumni seem to favor sports over academics. At a dinner during a conference in France a few years ago, I sat across from a faculty member from a large western state university. The school has never been a football power, but one year it surprised everyone by having a winning season and going to a bowl game. He said that alumni donations peaked that year and had never been that high again, and the school has not been to another bowl since that winning year. What can a college president do if the students, the alums, newspapers, magazines, and television all focus on athletics?

In other instances, it is not clear that football is funding the rest of the school's athletic programs. Rutgers is in a financial crisis with shortened library hours, staff reductions, and canceled classes. The school is eliminating six sports including crew, fencing, and swimming. The total savings from dropping these sports is $1.2 million. However, there was enough money to give the winning football coach and woman's basketball coaches 50 percent raises, to a reported $1.5 million and $995,000 respectively (*Wall Street Journal*, 8/9/2007). But Rutgers lost an estimated $3 million on football in 2005. Ironically, campus computer labs are shutting down early to save money, but the football team watches game films on a 42-inch plasma television in the locker room. The money Rutgers has allocated for recruiting academically distinguished students has been cut for next year, but both the football budget and the coach's salary will increase. Yes, the boosters club did raise $5.8 million, but the program still fails to cover its costs (*New York Times*, 10/1/2006).

Other schools make a lot from football. In 2005, football at the Naval Academy earned $16.6 million, of which $6.2 million was profit. Football is the only one of 31 varsity sports at the academy that makes money. The football coach's pay package is believed to be around $1.5 million, but the athletic director points out that it is not paid with tax-payer dollars. Funds for the coach come from the Naval Academy Athletic Association, not the school's budget (*Annapolis Capital*, 12/17/2006).

The emphasis on athletics creates major problems for the faculty and staff. How can a faculty member feel that her work is valued when, like Rutgers football, the pay packages for football and basketball coaches often exceed $1 million a year? How can an institution of higher education and research explain paying coaches more than the president of the school? Why should American universities be farm clubs for professional football and basketball teams, highly profitable organizations in their own right? Baseball runs its own farm system, why not other professional sports?

It is not clear how to reduce the emphasis on athletics when so many people want to maintain it! One approach is to eliminate athletic scholarships, as the Ivy League did decades ago. A second action would be to cap total compensation for coaches at some number like the average of a full professor's salary at the school. If higher education is going to send the right messages to young people aspiring to be its future students, then it needs to rein in athletics and return to its mission. The future demands well-educated, creative, and innovative workers, and all levels of our educational system have to focus on this objective.

COLLEGE AFFORDABILITY

Lack of college affordability is a major challenge for education in the United States. Two of the biggest college costs are faculty salaries and energy, and both of these tend to rise each year. Can technology help? Technology can make an individual faculty member more productive by teaching more students online. But as discussed above, there are reasons for having some classes meet physically and for having some limits on class size. It is safe to predict that there will be more online instruction in the future for both cost and accessibility reasons. Faculty can teach more classes, but competition for faculty and the demands of a research university to be a successful researcher make this a difficult solution to implement.

Technology has and will continue to make educational administration and research more efficient. I have access to a huge number of academic articles online from home or office. In the past, I had to go through stacks of journals in the library. Today I use Maryland's library research portal or Google Scholar to find copies of papers I need for research. Students receive better and more efficient services through online registration and grade reporting, and online instruction support systems like Blackboard improve class quality and dramatically reduce photocopying. This year, the massive packets of material required in the faculty promotion and tenure process will all be distributed electronically at the Smith School.

But college is still very expensive. Unfortunately Pell Grants, the major federal program for tuition assistance, have not been keeping pace with tuition increases. About $12.7 billion in Pell Grants was awarded for the 2005–2006 year, down 3 percent from the previous year. The average grant slipped to $2,354 from $2,474. The Bush administration changed the eligibility formula by reducing the assumption of how much families in a number of states were assumed to be paying in state and local taxes, thereby raising their after-tax incomes and making them ineligible for grants. The vast majority of the over 5.4 million students who have Pell Grants are from families with incomes less than $40,000 a year. The value of the maximum grant, $4,050, has not changed in three years. The maximum grant now meets 33 percent of the average price of tuition, room and board, and fees at a public four-year college, down from 42 percent in 2001 (*Wall Street Journal,* 10/25/2006). As a result, many low-income students are forced to attend a two-year college even though they are academically qualified to attend a four-year institution. The bad news here is that only about 23 percent of community college students go on to earn a bachelor's degree within six years. (As of this writing, the 2008 federal budget includes increases in Pell Grants to $5,400 over five years, hardly enough to keep up with rising college costs.)

Some states are trying to help low-income students attend in-state colleges. One concern is that many low-income students are discouraged in the early grades because they assume they can never go to college. One of the first states to tackle this problem was Georgia with its HOPE program. In its basic form, the program provides a scholarship for a student in a Georgia public college that covers tuition, mandatory fees, and a book allowance if the student has graduated from an eligible high school in the state with a "B" average. A colleague at Georgia whose wife teaches middle school remarked on how much difference this program made in her students' attitudes and aspirations when it first passed; there was now hope for them to attend college.

In 2004 the University of Maryland announced its Pathways program, which replaces loans with grants and jobs on campus for low-income students. Families with incomes below the federal poverty level are eligible, and the program guarantees that these students will graduate debt-free. State funds are combined with federal work-study funds; students are required to work eight to ten hours per week at on campus jobs. The school estimates that 12 percent of its freshmen are eligible for the program.

Maryland, the University of Virginia, and the University of North Carolina, Chapel Hill, all have similar programs, and it would be great if other states adopted this innovation. We can help reverse some of the negative attitudes toward education found in low-income areas by implementing and publicizing programs like this and by extending them to low-income families that are above the poverty level but still unable to pay for college.

THE BOTTOM LINE

There is a considerable amount that has been written about education and technology around the world, and it is hard to predict what the ultimate impact of IT will be as students and educators apply their creativity to taking advantage of what it offers. There are some applications and likely results of technology that stand out in stories about technology and education:

- Technology enables frequent communications among students, faculty, and parents. If you believe that the primary responsibility for education begins with parents, and then transfers to the student, keeping parents aware of student progress and student problems is an important objective. Computer conferencing systems, email, and class Web pages make this kind of communication possible, but people must adapt their behavior to improve communication. The technology will not accomplish this goal alone. Providing students with laptop computers, and going the next step of providing Internet access to families that lack it, will also encourage better communications.
- Education is going to be much more collaborative. Some authors envision students sitting at study carrels with their laptops instead of desks or tables. Collaboration will not be limited to students in the same physical classroom. The technology makes it possible to form student teams from around the world to work on a project together. Imagine an eighth grade class studying the environment with United States, Chinese, and Indian students trading experiences, news stories, and photographs to create a shared final report.
- For better or worse, children are excited and motivated by video games. This same technology can be turned into exercises and simulations for studying different

subjects. It is easy to envision a pollution game in which companies, policy makers, and regulators take different actions that impact the spread of air and water pollution. Students play the roles of different actors involved in the game and make decisions that affect the outcome.

- The nature of teaching will change as a result. Teachers will lecture less and will provide more guidance to groups of students who have been given an assignment to complete together. The teacher will answer questions, provide advice on how to undertake the project, and recommend sources of information. He or she will help the students organize their thoughts and prepare a presentation to the class. And of course, he or she will see that the presentations are posted to the class Web site so that parents and others can share the results of the work.
- With the need to lecture less and the ability to spend time with groups of students, learning will be more personalized. The teacher will be able to give students assignments and projects that are appropriate for their current stage of development and will find various online exercises to supplement the curriculum.

The technology is revolutionary when applied to education. But it is not the only component needed for producing knowledgeable, well-adjusted students. A student must know how to read and write and be competent at mathematics. There is also the issue of social relations with peers and others and ethical behavior to consider. From a middle school teacher:

> I taught middle school for about seven years. My experience with this age is that the social aspect of a student's life is much more important than the academic aspect. However, I also found that students were very willing to express themselves through writing. Along those same lines I thought that the students I interacted with liked to relate to characters in the stories we read.

She goes on to reply to my question of how schools can encourage creativity:

> It's important for students to comprehend concepts being introduced in the classroom, but it's also important for them to analyze and synthesize those concepts. For example, let's say I want students to understand how point-of-view affects the events of a story. After reading a short story, I'd have the class go through the events of the story in order to check for understanding. Then, I'd have them choose another character in that story and write an excerpt of it. This will get the students to see how the story might be changed when someone else tells "their side." I would say that this practice would be on the "comprehension" and "analyzation" levels of Bloom's Taxonomy. To take this concept to a high level perhaps I would have the students see how looking at an event in their own lives from someone else's point of view could be helpful.

The activities the teacher describes are not going to be replaced by technology though it may result in her undertaking them in a different manner. We will always need skilled, motivated teachers to guide the educational process.

REFERENCES

Bloom, B. *Taxonomy of Educational Objectives.* Boston: Allyn and Bacon, 1984.

Friedman, T. L. *The World Is Flat: A Brief History of the Twenty-First Century.* New York: Farrar, Straus and Giroux, 2006.

"Measuring UP 2006; The National Report Card on Higher Education." The National Center for Public Policy and Higher Education, 2006.

Project Tomorrow-Netday. "Our Voices, Our Future." Irvine, CA: www.tomorrow.org, 2006.

Silvernail, D., and D. Lane. *The Impact of Maine's One-to-One Laptop Project on Middle School Teachers and Students: Phase One Summary Evidence, Research Report #1.* 2004, http://www.usm.maine.edu/cepare/mlti.htm

11

The Tragedy of Resistance

This book has described some of the tremendous advances and revolutionary changes enabled by information technology. Our tone has generally been one of optimism about the potential of this revolution for individuals, organizations, and the economy. This chapter is less optimistic. It chronicles the extreme difficulties that Kodak has encountered as it tried to understand what going digital meant to its cash-cow film business. This story illustrates three of our rules:

Rule: *Every process is becoming digital, mobile, and virtual.*

Rule: *Products and services that can become digital will, and their physical representations will disappear.*

Rule: *Individuals, organizations, and countries who resist technological change and fail to adapt will be left behind.*

A SHORT HISTORY OF KODAK

George Eastman founded the Eastman Kodak Company in 1880 and developed the first snapshot camera in 1888. Eastman focused the firm on convenience and quality. It became clear early on that consumables provided the revenue. Cameras did not need to be expensive because their owners used large amounts of film. Kodak invested heavily in film, and, when color photography was introduced, it was one of the few companies that had the knowledge and processes to succeed. The company reached $1 billion in sales in 1962. By 1976, Kodak captured the majority of the U.S. film and camera market (90 percent and 85 percent, respectively). Kodak's photofinishing process

> ### Surviving
>
> The lesson from Kodak is that if you miss a giant technology transformation, the results are disastrous. Tens of thousands of people have lost their jobs at Kodak or been forced into early retirement.
>
> In the Kodak example, we see that management failed to drive change through the organization. We depend on senior management, and also on other managers in the organization, to get the message and respond. At Kodak, the challenge was to take a company that had been successful in producing film, an analog medium, for 100 years, and convince it to go digital. Senior management recognized the issue, but was unable to convince middle managers to go along.
>
> Kodak is not alone; the recorded music industry is a great case study of how not to respond to a technological discontinuity. Video content providers are doing a better job of exploring how to make the Internet competence-enhancing rather than competence-destroying, but they have not yet discovered a successful business model. Anyone facing the rules above has to recognize a transformation is coming and prepare a new strategy to deal with it. In some cases, there may be no strategy that will be successful, and you may have to find a new business model or a new business.

quickly became the industry standard for quality. As a result, most of the power of the corporation centered on its massive film-making plant, and historically CEOs came from manufacturing jobs at the factory (Gavetti, Henderson, and Giorgi, 2004).

When Polaroid's basic patents on instant photography expired in 1969, Kodak entered the field and announced its first instant cameras in 1977. Long years of disputes and lawsuits resulted in Kodak being forced to pay Polaroid for patent infringement and exit the instant photography market in 1985. Kodak's sales hit $10 billion in 1981, but then competitive pressures, especially from Fuji, hindered future increases (Gavetti, Henderson, and Giorgi, 1993).

Since the development of the first digital camera in 1972, Kodak exhibited three different strategies:

1. Diversify into non-photographic businesses like chemicals, pharmaceuticals, and photocopiers.
2. Defend market share in film photography and continue to invest in this high-margin business.
3. Offer a range of digital cameras and complementary products like printers.

In 1981, Sony came out with its Mavica camera, which used a floppy disk to store photos. In 1986, Kodak invented the fist megapixel sensor, capturing 1.4 million pixels to produce a high-quality 5x7 print.

In 1988 Kodak made two major acquisitions. The first was Sterling Drugs, which marked a major diversification, and the second was IBM's U.S. copier business. By 1989, Kodak had introduced more than fifty products that were tied to the capture or conversion of digital images. In 1990, Kodak began to sell its Photo CD system in which a consumer took a roll of film to a photofinisher who placed images on a CD-ROM rather than paper. The consumer needed a Photo CD player to see the images on a TV screen. However, costs were too high and the product never achieved the success Kodak had forecasted.

Kodak went through a total of seven restructurings during the period between 1983 and 1993. In 1993, Kay Whitmore, a Kodak insider, stepped down as chairman. He was replaced by Dr. George Fisher, the CEO who had turned around Motorola. The board saw Fisher as a "digital man."

One of Fisher's first strategic moves was to refocus Kodak on photography. He sold the companies in its health segment, collecting $7.9 billion he used to repay debt (Gavetti, Henderson, and Giorgi, 2004). He also went after Fuji and the Japanese government for restraining the sales of Kodak products. Fisher did not give up on film; he believed that China was an emerging market with great potential for photography and invested heavily there in a joint venture with the Chinese government. Fisher worked hard to improve quality at Kodak and to restore morale and pride in the company. By 1996, Kodak had cut $50 million from the cost of film and paper production and had reduced cycle times; what used to take months could be done in less than a day (Swasy, 1997).

By 1997, digital camera sales were increasing by 75 percent a year while film camera sales increased by only 3 percent. By this time, there were many new entrants in digital photography, mostly Japanese electronics firms. In 2000, the value of digital cameras sold passed the value of film cameras. That year George Fisher left as CEO and was replaced by Daniel Carp. In 2001, sales of analog cameras dropped for the first time.

In 2002, Kodak bought Ofoto, an online picture service, signaling a greater commitment to digital photography. In 2003, Kodak closed its film camera factory in the United States. Kodak's 2003 annual report chairman's letter stated that Kodak "implemented a digitally oriented strategy to support revenue and sustainable earnings." The 2004 chairman's letter reported on progress: "In the first full year of its digital transformation strategy, Kodak came out of the gate at a full gallop—and we continue to build momentum." In 2005, Carp stepped down early as chairman and was replaced by Antonio Perez.

Figure 11.1 shows employment trends at Kodak, and Figures 11.2 and 11.3 present financial results.

Since 1993, Kodak has reduced its labor force by retirements and layoffs by about half, a strong indication of the difficulties the company has encountered settling its suit with Polaroid, the rise of Fuji in the film business, and from sales lost to digital photography.

In addition to pressure from competitors, investors have been highly critical of the company and its management. Share prices in Figure 11.2 rose during

Figure 11.1
Kodak—Number of Employees Worldwide

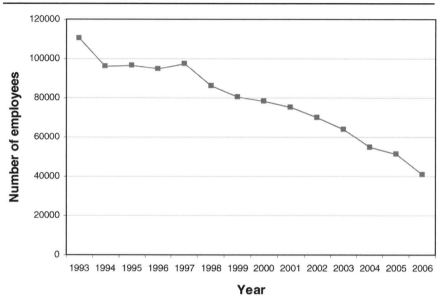

George Fisher's first few years of leadership and then began a precipitous decline during Carp's chairmanship.

Figure 11.3 shows that Kodak net sales hit $20 billion in 1992 and dropped to below $15 billion in the ensuing five years, though some of the decline was due to divestitures. This change is particularly dramatic when compared with Fuji's net sales, which have been growing rapidly since 2001. Fuji began its campaign in the United States in 1981 when it won the rights to the 1984 Olympics. Fuji and other brands began to compete heavily with Kodak, offering high quality film at 20 percent below Kodak's price. By 1993 Fuji had a 21 percent market share of worldwide film sales (Gavetti, Henderson, and Giorgi, 2004).

THE MOVEMENT TO DIGITAL PHOTOGRAPHY

The transformation from conventional photography to digital photography took about two decades. Conventional photography uses silver halides to record images by capturing light passing through a glass or plastic lens. The resulting image is developed through chemicals, creating a negative of the photograph, which is used to print the positive image on paper.

A digital camera is a computer with a lens. Unlike conventional photography, digital photography uses a sensor chip that captures light that sends the image

Figure 11.2
Kodak vs. Fuji (Monthly Share Price)

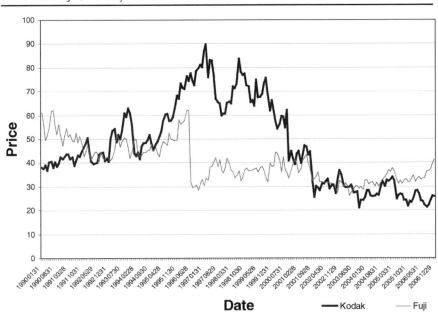

captured to a memory card. This memory card can then be read on other storage or viewing devices like the computer. Steve Sasson, the Kodak inventor of the digital camera, remarks on research at the company:

> Well, you'd be surprised at some of the breakthroughs and innovations that Kodak was doing. We were sort of in an odd position where we were certainly supporting silver halide photography for all our customers, but we were also doing advanced research into digital imaging. You know, Kodak made the first megapixel imager in the mid-1980s. We were doing image compression research and even making products using what we call DCT compression back in the mid 80s. And we made some of the first cameras. You might be surprised that a Kodak digital camera went aboard the 1991 space shuttle mission.

Paul Porter is director of design and usability at Kodak and is one of the people there with a clear digital focus:

> We were way ahead of the curve in digital even though we were pretty much a film and chemical company. We did a lot of research in digital because we knew at some point in time the world would change. We invented the digital camera. So, being the first ones there we continuously worked in the labs so to make sure when that change was made we were prepared for it. So we have the expertise in the research

Figure 11.3
Kodak vs. Fuji (Net Sales)

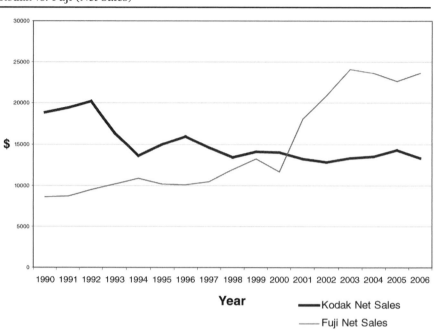

labs to generate these innovations that make our experience either more gratifying, more intuitive, or better connected than what other people do.

A major breakthrough in digital photography occurred when Kodak introduced a digital camera with the first megapixel sensor, capturing 1.4 million pixels to produce a digital photo-quality print. Soon, other companies like Sony introduced models of digital cameras. As prices fell and performance of digital cameras improved in the 1998 time frame, there was a dramatic increase in the sales of digital products (see Figure 11.4).

The movement toward digital photography had a huge adverse impact in firms that had historically been in the photography business. Traditional players such as Kodak, Fuji, and Konica Minolta found themselves caught in this transformation and have tried to reposition themselves in the market. After being in the photo industry for more than 100 years, Konica Minolta recently ended its traditional photography business and is now turning its focus on other businesses like photocopiers.

At Kodak, George Fisher was the CEO the board thought would convert the company to a digital mindset. Fisher separated the company's imaging efforts into a new division called Digital and Applied Imaging. Fisher himself observed

Figure 11.4
Sales of Digital Cameras

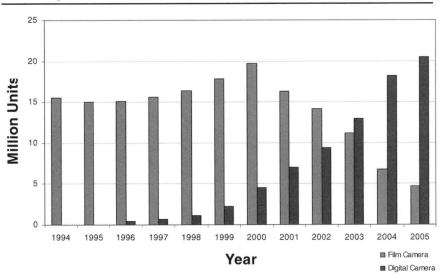

that he was able to change Kodak's culture at the top, but he was not able to convert the mass of middle managers; they never were able to understand the digital world (Interview, Gavetti, 2005). Eventually Fisher arrived at a "networks and consumables" model for Kodak. The company would be in the middle of the imaging business with customers sending photos, using Kodak print kiosks, and printing photos using Kodak printers and paper (Gavetti, Henderson, and Giorgi, 2004).

When photography moved from film to digital, it invited a whole new group of competitors into the marketplace. Companies like HP, Lexmark, Epson, and Canon suddenly became photofinishers with their color printers, some of which were designed to work easily with digital cameras to produce prints. Scores of online services like Ofoto sprung up. The costs of entry are very low for new companies entering this market.

WHAT HAPPENED AT KODAK (OR WHAT FAILED TO HAPPEN)

It is ironic that the company that invented the digital camera was unable to capitalize on its invention and the technology instead became competence-destroying for Kodak. Film was an analog business, and the digital camera was a once-in-a-hundred years event that required Kodak employees to embrace a digital mindset. What Kodak failed to understand was the huge change that the digital camera made in the process of photography, that consumers changed the process of taking and developing photos when they adopted digital technology.

Figure 11.5
Digital Photography Kodak Time Line

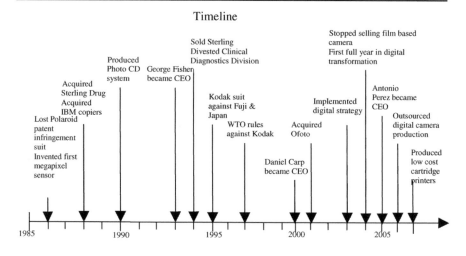

Instead of printing copies of several similar pictures, customers selected the best photograph before printing and deleted the others. Many did not print at all, but used the Internet to email digital photographs to multiple recipients. If the consumer wanted a print, he or she might use an inexpensive color printer, send the photo to a Web site for printing, or use a kiosk in a store. This story is a good example of how technology results in more than a change in a device; it leads to dramatic changes in the processes and behaviors associated with that device. Figure 11.5 describes some key events at Kodak.

Kodak managers were very successful in developing processes for manufacturing high-quality film and printing paper.

> "No matter what they said they were a film company," says Frank Zaffino (a Kodak executive). . . . Equipment was okay as long as it drove consumables . . . . Executives abhorred anything that looked risky or too innovative, because a mistake in such a massive manufacturing process would cost thousands of dollars. So the company built itself up around procedures and policies intended to maintain the status quo. (Swasy, 1997)

Kodak's strong market share produced a monopoly mindset according to John White, whom Kodak hired from the Pentagon to work on software. "As in many large old successful companies, people running it never created a business. They presided over the franchise . . . . That's not a good place to train people to be tough" (Swasy, 1997).

Kodak had a number of technological assets that were responsible for its success in the film business, including knowledge of chemistry, film production, and patents on its processes. There were also many complimentary assets in place, including one of the best known brands in the world and advertising programs. Its financial assets were strained by diversification into pharmaceuticals, a path George Fisher reversed.

Kodak's historical path was through film. Its foray into instant photography still involved film that could be developed easily by the photographer. It was digital technology that represented a completely new path to many employees. Fisher arrived after Kodak had spent $5 billion on digital imaging R&D with little coming from the labs. Product development and sales were scattered over more than a dozen divisions; at one point the company was developing 23 different digital scanner projects. In 1994 Fisher separated digital imaging from the silver-halide photographic division to create the Digital and Applied Imaging Division (Gavetti, Henderson, and Giorgi, 2004).

Kodak employees had a wealth of knowledge about making film. Some employees were knowledgeable about digital photography, but they tended to be new employees hired to create change. The traditional film managers were highly rigid in their adherence to this medium. Says John White:

> Kodak wanted to get into the digital business, but they wanted to do it in their own way, from Rochester and largely with their own people. That meant it wasn't going to work. The difference between their traditional business and digital is so great. The tempo is different. The kind of skills you need are different. Kay and Colby would tell you they wanted change, but they didn't want to force the pain on the organization. (Swasy, 1997)

Kodak had created a thriving film business, but it was challenged to develop managerial systems for digital photography. Kodak tried a number of different organizational structures for the digital business. For example:

> In the Fall of 2000 Kodak reorganized to bring digital and applied imaging and consumer imaging under one organization, in order to end the internal war between the film and digital segments. (*Rochester Business Journal,* 12/8/2000)

Kodak was a company that valued harmony, so a manager might think that there was support for a new innovation because people failed to speak out against it even though they opposed the idea. Kodak executives were polite and did not like confrontation. Employees valued hierarchy and authority:

- "It was so hierarchically oriented that everybody looked to the guy above him for what needed to be done." (*Business Week,* 1/30/95)
- At Kodak this arrogance fueled the growth of a nightmarish bureaucracy so entrenched it could have passed for a government agency . . . . There was an emphasis on doing everything according to company rulebooks. . . . Meetings were held prior to meetings to discuss issues and establish agreement in order to avoid confrontations, which were considered un-Kodak-like. (Swasy, 1997)

Fisher converted those at the top of the organization to believers in the future of digital photography. In an interview, Fisher said that he realized later that the belief in digital did not extend throughout the organization:

> The old-line manufacturing culture continues to impede Fisher's efforts to turn Kodak into a high-tech growth company. Fisher has been able to change the culture at the very top. But he hasn't been able to change the huge mass of middle managers, and they just don't understand this [digital] world. (*Business Week,*10/20/1997)
>
> I think that the fear drove paralysis that manifested itself as time went on, to rigidity with respect to changing our strategy and I didn't see that at the start . . . we really had to work very aggressively to get middle management, first of all, understanding what we were trying to do and believe that this was a story of opportunity, that we were in the picture business, that digital was just a technology just like film was, and that picture business opportunity was gigantic, and there was a future for them. . . . Their arguments would be all over the map: . . . Kodak can't succeed in this market. We've tried some consumer products before and failed miserably. There is no money in this business; it's all low margin . . . There is a new set of competitors . . . we don't know anything about them. (George Fisher interview, Gavetti, 2005)

Managers at all levels in Kodak also consistently underestimated the growth of the market for digital cameras. Kodak was convinced that the professional photographer would be the first adopter and that amateurs would move more slowly. As seen in the sales statistics in Figure 11.4, this prediction was seriously in error.

It is clear that Kodak chose to pursue its high-margin film business in light of declining market share and sales. High margins and a large stream of revenue are difficult, if not impossible, to give up. It is unlikely that a board of directors or shareholders would suggest that Kodak exit the film business or spin it off as a new firm. However, the focus on film and its margin made it easier for doubters to reject digital as a disruptive technology. This focus became a core rigidity for many Kodak employees.

> "We're moving into an information-based company," Leo J. Thomas, SVP and director of Kodak research. . . . "[But] it is very hard to find anything [with profit margins] like color photography that is legal." (*Wall Street Journal,* 5/22/1985).

Two events helped distract Kodak in recent history. The first was the suit, which it lost to Polaroid after it entered the instant photography market. In addition to a lost investment and damages Kodak had to pay to Polaroid, this episode alienated photofinishers who thought Kodak was trying take away their business with an instant camera and film. They started to divert some of their traditional Kodak business to Fuji and other finishers.

A second serious distraction was the ongoing battle with Fuji film for market share. In 1976, Fuji was the first to introduce 400-speed color film which was faster than any of Kodak's products. Kodak's photographic paper was about 20 percent more expensive than Fuji's (Swasy, 1997).

Fisher commented on the history of the Fuji battle:

> I remember over a 20 year period, they (Kodak) were averaging losing a point to a point and a half of market share a year . . . but there was a gradual erosion of market share from 95 percent at one time to . . . I think it was around 65 percent in the U.S. consumer market. [Kodak] explained the market share loss largely by price aggressiveness of competitors including Fuji. Whether or not that was all true I don't really know; I think it was mostly true. But in fact there were some product differences where Kodak had slipped in product in some significant ways . . . and we had to catch up from some serious holes in our product line. And I think part of the erosion had to do with Fuji having some actually better products than we had. (George Fisher interview, Gavetti, 2005)

A 20-year struggle with a major competitor in film would make it easy for Kodak managers to ignore the coming threat of digital photography.

CONCLUSIONS

Kodak developed many of the major advances in photography and was a leader in producing quality films and cameras. Kodak has one of the most recognized brand names in the world. Management was unable to marshal these dynamic capabilities to create an effective response to digital photography. Kodak's core competencies in the knowledge and skills of its employees, technical and managerial systems, and values and norms worked against the objectives of senior management to respond vigorously to the threat and opportunities of the digital world.

While management, and especially George Fisher, announced new strategies from the top, senior managers were unable to change the cognitions of a powerful group of middle managers. Their mental models were fixed on the high margin film business and could not adapt to the changes coming from digital photography. Senior managers did not help their own cause by diversifying into pharmaceuticals, engaging in a price war with Fuji, and fighting a lawsuit by Polaroid.

What might Kodak have done differently? Kodak would be in a better position today had it followed a different path.

(1) Marshal and organize capabilities for change

- The board of directors and CEO needed to demonstrate a commitment to the digital business, and expect that it would not be immediately profitable. The message should have reached all of Kodak that the company expected digital photography to be the wave of the future and was committed to serving this market. It is instructive to note that the CEO's letter in the Kodak annual report first talked about a digital strategy for the company in 2003.

- Kodak should have created and maintained a separate organization to develop digital photography prior to 1994, as suggested by Christensen (1997), when a traditional firm is trying to be innovative. Kodak had several structures in place for digital photography and restructured the company a number of times, sending mixed signals.
- The company failed to deal quickly with distractions and allowed the ongoing competition with Fuji to encourage an emphasis on the film business.

(2) Attack rigidities

- Kodak yielded to the temptation to keep a strategic focus on the high-margin film business and discounted evidence that this business was shrinking. The challenge for Kodak and other companies in a similar situation is how to continue to exploit a "cash cow" line of business while simultaneously moving resources to support new, technological-based products.
- The task of changing the cognitions of middle managers was immense, and according to George Fisher, he and Kodak were not successful in this effort. We need to develop better strategies for bringing about extensive organizational change when companies are confronted with transformational technologies.
- The company should have done a better job of anticipating how rapidly digital technology would transform amateur photography. We do not know if Kodak used outside experts to predict this transformation or conducted focus groups and customer surveys to assess how rapidly photography would become digital. However, it is clear that the company seriously overestimated the demand for film and film cameras and underestimated the demand for digital photography.

What can be generalized from Kodak's experience? The most important observation is to recognize the threats and opportunities of a new technology and marshal capabilities for change. Managers have to incorporate a response to the new technology in corporate strategy, and take advantage of the dynamic capabilities of the organization. Kodak had many such capabilities, including a strong brand, excellent research in general and on optical technologies specifically, and talented staff, among others. One must also avoid distractions that take attention away from the new challenges their organizations is facing.

This chapter has presented a history of Kodak's response to the technological transformation that digital photography created in the marketplace. As with any complex history, it is virtually impossible to assign the blame for Kodak's poor performance to one factor. A combination of events contributed to the company's path over time.

What of the future? Carly Fiorina observes:

Conventional photography . . . was a physical, chemical process . . . Less than five years later (post 1999) that physical process had become virtually completely digital. IT has also become mobile. . . . along the way Kodak protected its franchise for as long as it could. And when Kodak finally declared that it would enter the realm of digital photography in a big way when it was completely obvious to everyone that the old model simply would not survive. The resulting strategic about-face was applauded as necessary but was accompanied by massive write-offs and losses because the obvious move was overdue. It is still not yet clear what Kodak's role or success will be in the new digital age. The brand survives, but will the company? (Commencement Address, Smith School of Business, University of Maryland, May 22, 2006)

And in a 2007 interview:

Well, it's ... difficult when businesses are very successful to take a risk and try something new. ... Kodak sat on a mountain of cash and profitability in their traditional photography business, and I believe their thinking was: "Digital photography will eat into my traditional most profitable business. I don't want that to happen." What I think Kodak miscalculated about was they weren't in charge of whether that would happen. Consumers were in charge. Individuals were in charge. And an individual will always choose ... what gives them greater control, flexibility, freedom, choice. ... So suddenly consumers had a new way of taking pictures that gave them more control, more freedom, more flexibility and more choice. The consumer became in charge of how fast Kodak's traditional business would be eaten away. And Kodak unfortunately didn't see that in time. And so now they're attempting a transformation in a very weakened state and they may have missed their season of change.

The *Wall Street Journal* (8/2/2006) reported on Kodak's second-quarter, 2006 results with the headline "Kodak's Loss Widens as Revenue Declines 8.8 percent."

Eastman Kodak Co., underscoring the difficulties it is having moving to the digital age, reported a widened second-quarter net loss on a revenue decline and said it will stop making digital cameras. Kodak said it would contract with Singapore-based Flextronics International Ltd. to handle camera manufacturing and some of its camera-design work. The decision marks a turning point for Kodak: The company founder, George Eastman, started making cameras in 1887 in Rochester NY...Kodak will continue selling digital cameras under its brand even though it is outsourcing the manufacturing.

Even the shape of Kodak's campus is changing. Ten years ago, Kodak park encompassed 1,600 acres and was the biggest industrial complex in the Northeast. By the end of 2007, the park will be reduced to 700 acres. The factories where film and paper were produced by thousands of workers are disappearing. The company used explosives to destroy three huge buildings in the summer of 2007, including a four-story paper-products plant constructed in 1918 (*Wall Street Journal*, 10/31/2007). It is hard to imagine a more graphic portrayal of the impact of digital technology than four buildings imploding with the help of well-placed explosive charges.

It appears that Kodak is finally committed to digital photography. It is a much smaller company today with fewer employees and lower sales. The company is working on a strategy that brings its digital print technology to the commercial printing market (*Business Week*, 9/4/2006). Kodak is developing a new inkjet process that is extremely fast so that custom digital presses can perform with the speed of offset presses, up to 24 miles an hour. This breakthrough would allow companies to produce custom catalogs designed for the habits of each customer.

For the fourth quarter of 2006, Kodak reported its first profit in nine quarters on higher revenue from photo kiosks and its savings from laying off workers. The company reported fourth-quarter net income of $16 million, though sales fell 9 percent to $3.82 billion for the quarter. "2006 was the first year when the earnings growth in digital products exceeded the earnings decline in traditional products," Antonio Perez said in a conference call with investors and analysts. "We have continued with the transformation to make significant progress against important and challenging goals" (Bloomberg.com, 1/31/2007).

Perez, the current Kodak CEO, is a printer veteran, having run HP's printer business before assuming his present position. In early 2007, Kodak announced a new, low-cost inkjet printer. The printer is designed to print high-quality photographs that should last for 100 years, better than the current 15-year life of a print. Replacement ink cartridges will cost half of what we are used to paying (*BusinessWeek*, 2/19/2007). The news of the new printers was accompanied by an announcement that Kodak would cut another 3,000 jobs in addition to the 25,000–27,000 it had already planned to cut by the end of 2007. At the end of 2007, Kodak is expected to employ about 30,000 employees, half the number of three years before, and a small fraction (21 percent) of the 145,000 it once employed when it dominated the film business (*Wall Street Journal*, 2/9/2007).

Carly Fiorina comments on the printer strategy:

> Kodak is going back to old technology, printing, where another company, Hewlett-Packard, dominates, and they're trying to attack that hill, and I don't think that will work because now they're in a very weakened state attacking a very strong competitor. If they're going to win, they've got to win by doing something new, not by copying someone else. But doing something new is hard for companies. Really hard.

The questions remain: Has Kodak shed enough core rigidities to survive in a digital world? Can it now marshal its technological skills, brand name, and historical relationship with customers to once again become a leader? If so, it will be an example of a firm and employees that suffered greatly from a major technological disruption but in the end managed to meet the challenge? Time will tell.

REFERENCES

Anderson, P., and M. Tushman. "Technological Discontinuities and Dominant Designs: A Cyclical Model of Technological Change." *Administrative Science Quarterly* 35, no. 4 (December 1990): 604–633.

Barney, J. "Firm Resources and Sustained Competitive Advantage." *Journal of Management* 17, no. 1 (1991): 99–120.

Gavetti, G. Interview with Dr. George Fisher (DVD). HBS Publishing, 2005.

Gavetti, G., R. Henderson, and S. Giorgi. Kodak (A). HBS Publishing, 2004.

Swasy, A. *Changing Focus.* New York Times Business, 1997.

———— 12 ————

The Evidence for Transformation

C hapter 2 presents a framework for thinking about IT-enabled transformations and suggests several criteria for determining when a transformation
has taken place. Three indicators of transformation include technology
that:

- Fundamentally alters traditional ways of doing business by redefining business capabilities and/or (internal or external) business processes and relationships.
- Potentially involves strategic acquisitions to acquire new capabilities or to enter a
  new market space.
- Exemplifies the use of IT to dramatically change how tasks are carried out . . . is the
  move recognized as being important in enabling [the] firm to operate in different
  markets, serve different customers . . . gain considerable competitive advantage by
  doing things differently (Dehning et al., 2003).

We have been concerned with more than just business transformations because
of an interest in how IT changes our lives, so the criteria above can be simplified
to "fundamentally altering traditional ways of doing things," and "exemplifies the
use of IT to dramatically change how familiar tasks are carried out."

IS THERE REALLY TRANSFORMATIONAL IT?

Have the examples in the book made a case for transformation? See Table 12.1.
Is there something going on with technology that constitutes a "quiet revolution"?
It is likely that people living in the middle of the Industrial Revolution were
oblivious to its historical significance. Lives changed as workers moved from
rural areas and agricultural jobs to factory jobs in cities, but some people continued to farm or remained as shop keepers and merchants. A banking system was
already in place, and it helped provide the capital needed in England and other

> ### Surviving
>
> You need not worry about surviving if there are no transformations going on. And one man's transformation may be another's incremental change. This chapter presents a summary of the evidence in an effort to convince the reader that the technology revolution is ongoing and that we need to be aware of it.
>
> Is the evidence enough to be convincing? For those who are still skeptical, talking to an ex-employee of Kodak or a current worker in the recorded music industry may be enough to create awareness and concern. Or you can look carefully at articles in the business press that every week describe a different company or industry that is facing the challenge of a disruptive technology. The evidence is all around, and people who manage to ignore it do so at great peril.

countries to finance new industries. Did banking change dramatically one day as a result of the Industrial Revolution? Banking evolved and increased in scale, but bankers did not walk into their offices one day and find a different world than the day before. Transformations do not take place overnight; they require time to manifest themselves.

What is the picture that emerges from Table 12.1? To me, it is one of transformation, of major changes in the way in which people work and play. I make my own airline reservation, print a boarding pass, and check in at the airport with it. A consultant at Accenture finds that it is impossible to be promoted to the corner office with a lot of windows because the consultants in the firm do not have permanent offices. I buy a product from Cisco, but Cisco did not manufacture it. Instead of calling a broker, many people trade securities online and pay far less in commissions than they used to when brokerage services were bundled. At EarthColor, there are new workers using computers in the prepress operation; workers with expertise in handling film are no longer there.

It is likely that your children are registered with MySpace. They have friends that they see physically and many more friends that are part of their online community. When you need to find out information about your government and community, you do so online. If you live in a state that has transactions capabilities built into its Web site, you renew your auto registration and your driver's license online. Depending on your tastes in music, you have an iPod and download music from iTunes instead of buying CDs. You are starting to download movies from Amazon.com. You routinely shop online for yourself and for other people, and of course, you take pictures with your digital camera. Some days you go to a photo kiosk to print pictures, while other times you upload your pictures to one of the services on the Web and have them printed and sent to you.

If you are a veteran or a member of Kaiser Permanente there is an electronic medical record that contains your medical history. Doctors access this record

Table 12.1
Discussion Summary

Industry	Example	Technology Innovations	Impact of Technology
Airlines	American, United	Computerized reservations systems, Internet, e-tickets, boarding passes	Move to customer self-service, strong negative impact on travel agent business
Services	Accenture	"Hoteling" instead of permanent offices	IT helps coordinate employees who are constantly traveling
Manufacturing	Cisco	Internet for taking customer orders, providing customer service, routing orders to contract manufacturers	Customer self-service, reduced cycle times, greater efficiencies
Brokerage	eTrade, Schwab	Online retail stock trading	Forced unbundling of trading, reduced prices for investors
Securities markets	Archipelago and NYSE	Electronic marketplace for trading securities	Facilitated online trading, put pressure on physical exchanges to change
Commercial printing	EarthColor	Processes go digital: prepress, plate making, private network	EC able to reduce employment and costs in order to succeed in a highly competitive business
Multiple industries	Wal-Mart	RFID	Product tracking and remote payments
Multiple businesses	eBay, MySpace	Feedback via the Internet, community software	Power transfers from businesses and formal organization to groups and individuals
Government	Montgomery County, Firstgov.gov	The Web as a source of information about government and a place to execute transactions	Customer self-service, better informed citizens, reduced cycle times, more government transparency, bringing government and the people closer together
Hollywood	Walt Disney Studios	The Internet, file sharing software, downloading software	Violation of copyright and loss of revenue, need to find new distribution models to provide freedom of place and time for viewers

Health care	Department of Veterans Affairs, Kaiser Permanente	Electronic medical records, electronic prescribing, electronic payments systems, Web interfaces for patients	Improved quality of service, fewer medical errors, ability to practice evidence-based medicine
Telecommunications	Verizon, Comcast	WiMax, fiber, convergence of PC and video	Competition for pipe to the home, services like Internet and video
Recorded music	Recording studios	File sharing software	Violation of copyright, forced unbundling of songs in an album, forced reduction in prices, bankruptcy of retail music chains
Retailing	Amazon, L.L. Bean, Lands' End	Online shopping via the Internet	New sales channels, reductions in travel, customer self-service
Newspaper	*Philadelphia Inquirer, New York Times*	Web news sites, Web advertising, search advertising, eBay Motors	Reductions in newspaper ad revenue, size of papers, and news staffs
Multiple	Wikipedia, Linux	Open source development, shared projects	Cooperative projects produce high-quality output through the contribution of expertise
Education	K-12, College	Laptops for students, Internet access, email for all parties	Remote access to resources, collaborative learning
Photography	Kodak	Digital photography	Loss of market share, reduced share price, multiple rounds of layoffs and retirements

and post their findings to it so that whenever you need treatment, the doctor, nurse or paramedic has access to your medical history. Physicians enter prescriptions electronically, reducing the chances for errors. Researchers look at the database of electronic medical records to learn what treatments are working best so that your treatment is based on evidence from many patients.

What is striking about Table 12.1 is the transformation of a wide variety of businesses and processes. There is little that is likely to be untouched by this technological revolution. It affects all of us at work and at home. The technology invades our leisure time, for better or for worse. The revolution in technology is quiet, but it moves quickly once it finds a new application. Internet connectivity, Napster, the iPod, and MySpace grew like wildfire, and nothing will be the same again.

THOSE RULES OF THE REVOLUTION

Rule: *Every process is becoming digital, mobile, and virtual (Carly Fiorina).*

Products like digital cameras illustrate this rule; photography is no longer an analog, chemical process. Your pictures are not recorded on film, but instead as bits in the camera's memory. Many people keep their photographs in electronic form on a computer. You can convert the pictures to a physical form in a kiosk, using a home printer, or by sending them to a Web site. The airline reservations process is virtual and requires no ticket agent; you can make a reservation anyplace you have an Internet connection. Consultants at Accenture have virtual offices; they can choose to conduct business from an office "hotel" or from a client's site. You can place an order online at a virtual store for a vast array of merchandise, including industrial goods like routers and switches from Cisco. Listening to music is possible anyplace and anytime, music that came to your iPod from the Internet.

Rule: *Products and services that can become digital will, and their physical representations will disappear.*

Digital goods are a natural for the technology; information of all types, music, and video all migrate easily to the Internet. Soon there will be no CDs, and the development of a new DVD format will turn out to be unnecessary. Video content is a natural for the Internet just as it is for music. Newspapers are facing a double threat: advertising is migrating rapidly from newspapers to Web search engine sites like Google, and the news itself is available on the Web as it happens.

Rule: *Physical products will be marketed with information components.*

Automobiles are major consumer purchases and used to be thought of as hardware. Auto manufacturers have built-in information capabilities to enhance the driving experience and to market their products. A common option on a new car is a navigation system, an application that uses GPS hardware and a dedicated computer and database to compute routes and provide directions. General Motors developed the OnStar system to enhance safety. The system contacts a service center if the airbags in the car deploy, and an agent at the center tells the police where the car is located. The agent can also remotely unlock the car's doors, and the service has been extended with a number of optional features. In health care, prescription drugs are an information product as well as a physical one. Systems in the pharmacy check to be sure the prescribed drug does not have an interaction with a drug the patient is already taking. Drug companies and independent researchers publish the results of trials and experiments with drugs to help the physician use the drug most appropriately. The iPod is a physical, consumer product while iTunes sells the "information" that accompanies the product.

Rule: *Organizations are shifting as much work to consumers as possible. The age of customer self-service is here.*

Many of the examples in the book feature customer self-service such as making airline reservations, trading securities online, dealing with the government, downloading music and videos, and shopping. For consumers, the advantages of customer self-service include speed, convenience, and the ability to search and compare offerings from different vendors. For the organization offering self-service to its customers, the great advantages are labor and space savings. Every customer that orders something online, makes a reservation online, or who answers his or her own question means that a company employee is not needed for the interaction. With fewer employees dedicated to customers, the firm needs less expensive office space. This looks like a case where everyone wins!

Rule: *People want freedom to set their own schedules and to work and engage in leisure activities from a location of their choosing.*

If you wake up at 3:00 in the morning with a great idea for buying a stock, you can go to your computer and put in the order. For the most part, it will not trade until the U.S. market opens in the morning, but that is likely to change. You can make an airline reservation anytime of the day or night. TV networks are finding that viewers want to choose what to watch as well as when and where to watch it. Viewers do not want to be constrained by a network broadcasting schedule or the need to be tethered to a television set. Movies are likely to follow suit.

Rule: *Technology enables powerful online communities: power to the people.*

Buyer and seller reviews on eBay are extremely important in making the market transparent. Book and product reviews at sites like Amazon have a great influence on sales. Web communities like MySpace are wildly popular, and Facebook has replaced collections of bad photos distributed by college administrators. Online communities quickly grow to be much larger and more influential than one's circle of friends who interact in person. Politicians are finding that online communities are changing the nature of campaigns and the legislative process.

Rule: *Some services are better bundled, some are better unbundled, and the market will choose the winners.*

The biggest news here is about unbundling because it favors consumers. The advent of electronic brokerages broke the bundle of services and trade execution that was the norm in the brokerage business. Online entrants came into the industry offering just one part of the bundle, the trade execution, at a substantially lower price. Napster did the same thing for the music fan; he or she does not have to buy an entire CD with 15 songs to get the one song he or she really likes. While the brokerage industry responded with full-service firms offering online trading, the music industry is still in turmoil over how to proceed. It is supporting legal download sites where the recording companies are compensated, but it is not clear that the industry is ready to embrace total digital distribution of music.

Rule: *Technology will speed up every process, reducing cycle times and driving inefficiencies out of the economy.*

Customer self-service is just one of the many places for dramatic savings and productivity improvements. The firm offering self-service saves on labor and handles a larger volume of customers, a clear increase in efficiency. UPS continues to drive inefficiencies out of its business with information technology. Cisco has discussed its savings from intensive use of the Internet in speeches by senior executives, and the amount claimed is well over $1 billion. The reasons for outsourcing manufacturing are cost savings and quality; the technology makes it possible to quickly route orders to outsourcers. The outsourcers in turn use the technology to manage their supply chains, reducing cycle times for production. Potential savings are there for new innovations: Hollywood spends an estimated $1 billion a year making copies of movies and distributing them to theaters. Some players in the industry are trying to eliminate film and move to digital distribution to theaters. Each copy would be a perfect match to the original and film could not break in a projector. It would be easy for a multiplex to show the same movie in several theaters at the same time.

Rule: *Local markets will become national and international.*

Securities markets are in the process of becoming global, and it is likely that restrictions on trading outside of local market operating hours will go away. The merged NYSE and Archipelago has bought EuroNext, which will make it possible to expand trading hours. For years, financial firms have been "passing the book" around the world, completing trading in one location while moving their positions to the location where the market is opening next. With the Internet, anyone can set up a Web site and take orders from around the world; with online commerce there are no borders.

Rule: *Technology will continue to accelerate globalization.*

Technology is an enabler and a driver of globalization. IT provides the backbone for communications among different physical locations. Any company that outsources call centers and manufacturing to another country is enjoying the benefits of globalization. Contract electronics manufacturers are located around the world, with many having plants in Asia. TAL is a Chinese partner of Penney's and manages its dress shirt lines from product design through manufacturing and inventory management in each retail store. Globalization has its downsides as well; some parts of the world do not seem to have gained much from this growing trend while others have done very well. The U.S. trade deficit is also a major concern that certainly has not improved with globalization.

Rule: *The spoils go to innovators and those who can execute.*

Companies like EarthColor that figure out how to take advantage of technology are highly successful. The company has managed to increase its market share during a time of great cost pressure and changes in the nature of customer printing needs. Much of its success is due to the integration of three key technologies in its business. Cisco has a reputation as an innovative company both for the products it sells and for the way it runs its business. The iPod is one of the most successful innovations of the last decade, and it, combined with iTunes, has reversed Apple's decline, creating a much more competitive firm.

Rule: *The rapid development of new technology-based business models is responsible for a hyper-competitive economy.*

It is unlikely that anyone in business today would suggest that competition is lessening. Globalization means that many more individuals and firms are after the same customers. As a high wage country, the United States is highly susceptible to market entrants from other countries who have a significant wage advantage. The typical business today is faced with competition in the United States and competition from companies in the rest of the world. With the Internet providing a global information infrastructure, it is easy for firms to participate in global markets, increasing the amount of competition.

Rule: *Individuals, organizations, and countries who resist technological change and fail to adapt will be left behind.*

This last rule may be the most controversial of all. For the United States and its services economy, it is highly relevant. What kind of capital investment is there to improve productivity in the services industries? The obvious answer is information technology. All you have to do is look around and see the extent to which the technology is a part of everyday life, from collecting tolls automatically at tunnels and bridges, to verifying credit cards and processing debit transactions, to downloading music and movies to a PC or mobile device.

I am convinced that unless we make major reforms in our education system as discussed in Chapter 10, the United States is at great risk. That chapter argued for an education system that stresses innovation to continue the historical trend of creativity and invention that has characterized the U.S. economy. In addition to innovation, we need educated citizens who are able to use the technology around them in daily life and who are capable of working with the technology in their jobs. There will always be a need for jobs that do not involve technology, but the number and scope of those jobs is declining. Today's auto mechanic plugs a diagnostic machine into the car to retrieve onboard diagnostics that tell him what has malfunctioned. McDonald's is experimenting with self-service kiosks for food distribution; one cannot count on employing the under-educated in hamburger chains for the indefinite future.

CAN DEVELOPING COUNTRIES CATCH UP WITH THE REVOLUTION?

What about countries in the process of development? There is little consensus on why some countries have fallen so far behind others. In the 1960s, Africa's future seemed bright. During the first half of the 1900s, for example, Africa had grown more rapidly than Asia. However, since 1980, aggregate per capita GDP in sub-Saharan Africa has declined at a rate of about 1 percent a year (Collier and Gunning, 1999). In fact 32 African countries are poorer today than in 1980. It is very hard to identify the causes of poverty versus the effects of poverty. Once a country begins to fall behind in growth and development, things tend to get worse rather than better. No one wants to invest in a politically unstable country; the lack of investment increases poverty, which, in turn, fuels instability.

A number of experts have offered explanations for Africa's lack of growth ranging from a tropical climate that encourages diseases, large families, AIDs, ethnic diversity and strife, dictatorships, government policies, lack of infrastructure, farm subsidies in Western countries that depress local prices, lack of contract enforcement, ineffective support for exports, and low productivity (Collier and Gunning, 1999). It is likely that all of these factors interact to create the kind of downward spiral that makes it so difficult for countries to reverse negative growth.

Will developing countries be left further behind if they fail to adopt technology? The world economy is competitive, and if countries are to participate in global markets, then they will need to be technologically capable. Technology alone will not lead to economic development; economic growth needs to be treated as a package or system of variables. In looking at the "East Asian Miracle" of growth, Stiglitz identified a number of drivers. "East Asia's success was based on a combination of factors, particularly the high savings rate interacting with high levels of human capital accumulation, in a stable, market-oriented environment—but one with active government intervention—that was conducive to the transfer of technology" (Stiglitz, 1996, p. 151). He identified four policies that promoted growth:

- The support for education, especially in engineering and science, along with policies to ensure universal literacy, and support for educating women.
- Financial market regulation to discourage the allocation of capital to areas like real estate, channeling capital instead to plants and equipment.
- A policy to encourage exports, including programs to build infrastructure.
- Promotion of technology programs and science centers in selected industries.

Two of these four drivers of growth are education and technology. Barro (2001) also focuses on human capital and education as a means for growth, emphasizing both the quantity and quality of education.

We know that technology can help improve the reach and content of education. As an example, one innovator is developing a system to deliver textbooks and other materials across Africa via one-way satellite radio transmission (*Technology Review,* September/October 2006). Chapter 10 discusses a number of ways in which technology interacts with the educational system and stresses the need to prepare students to use technology in order to obtain its benefits. Technology is an enabler. Its success in contributing to economic development and growth depends on an educated work force and policies that set the stage for transformations.

THE COMPETENCE QUESTION

The framework for transformations in Chapter 2 focuses on competence-enhancing and competence-destroying change. For EarthColor, the overall adoption of three key technologies was competence-enhancing, just as was the move to the Internet for orders and customer service at Cisco. These technologies built on existing competencies in the organizations, resulting in very positive outcomes. But at EarthColor, there were individuals who did not adapt, people who were not a part of the technology revolution. For them, changes were competence-destroying.

In any transformation, it is likely that for some the changes are competence-enhancing and for others, competence-destroying. The digital distribution of movies would be competence-enhancing for theater owners and operators and for theater-goers, but it would be extremely competence-destroying for those who benefit from selling film and making copies of movies. Judging whether a transformation enhances or destroys competence requires an in-depth analysis of what is changing and how the people involved are affected.

The competence issue suggests a strategy for accommodating transformations—you want to look for opportunities that are competence-enhancing. Beyond that, you should seek ways to turn potential competence-destroying changes into ones that are competence-enhancing. Our advice to Technicolor would be to invest in digital distribution of films since the company has competence in the overall process already with physical film. (And that is exactly what Technicolor is doing.) To the prepress operators at EarthColor, the message would have been to take evening classes to learn how to use a Mac and associated software for printing operations.

CONCLUSIONS

As someone who has worked with technology for many years, I am an enthusiastic proponent of IT. It is not the solution to every problem, but the technology has become so pervasive today that ignoring it is dangerous. I believe that historians will look back at the last half of the twentieth century and the present century as the time of the technology revolution, a time in which technology enabled massive transformations of business and the way we live our daily lives. The evidence gathered for this book only reinforces my belief, and I hope that the text has stimulated the reader to think more deeply about IT-enabled transformations. Change brings with it great risks but also the potential for huge benefits. The choice between these outcomes is up to individuals and the decisions they make about the technology. Ask yourself: Am I ready for a future filled with technology-enabled transformations?

REFERENCES

Barro, R. "Human Capital: Growth, History and Policy—A Session to Honor Stanley Engerman." *AEA Papers and Proceedings* (May 2001): 12–17.

Collier, P., and J. W. Gunning. "Why Has Africa Grown Slowly?" *The Journal of Economic Perspectives* 13, no. 3 (Summer 1999): 3–22.

Dehning, B., V. Richardson, and R. Zmud. "The Value Relevance of Announcements of Transformational Information Technology Investments." *MIS Quarterly* 27, no. 4 (December 2003): 637–656

Stiglitz, J. "Some Lessons from the East Asian Miracle." *The World Bank Research Observer* 11, no. 2 (August 1996): 151–177.

PART III

How to Survive

———— 13 ————

Barriers to Change

There is nothing more difficult to take in hand, more perilous to conduct, or more uncertain in its success, than to take the lead in the introduction of a new order of things.
—Niccolo Machiavelli

What I know is that certain things about change are always the same. They're universal. One of them is change is always resisted. Always. It doesn't matter where you try it. It's resisted because of human nature. People are afraid . . . to try something new. They're afraid to fail. They're afraid to take a risk. People who have positions of power and influence in an organization want to keep them; it's human nature. So the natural momentum of an organization is always preservation of the status quo. Let's just stay the way we are. And so change takes more energy, more will, more discipline than the status quo. Otherwise, change fails.
—Carly Fiorina interview, 2007

Rule: *Individuals, organizations, and countries who resist technological change and fail to adapt will be left behind.*

Transformation is all about change, and as Machiavelli argues, nothing is as difficult to accomplish as change. The description in Chapter 2 of the IT transformation process distinguishes between competence-enhancing and competence-destroying change. One would predict that change is easier to bring about in the case of a competence-enhancing technology. Individuals and organizations faced with competence-destroying change are likely to resist, to fight change, and to try and maintain the status quo. This behavior is even more likely if large amounts of money are at stake.

Resistance to new technology has been a constant in history as exemplified by the Luddites. This group is named from a real, or perhaps invented person,

> **Surviving**
>
> This chapter is about survival. It explores the barriers to recognizing and confronting an IT-enabled transformation. Skepticism and resistance to change are not new. They have been around for centuries. Given the speed at which change is occurring, we have less time than ever to overcome these barriers and adapt to a technology revolution. We have to learn how to change ourselves and to bring about change in others. The failure to identify barriers to change and to overcome them means that you and your employer are going to be left behind, and the evidence we have presented so far suggests that is a very undesirable outcome.

named Ned Ludd, reportedly of Sherwood Forest. The Luddites smashed industrial machines used in the textile industry to save their jobs. The Luddites destroyed stocking-frames and cropping frames among other equipment, fearing that these machines would destroy their livelihoods. A local worker would rent a frame from a master and work at his own shop with thread from the master; the finished stockings went back to the master to sell. Because the frames were located in many different places, it was easy for the Luddites to find and destroy them. In 1811 and 1812, they destroyed about a thousand machines (http://www.historyhome.co.uk/c-eight/distress/luddites.htm).

Since the early days of computers, we have been concerned with successful implementation. It is an accepted fact that many information systems fail partially or completely. For example, there are estimates that 50 percent of ERP installations (Enterprise Resource Planning packages) do not work in their initial implementation effort. And here we are talking about planned change, one in which an organization decides to invest in new technology. What happens when change is forced on organizations or individuals because of a change in technology or a new innovation? Resistance is going to be even stronger in these conditions since it is also likely that the forced change is competence-destroying.

In addition to planned change, one of the keys to success in the technological revolution is innovation. Organizations must innovate to continue to grow and have a leading role in the world economy. David Berlind of ZDNet gives a good example of how his company responds to innovation:

> New technology comes along and we look at it right away. Podcasting is a really good example. Between the time it showed up and the time we had our first official recurring podcast on ZDnet was a matter of a couple months. We looked at podcast and said, "Well, we're not sure what it is, we're not sure whether we should be doing it or not in terms of if it's good for our audience or not, but we do know is if people are driving in their cars and they're able to listen to our competitors' content, then we need to be a channel they can select as well. [We said] let's do it, let's see what happens. If in the end it works out it wasn't a good idea, we can stop. But

we can't sit there, rest on our laurels and say, okay what we've got is great and none of this other stuff is going to pose a threat to us or cause people to change the channel." We have to be very aggressive in embracing new technologies to . . . continually give our audience ways to tuning into our content.

More broadly, Berlind talks about disruptive technologies:

> Innovation in many cases is about disruption, so it has to be a part of the company's culture to be willing to disrupt something about their existing business before they're going to be able to openly innovate. The culture is important at the company and I think also you need to have several heavy-duty disruptive forces within the company and I'm talking about people. People who are willing to go against the status quo, go against the grain, because if you have a company full of people who don't like change . . . and who just want to kind of go about doing business the way they've been doing it, your company is sooner or later going to find itself at a disadvantage to its competitors who embrace technology and innovation. If you don't disrupt yourself, somebody will come along and do it for you, so the big question is do you wait for somebody else to come along and motivate you to do it as matter of survival, or do you take the lead.

Disruptive technologies lead to innovation and change. How can we motivate individuals and organizations to see that they happen?

THE POWER OF THE STATUS QUO

Recording Companies

Chapter 3 presented the saga of the recording industry versus music downloading. The industry fought downloading with lawsuits against file sharing sites, in particular winning a judgment that shut down the original Napster. Over time the industry acquiesced and partnered with legal download sites that sell subscriptions to music while paying royalties to the recording companies. When the innovative iPod hit the market, downloading took off and is likely to become the dominant mode for distributing music. Sam Goody and Tower Records filed for bankruptcy; this sea change was clearly competence-destroying for them.

You have to wonder if the recording industry had lost touch with its customers. Did these companies not know that consumers were angry about having to buy a bundled album when they wanted one or two songs from the album? Did industry executives ignore the articles and discussions of the Internet and its likely impact on digital goods like music? What might have happened if the industry joined together to buy the original Napster and turn it into a subscription service?

Health Information Technology

One of the most challenging implementation environments has always been medicine. There are many reasons for difficulty in bringing information technology to this domain, and it is ironic to compare those efforts with technology used directly in treatment like scanning and imaging machines. Doctors and hospitals are quick to adopt exotic treatment technology because it is almost always revenue-generating. Health information systems usually do not generate revenue; the benefits that come from health IT often accrue to the patient, the hospital and/or the insurance carriers, with little benefit and almost no revenue for the doctor. Medicine is a highly fragmented industry with doctors, hospitals and outpatient sites, payers, the government, and others each having an interest in the outcomes of any initiative.

In some cases partial implementation of a health information system may be worse than no system at all. The Department of Defense (DOD) developed a digital medical record system for tracking wounded soldiers in Iraq and Afghanistan. But the Department has only been able to get 13 of 70 military treatment centers in the United States to adopt the system despite the fact that the Pentagon mandated its use two years ago. The system, which is Internet-based, was designed to allow doctors to track the medical care given a soldier from the moment he or she arrives at a field hospital in a combat area through a stay in a military hospital in the United States. The slow pace of adoption has forced thousands of wounded soldiers to endure long waits for treatment and exposed many of them to medical tests that duplicate ones they have already had (*New York Times*, 3/30/2007).

Three case studies illustrate different kinds of resistance to health information technology. The first case is described below (Lapointe and Rivard, 2005):

> Case 1 is an acute care hospital where physicians are remunerated on a fee-for-service basis. This new hospital was to serve as a model "paperless hospital." As they were recruited, nurses and physicians were informed that they would be using an EMR. However, when the hospital opened, the system had not yet been installed. Implementation of Alpha began two years later. Five years after system introduction, only the first module (Phase I, test requisitions/test results) was still in use. The second module (Phase II, nursing care) had been withdrawn after major conflicts, first between the nurses and the physicians, then between the physicians and the administration. Workstations installed at bedside, which had almost never been used, had been removed. The system was running at 25 percent of capacity, and there were no plans for expanding its use. . . . resistance behaviors initially consisted mostly of apathy and lack of interest, they later became more aggressive. The project was ultimately abandoned and the Department of Health put the hospital under trusteeship.

The authors report that in Phase I doctors did not participate in training sessions nor did they attempt to learn to use the system. This first phase replaced paper hospital files with an electronic record, representing a significant change in the interface between the physician and patient files. Instead of the familiar paper format, physicians had to navigate from window to window to find information, adding between 1.5 and 2 hours of work every day. Doctors in the hospital were compensated by procedure, so they incurred an opportunity cost for using the new system. In Phase II of the system, doctors had to enter orders electronically instead of giving verbal instruction to nurses; only doctors could use the prescription modules of the system. It took physicians longer to use the system since they often had to go through multiple screens, and the doctors felt they were performing clerical tasks inappropriate to their profession. The hospital board tried to force doctors to use the system; they identified six change resistors and removed their admitting privileges. Some doctors resigned, and the hospital could no longer staff its emergency room. The state Department of Health removed the CEO and put the hospital in trusteeship. Clearly the benefits of this system for the doctors did not outweigh the costs of using it.

The second case is described in this manner:

> Case 2 is a university hospital where physicians are partly salaried and partly remu-nerated on a fee-for-service basis. Implementing an EMR was a way to prepare for the twenty-first century. As in Case 1, Alpha was the selected software. Initially the system was well-received by physicians, who liked the idea of using IT in their work. However, a crisis occurred after a few months when the pharmacy module was installed and the residents formed a coalition. In response, the administration had the system modified. Four years after implementation, the project was consid-ered a success, with 65 percent of system's functionality operational and plans to have 75 percent of them in function within a few months. Case 2 had agreed to col-laborate with two other hospitals that were considering implementing the same software.

The initial reaction to the idea of the system was very positive. Physicians wanted to have the ability to retrieve information quickly and easily. Some doctors did resist the prescription features because it took them longer to enter a prescription online instead of writing it on paper. Resistance became active due to slow response time and the threat to patient care. Administrators slowed implementation and removed the modules until they could be improved. With a few years all of the staff was using the system, and it is considered a success.

Case 3 is described as:

> Case 3 is a university hospital where physicians are paid on a fee-for-service basis. When the time came to change its laboratory, admissions, radiology, and pharmacy systems, the hospital opted for an EMR. The Delta software was chosen, and the surgery units acted as a pilot site. As implementation began, the surgeons had a pos-itive attitude toward the EMR; indeed, they showed exceptional enthusiasm. This quickly changed as they developed reservations about how well the system met their needs. Soon they demanded, to the great disappointment of nurses, that the system be withdrawn. They agreed to use the system again only when the hospital appointed a nurse to enter data for them. Even with this support, the surgeons felt that the system was inadequate and demanded a return to the paper file.

One of the first pieces of the system to be implemented was the module for pre-
scribing tests, which doctors had to enter online. However, the results of the tests
did not come back from the laboratories in electronic form. There was little benefit to them from the efforts to use a complex system for data entry. They had to
spend more time, which reduced their income as pay was by the procedure. Disputes broke out between physicians and nurses, with doctors feeling they were
doing nursing work entering data and nurses refusing to enter data when asked
to do so by a doctor. After a patient did not receive prescribed medicine, the sur-
geons met and demanded that the hospital withdraw the system. A fight ensued
between physicians and hospital administration with the administration eventually withdrawing the system for the surgical units. Again, a system provided few
benefits to the people who had to bear the major costs of using it, both in time
and in opportunity cost.

These stories are primarily about physicians and hospital attempts to implement aspects of health information technology, specifically electronic medical
records and prescription systems. Appeals to the quality of patient care were
not enough to win over doctors and even became a weapon to use against the system in one case. The case is far from hopeless because of government pressure to
use electronic medical records and the fact that some physicians do see the positive side of the technology. My internist, a doctor with his own practice, told
me that he invested $10,000 to install a computer system in his office that pro-
vides connectivity among doctors and the major hospital in the area.

There are also technical problems that have to be overcome before health IT
can transform medical care. Competition means that there will be more than
one electronic medical records system in the United States. Therefore, it is imperative that any systems interoperate. You want a physician, emergency medical
worker, and hospital in any part of the country to have access to your medical
record. They should be able to retrieve the record and post any diagnosis or treatment to it. The second technical problem is that hospitals have long had information systems they developed themselves or purchased from a software vendor.
These applications fall into a category called "legacy systems," old software that
may not be supported anymore and that is likely to be incompatible with new initiatives that are being developed. Hospitals and insurance companies in particular have to figure out what to do with their incompatible legacy systems. The
final technical problem is to develop sufficient access security so that individuals
will not be afraid that their data in electronic medical records will be misused; it
is the privacy issue.

Kodak

Kodak employs a lot of capable people, many of whom have scientific and
engineering backgrounds. Why did Kodak employees resist the move to become
digital instead of embracing it as the future for the company? It appears to be easy

for people to minimize the threat from a forecast. The data from Kodak indicates that everyone in the company misjudged how quickly digital photography would become popular and displace film sales.

The problems at Kodak stem from profits, organization structure, and culture. It is hard to look past a highly profitable, cash-cow business like film. Kodak had a highly bureaucratic culture; our analysis in Chapter 11 described a practice of having a pre-meeting to work out the issues that would be discussed in the official meeting, thus reducing the chances for conflict (or meaningful discussion?). In a bureaucracy, one is rewarded with salary increases and promotions by not rocking the boat. If you started a campaign to say that film photography was going to die and that Kodak had to become a digital company, you would certainly have been making major waves. George Fisher tried but was not successful, by his own admission, in convincing middle managers to go along with a digital future for the company. Bureaucracy and a culture of non-confrontation, combined with profits, served to minimize the perceived threat from digital photography to Kodak and to weaken its attempts to counter the threat.

CONCEPTUALIZING CHANGE

The trouble with transformations is that they are obvious after the fact, but often are hard to discern in advance or when undergoing one. Some of it is that vision thing: how many people are reliably able to forecast the future impact of technology? Many portable MP3 players were on the market, but did anyone foresee the huge success of the iPod? Beyond the device, did anyone forecast how attractive iTunes with its wide access to music (and now videos and various podcasts) would become and see its impact on the music industry? It is easy to discount a visionary or a futurist, but we do so at great risk. Lars Kolind, a CEO who rescued Oticon, a Danish hearing aid company, liked to say "think the unthinkable." What could technology do to me, my work, and/or my family? Could the most outlandish scenario come true? If so, what must we do to prepare for it?

If you believe that a technology-enabled transformation is coming, what can you do to influence people's behavior to adapt to the technology and flourish during and after the transformation? There are two approaches to understanding change that I have found helpful: a kind of cost/benefit analysis and something called force-field theory.

Cost/Benefit Analysis

A cost/benefit analysis is pretty simple. The question is who benefits from a change in behavior and who pays? This notion first came up in a study I did many years ago of a sales information system. The purpose of the system was to obtain better information for sales management on the calls the sales force made

Figure 13.1
Change as a Force Field

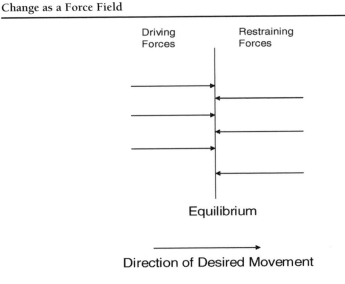

Equilibrium

Direction of Desired Movement

on customers. Sales representatives were supposed to submit detailed call reports to a system, which produced a number of reports for management. The problem was that there was no benefit for the sales representative who incurred all of the cost of using the system. The company paid the sales force on commission, so taking time to complete reports was costly to the sales rep in terms of lost compensation. The problems with the examples of failed health IT implementations earlier in the chapter illustrate this same concept: doctors bore the cost, and perceived few benefits for the system for them, even though there were obvious benefits to the hospital.

Force-Field Theory

A famous psychologist named Kurt Lewin studied communications extensively to understand better how communications might influence behavior. He conceptualized a three-step change process in which individuals first had to unfreeze old behavior, adopt or move toward a new behavior, and then freeze that new behavior. Along the way he developed the force-field analysis of a change situation (see Figure 13.1). This analysis shows a vertical line, which represents the status quo. A change agent is trying to move the line in one direction. In Figure 13.1, the desired movement is to the right. But forces act on the line to push it left, to keep people from changing their behavior. The forces on the left are driving a change in behavior. If one is trying to bring about change, there are two places for leverage: you can reduce the restraining forces and/or increase

Figure 13.2
Force Field Analysis of Medical Cases

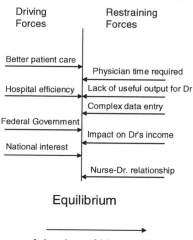

Driving Forces | Restraining Forces

Better patient care

Physician time required

Hospital efficiency | Lack of useful output for Dr

Complex data entry

Federal Government

Impact on Dr's income

National interest

Nurse-Dr. relationship

Equilibrium

Adoption of Health IT

the driving forces. Change is easier if you can accomplish both objectives. Reducing the restraining forces makes movement easier and creates less stress and tension.

Once you have started moving in the desired direction, it is necessary to keep applying forces for change to keep up momentum and solidify the results of the change. The good news here is that once accepted, new technology tends to become the norm. People become quite comfortable with it; I hardly ever hear anyone reminiscing about the good old days of paper airplane tickets or how nice life was before we had email. If we can implement electronic medical records in teaching hospitals, each graduating class of physicians will have been introduced to these records instead of paper and will expect to have them available throughout their careers.

Figure 13.2 shows how one might use a force field analysis to understand better the three medical cases described earlier in the chapter. The driving forces for change were better patient care and improved efficiency in the hospitals. The federal government is also strongly promoting electronic medical records and other health information technology to reduce cost and improve patient care. There is great national interest in an electronic medical records system that would interoperate across the country, as one example.

Restraining the adoption of health IT are three aspects of the systems in the cases: complexity, the time required for data entry by the physician, and the failure of at least one of the systems to provide any significant benefits to the doctor. In fact, the largest impact on the doctor as a result of using the system was a decline in income; the technology required more physician time, and doctors

Figure 13.3
Force Field Analysis of Kodak

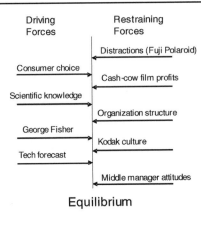

Making Kodak a Digital Company

were paid by the patient/procedure, not by a flat salary. As doctors resisted the input requirements of the system, they turned to nurses who did not want to take that effort on. The result was much worse relationships between doctors and nurses.

Figure 13.3 presents an analysis of Kodak and its attempts to move toward becoming a digital company. Consumers were rapidly demonstrating their choice for digital over film cameras, a message which should have come through to Kodak. There were a number of articles and stories talking about the benefits of digital photography and forecasts about its likely success. Kodak held patents on aspects of digital photography and had good in-house scientific and engineering skills. The board brought in George Fisher from Motorola to help turn Kodak into a digital company.

Acting against these forces for change were two distractions at Kodak. The first was the suit it eventually lost to Polaroid on instant photography and the necessity of paying a fine and exiting the business. The second distraction was the intense competition of Fuji resulting in a loss of market share in film for Kodak. Yet Kodak was still very happy with the film business and its cash-cow profits. The structure of Kodak, a benign bureaucracy, interacted with a culture of non-confrontation to dampen the impact of those who called for change. As George Fisher found, it was a Herculean task to change the mindset of Kodak's middle managers, to get them to reduce their emphasis on film and become enthusiastic supporters of Kodak's digital efforts.

CONCLUSION

The point of this book is that technological transformations are inexorable. There are too many exciting opportunities for positive change, better lives, greater efficiencies, and the creation of wealth. You can fight a delaying action in the spirit of the Luddites, but all that will happen is that you slow down benefits and run the risk of alienating employees, customers, and bystanders. Delaying may cause you to miss out on the first set of benefits from a transformation and let someone else's business model triumph. On a personal basis, refusing to change may doom your employer and your job. The people who fought digital technology at Kodak and the company's failure to respond to the digital challenge resulted in a workforce targeted at 71 percent smaller than the company's peak employment. Technology-enabled transformations are the norm for the twenty-first century. The challenge is to recognize that a transformation is underway and figure out how to take advantage of it.

REFERENCE

Lapointe, L, and S. Rivard. "A Multilevel Model of Resistance to Information Technology Implementation." *MIS Quarterly* 29, no. 3 (September 2005): 461–491.

How to Flourish

THE NATION

The United States really did invent the Internet (and Al Gore actually helped get funding through Congress for it). The United States has dominated the information revolution and the creation of new innovations from the technology. IT-enabled transformations have largely started in the United States and spread to other countries. However, this is all history. What will the story be in the future? For the United States to remain competitive, it must continue to renew itself with new innovations. We must constantly be reinventing how people live and work to take advantage of IT-enabled transformations. Why? If we fail, others will take the lead, and we will be left behind. The United States is not likely to see a resurgence in manufacturing, and only a small percentage of the population earns a living through agriculture. We are a services-based economy, and we can use technology to create innovations that will insure a healthy economy in the future.

Unfortunately, many of our resources are not being applied with this objective in mind. We spend lavishly on politically popular programs, wars, and defense, while speaking highly of education and under-funding it at every opportunity. Cities will spend millions to entice a professional sports team to move in and will heavily subsidize a new stadium. Meanwhile their schools are falling down. The *Wall Street Journal* (8/28/2006) described how one of the top high schools in the country in Alexandria, Virginia, has faced a severe mold problem and experienced falling ceiling tiles and duct work. If a leading suburban school that sends many graduates to the Ivy League and M.I.T., and has had guest lectures by U.S. presidents, is in this condition, what shape are less successful schools in? How can a country as wealthy as the United States allow its education system to sink to this level?

We need to reorient our priorities as a nation. Christa McAuliffe, the teacher who died in the *Challenger* explosion, said, "I touch the future; I teach." As a country we can afford to defer some current consumption in order to invest in our future. We need to create an environment where education is valued, where it is seen as a way to a better life. In my fantasies I see a pep rally complete with cheerleaders for a team of top high school students, a gathering of Rhodes Scholars in the White House instead of the top college basketball team, and leading professional athletes visiting schools to tell students to study because there is little chance they will succeed in becoming professional athletes.

THE GOVERNMENT

For us to continue to enjoy the rewards of innovative technology, to lead the world in transformations to improve all aspects of life, we need to do the following:

Provide Adequate Funding for Education

This call is hardly original. Others have bemoaned the financial state of American education. You cannot buy an educated population, and it is possible to overspend on education. However, I do not think that the United States is in danger of overspending any time soon. Our children deserve schools that are in decent physical condition with laboratories and equipment for their education. Preparing children is an investment for the future, and we may have to sacrifice current expenditures to prepare the next generation. Education funding comes from taxes, and no politician likes to increase taxes. But who represents the children? There are few jobs in a knowledge economy for those without high school diplomas. Innovation will come from a highly educated workforce made up of people challenged by school to learn how to think and solve problems.

Stress Innovation and Creativity at All Grade Levels and in All Activities

My biggest fear for education is that we become obsessed with standardized tests to the exclusion of the activities that lead to creativity. Certainly a child has to be literate in both reading and mathematics, but there is much more to education than rote learning. If we judge and reward teachers on student test scores, and if we punish schools for not improving, then there is no question that teachers will teach how to take tests. After finishing school, there aren't any standardized tests in life, and usually there is no teacher to provide guidance.

One psychologist who has studied creativity extensively suggests that there are three intellectual skills that are particularly important:

1. The ability to see problems in new ways and escape the bounds of conventional thinking.

2. The ability to recognize which ideas are worth pursuing.
3. The ability to know how to persuade others, to sell other people on the value of your ideas (Sternberg, 2006).

He goes on to suggest that creativity is helped if people are willing to overcome obstacles, take sensible risks, tolerate ambiguity and have self confidence. A person also needs an environment that is supportive and rewarding of creative ideas.

I believe that creativity leads to innovation, which is a non-routine change including a new idea that is likely to be frame-breaking. An innovation is also inconsistent with current ways of thinking (Glynn, 1996). The challenge is to find ways to encourage creativity and innovation, in schools, organizations, and all aspects of life. Innovation is the spark plug of technology-enabled transformations.

Carly Fiorina comments on innovation in a business context:

Technology and innovation are not the same things. Just because you sell technology or build technology or love technology doesn't mean you're innovative. Innovation is about new ideas. Innovation is about risk taking. Innovation is about creativity. And that's a human spark. Tech(nology) can accelerate it. Tech(nology) can be used to drive it, but ultimately, people have to be innovative. So some of the most innovative companies in the world are consumer products companies that are doing prosaic things like diapers and toilet paper.

When I arrived at Hewlett-Packard, one of the values that was part of the HP way was innovation. So I asked, "How do we measure innovation?" We didn't. How many patents do we produce? Nobody knew. There's a list that comes out once a year, the top 25 innovators in the world. We weren't on it, although we were one of the very few companies that had a central research lab left. I said what percentage of our revenue stream each year comes from brand new products? We didn't know. Well when you don't measure innovation in any way, in a business [it is] guaranteed you're not innovating. Because in business . . . you need to measure and value and track and reward for [innovation]. So part of what you have to do to foster innovation is to say, "it's actually important, we will measure it, we will reward people who deliver it, and we'll set goals and objectives for it." So we started measuring patents. By the time I left, we were generating 11 patents a day, and we were the number three innovator in the world.

A big part of innovation is to recognize that, at its heart, it's about taking risks. So you not only have to measure it and value it and reward it, you have to accept that risk-taking is required. And taking risks means people will make mistakes and some things will fail. And you have to be okay with that as a business. (Carly Fiorina interview, 2007)

Provide Laptop Computers for All School Children

The cost of computing has dropped sufficiently that schools should provide inexpensive computers so that every student in the United States has a laptop for school and home. There should be a home connection so that parents can be connected with teachers and administrators at the school.

Secure Resources for Every Class to Have a Web Site

If students have laptops, then it is only natural that classes should have Web sites where teachers can post information about their class and student projects. Teachers can use the Web site and Internet to coordinate joint projects with students in other schools and other countries. Funding for this effort will be allocated to a staff person who can be the Webmaster for a school, helping teachers set up and maintain class Web sites.

Establish a National Academy of Technology

The U.S. government has a number of academies to promote medicine, science, and other disciplines. It is time for there to be a "National Academy of Technology" to promote interest in information technology and to study its prospects and impact. The research of the national academies has informed policy-makers and politicians in the United States. We need an academy to play this role for technology since it is rapidly changing the way we live and work.

Make Universal Broadband Access a National Priority

There is an incredible difference between dial-up and broadband connections to the Internet. To me, much of the Internet becomes unusable at slow speeds. It is hard to imagine students being inspired by the resource of the Net with a slow connection. As more commerce and more activities move to the Web, universal broadband connectivity will stimulate the kind of transformations we have been talking about in this book.

YOUR EMPLOYER

Exercise Leadership by Constantly Looking Ahead

As Carly Fiorina observes from her perspective as a senior manager:

One of the big challenges, of course, is how do you see what's coming so that you can lead an organization to adapt. A colleague of mine once said a leader's job is to sense danger and opportunity and to lead their organization to adapt to both. And I think it's a wonderful definition. So to see things, you have to be open to a whole bunch of different points of view. Which is to say, in another way, one of the things businesses do sometimes is start listening to themselves a lot. They get internally focused. I think the most effective way to stay on top of what's coming is to talk to customers all the time. I think it's really useful to understand what your competitors are doing. What do they do well? What could we maybe do better? In other words, I think it's really important to seek different inputs all the time and, that's not habitual for organizations. (Carly Fiorina interview, 2007)

Prepare for Competence-Enhancing and Competence-Destroying Change

Technology is advancing and changing so much that it hard to keep up. Whoever plays the role of the chief technology officer needs to look at current and emerging technologies and predict how they will impact you and your employer. This suggestion is not just an academic exercise; it is a serious effort to understand and forecast trends so that you will not be blind-sided as the recording industry was by the technology of peer-to-peer file sharing. Do you have specific competencies to take advantage of new technology?

Experiment with New Technologies

America is famous for a "can do" attitude. I remember seeing a sign in the machine shop on a Navy ship that said something like, "Difficult requests require a couple of hours and the really impossible may have to wait until tomorrow." Take a new technology and see what it might do for your business model. Five years ago it might have been GPS, today it might be experimenting with RFID, tomorrow it might be mobile broadband.

Look for New Business Models

To me, the most exciting part of the Internet boom of the 1990s was the huge number of new business models that emerged from creative entrepreneurs. Some of these models probably did not have a chance of success, but they were clever and innovative. WebVan is a good example of a model that did not have a hope but attracted billions of dollars of venture capital. WebVan delivered groceries that customers ordered online. Rather than form an alliance with an existing store, WebVan set out to build grocery distribution warehouses in cities where it did business, and in addition set up a fleet of trucks to deliver the groceries. Most Internet firms tried to limit their investment in physical facilities; it took Amazon a number of years to build distribution centers. All the Internet businesses used existing logistics systems for delivery, UPS, FedEx, and the Postal Service being prime examples. So WebVan was a disaster. But the model is back, this time refined to work with existing grocery chains. A few months ago I followed a truck for Safeway Online as it drove into our neighborhood, presumably with a delivery. The point is that the first pass at a business model may not work, but version two or three may turn out to be a great success.

Keep Up Your Technological Infrastructure

It is really hard to catch up if you are far behind on the technology curve. In the 1980s UPS invested in information technology to do the basics while its arch rival, FedEx, figured out how to use technology to offer superior service. It cost UPS about $1 billion to rebuild its infrastructure and to offer services like online package tracking. Now the company spends $1 billion a year to innovate with technology, both to improve efficiency and to provide better customer service. In the early 1990s, Cisco invested in an Enterprise Resource Planning (ERP) system to standardize all of its applications. When the Internet opened up for profit-making activities in 1995, the company was ready to interface its internal system with the Net. As a result, Cisco became the prototypical Internet company and has saved billions in costs by taking advantage of this technology.

Be Open to the Unthinkable

Consider radical ideas like outsourcing part of your business, relying on network partners for key tasks, sharing information with suppliers, and/or turning over some of your business activities to suppliers. Since the early days, for companies like GM, the trend was vertical integration. Buy companies ahead of you in the supply chain to assure a constant supply of needed goods. If you made steel, buy coal mines to provide fuel and iron mines to supply raw materials. Then create a distribution business so that you control the sale of your products. The trouble is that these huge vertically integrated firms became inefficient. They lost the benefit of comparing their costs, often well obscured, with a market price. They also did not trust business partners. Today, there are many high-quality providers of different kinds of services as well as manufactured goods. The technology exists to closely coordinate with outsourcing partners, so the unthinkable may in fact turn out to be your best way to operate.

YOU PERSONALLY

Develop an Understanding of the Capabilities of Technology

Understanding the capabilities of technology and how to apply it is critical to living in the twenty-first century. But what constitutes such an understanding? Do you have to become an electrical engineer or a programmer? The answer is most assuredly "no." It is easy to understand the capabilities of a technology without knowing the details. The use of the Geographical Positioning System (GPS) is a good example. Thousands of vehicles, ships, planes, cars, and trucks have GPS receivers. These receivers provide the latitude and longitude of the vehicle with an accuracy of three meters. The navigation system in your car or on a ship plots this information on an electronic map or a nautical chart in the case of a ship. Navigation programs use a database associated with the map to compute the best route to a destination the user has entered into the system. The program plots the track of the vehicle on the screen from the changing GPS coordinates and gives directions to the driver to follow the computed route.

Schneider National was one of the first trucking companies to apply GPS to plot the location of all of its trucks. Today it is common for companies to use GPS to track vehicle fleets using GPS, cellular, and satellite technologies to transmit location data to a central dispatching site. We do not need to understand the details of how the GPS system works in order to take advantage of it. One can accept the claimed accuracy of the system without understanding that the system uses more than two dozen low earth orbit satellites that continuously broadcast data to earth. The GPS receiver calculates the time it takes for the signal from a satellite to reach it and computes the distance to the satellite. Given the precise position of the satellite, the receiver can calculate a line of position on which it must be located. By using at least four satellites, the receiver can triangulate to an exact position. Without knowing these details, one can still figure out a myriad of ways to use the GPS system just as Schneider National, as well as other fleet managers, did. Automobile manufacturers saw an opportunity to provide navigation systems in cars, and a number of entrepreneurs started companies to provide these systems. Similarly, there are over a half dozen companies that sell navigation programs for commercial and recreational boaters.

The individuals who innovate, who come up with new ideas on how to apply a technology, need to understand what the technology is capable of doing, not *how* the technology works. Do not be afraid of technology because it may be hard to understand; you want to focus on its capabilities and on how it can be applied to create new products and services.

Do Not Attempt to Suppress or Ignore Technology, a Guaranteed Losing Strategy

It is hard to keep technology down. The Luddites tried but had no success in stopping the Industrial Revolution. Remember:

Rule: *The rapid development of new technology-based business models is responsible for a hyper-competitive economy.*

Rule: *Individuals, organizations, and countries who resist technological change and fail to adapt will be left behind.*

If your employer decides not to use technology, the firm will eventually lose out to competitors who do take advantage of it.

On a personal level, you can choose to ignore technology without incurring serious damage. You may miss out on some opportunities that would enrich your life or make work easier, but that is a personal choice. I confess to liking CDs and to not owning an iPod, but I do have a half dozen GPS receivers—fixed units in cars and a boat and several hand-held portable units for outdoor activities.

Be Prepared to Change the Way You Work

If you have been successful in what you do, there is often little incentive to change how you work. Technology, however, forces many changes on us. For better or worse, I now do many tasks that a secretary used to do. I used to ask a secretary to type research papers and book chapters. Since the PC and viable word processors, I have done all of this work myself. I used to make transparencies, and students would copy key points from them in class. Then we started to use Powerpoint and a projector in class, and I made copies of the presentation for the students. Now we post our Powerpoint slides and other materials to a system called Blackboard, and students download them to their computers. Some employees at EarthColor were able to adapt to changes in the printing business, but others ended up leaving the company. The pace of technological change is so great that you can expect change to be a constant aspect of work in the twenty-first century.

YOUR FAMILY

Learn As Much About Technology As Possible

While it is not necessary to understand the intricate details of a specific technology, students will benefit greatly from an overall awareness of technology and its capabilities. Providing school children with a computer opens up the Internet to them, one of the world's great repositories of knowledge. They quickly learn how to search and they take naturally to electronic commerce transactions when they download songs from iTunes for their iPod. The more experience members of your family have with technology, the better able they will be to take advantage of it and to flourish in an increasingly technological world.

Look for a Career in a Field Where Technology Is Competence-Enhancing

If a young person asks about careers, there are a number I would be hesitant to recommend based on what we know now about competence-destroying technological transformations. Fields not recommended include:

- The recording industry
- Video rentals
- Satellite television
- Travel agencies

Where has technology proved competence-enhancing?

- Retail stock brokerage
- Securities markets (electronic exchanges)
- Airline operations
- Overnight package delivery
- Start-ups (Google, Amazon, eBay, etc.)
- Education
- Outsourcers

With a knowledge of the capabilities of technology, can you forecast the fields in which transformations will be competence-enhancing and avoid the ones in which they will be competence-destroying?

THE MAIN MESSAGES TO THE READER

In closing, I have a few words that sum up the messages in this book.

1. There is a revolution in technology that is responsible for the transformation of business and the way individuals live and work.

This is the main message of the book. All of the evidence presented is intended to build the case that transformations are all around us and are ongoing. Few areas of our personal or work lives are omitted from the revolution. Economic efficiency, the quest for new products and services, and global competition mean that new technology will continue to be introduced at a rapid pace.

2. We have to adapt to change; resisting technological advances is futile and leaves anyone resisting change at a huge disadvantage.

The Luddites have not all gone away, but they suffer the same fate every time they try to stop technology. We have stressed education because it prepares one to adapt to change and to integrate new ways of doing things into established routines. People who live in post-industrial countries largely work in services; they perform knowledge work. Technology is the engine that supports and drives this kind of work

3. Individuals, companies, and countries that fall behind in technology may never catch up.

We have seen many examples of what happens when you fall behind. Developing countries present a real challenge. They often fail to provide universal education, and their economies fail to attract investment. With little preparation for applying technology, and limited investments in it, it seems they are destined to remain behind the developed world unless provided with outside assistance. I do not want to claim that technology can somehow bring a huge improvement in the economies of countries in, say, Africa. However, the lack of a viable technology infrastructure and education will make it very hard for these countries to develop their economies.

4. The United States needs to prepare current and future workers for an economy that incorporates technology in every business process, in which there are almost no constraints from time and place, in which most hierarchical organizations disappear, and in which employees work with groups of colleagues in networks of firms.

This item is the real bottom line of transformation. Remember our first rule:

Rule: *Every process is becoming digital, mobile, and virtual.*

We argue that the way in which businesses are organized and operate is changing. Many people do not have 9-to-5 jobs. JetBlue employs housewives in Utah as the bulk of its reservations agents. They work from home during hours that are convenient for them. There is no physical reservations center; communications technology makes it easy to route calls to the next available agent at her home. The hierarchical organization is becoming more and more dysfunctional. To replace it, people are working together on teams to solve problems and develop new ideas. Videoconferencing and conference calls are reducing the amount of travel required and allowing a firm to have team members in different locations. These dramatic changes will continue, and we need to prepare current and future workers to adapt to changing times.

5. The future competitiveness of the country depends on our ability to innovate and implement change enabled by technology.

A number of our rules confront changes in the world that increase competitiveness:

Rule: *Local markets will become national and international.*

Rule: *Technology will continue to accelerate globalization.*

Rule: *The spoils go to innovators and those who can execute.*

Rule: *The rapid development of new technology-based business models is responsible for a hyper-competitive economy.*

Rule: *Individuals, organizations, and countries who resist technological change and fail to adapt will be left behind.*

Our economic system is based on competition among companies for market share and profits. Technological transformations are focused on efficiencies, greater productivity, and on direct revenue generation. Since the dramatic political changes in the former Soviet Union and Eastern Europe, more and more countries have adopted free and competitive markets. These countries want to participate in the global marketplace and will compete to do so. Technology is one of the key drivers of competition in global business, especially in the service and knowledge-oriented U.S. economy.

In closing, one final rule. Heed it well:

Rule: *To remain competitive in the world, we must continue to innovate and successfully initiate technological transformations. You don't want to be left behind.*

REFERENCES

Glyn, M. A. "Innovative Genius: A Framework for Relating Individual and Organizational Intelligences to Innovation." *The Academy of Management Review* 21, no. 4 (October 1996): 1081–1111.

Sternberg, R. "Creating a Vision of Creativity: The First 25 Years." *Psychology of Aesthetics, Creativity, and the Arts* 8, no. 1 (2006): 2–12.

Index

About the Author

HENRY C. LUCAS, JR., is the Robert H. Smith Professor of Information Systems in the Robert H. Smith School of Business at the University of Maryland and Chairman of the Decision, Operations and Information Technologies Department. He is the author of a dozen books and more than seventy articles in professional periodicals on the impact of technology, information technology in organization design, and information technology and corporate strategy. His most recent books include *Information Technology: Strategic Decision Making for Managers, Beware the Winner's Curse: Victories That Can Sink You and Your Company,* and *Strategies for E-Commerce and the Internet.*